DRUM and CANDLE

Books by David St. Clair

CHILD OF THE DARK
SAFARI
THE MIGHTY, MIGHTY AMAZON
DRUM AND CANDLE

DRUM and CANDLE

DAVID ST. CLAIR

DOUBLEDAY & COMPANY, INC.
GARDEN CITY, NEW YORK
1971

Library of Congress Catalog Card Number 79-131103
Copyright © 1971 by David St. Clair
All Rights Reserved. Printed in the United States of America
First Edition

For JUREMA TAVARES
my Brazilian mother

Para JUREMA TAVARES
minha mãe brasileira

DRUM and CANDLE

1

Brazil is a mystical land, a land of the unknown, of the improbable, of the incredible. I saw this almost as soon as I arrived.

First there is their language. While their Central and South American neighbors speak Spanish, the Brazilians speak Portuguese. It is a very important and touchy point with them. They are proud of this difference and don't appreciate it at all when a stranger addresses them in Spanish. This Portuguese heritage is responsible for many of their differences from their neighbors.

Second is their vast distance *away* from everybody. While Peruvians can go north and cross into Ecuador, south and enter Chile or southeast and visit Bolivia, for example, the Brazilians have to travel for days or even weeks by land or river before leaving their own boundaries. Brazil's southern states that border on Uruguay, Argentina and Paraguay have hardly been affected by the Spanish influence, and Brazilians appreciate these close countries because of the marvelous smuggling that can be done—but for no other reason. Brazil was first settled on the east coast (it has yet to be settled on the western borders), and this geographical fact kept local traditions pure and foreigners at a distance. Its former capital, Rio de Janeiro, was isolated from the rest of the world for generations from everybody but the hardiest ocean-vessel passengers. Even Brazilians born in the interior, because of the

Drum and Candle

terrible roads and the lack of communications, considered a trip to Rio with almost as much trepidation as if they were readying to go to the other side of the earth. In the days of the rubber boom along the Amazon River, the nouveau riche found it easier to go to Paris for their vacations than to Rio, and women sent their dirty clothes to be laundered in London.

Third is their warmth and sense of humor. The Brazilians greet each visitor as if he were a long-lost relative (customs officials excluded, however), and soon the newcomer is invited into their homes, to sit at their tables and to hear the latest joke about the President of the Republic. This is one more trait from the Portuguese, who were an easygoing people, much more so than the Spanish. Travelers in black Africa say that tribespeople offer food and shelter to everyone, and this sense of "southern" hospitality is carried over into the Brazilian Negro of today. There are more Negroes in Brazil than in all the other South American nations combined. They came as slaves but ended up as members of the family—and some of the *very best* families too! It is this easygoing Portuguese attitude and this broad-grinning African attitude that make the visitor feel at ease almost immediately. I know. I arrived in Brazil to spend just six weeks and ended up spending twelve years!

And fourth are their religious beliefs. Like all good descendants of the royal house of Portugal, they are Roman Catholics. In fact, the Pope often comments that Brazil is the world's largest Catholic nation. It's true. What His Holiness does not add is that it is also the world's largest Spiritist nation. Churches may be full for Sunday Mass but spirit centers are jam-packed the night before. All babies may be baptized in the name of the Father, Son and Holy Ghost but a large percentage of them also get blessed in the name of Oxalá, Ogun and Yemanjá. Cowled Catholic nuns may administer injections and hand out pills in urban hospitals but very often the same patient may ask a scowling spirit medium to chase away the curse and placate the devil.

You doubt this? I'm exaggerating? Only ignorant Negroes believe in this? Ask any white Brazilian what he thinks about Spiritism and spirit healing and after he gets red in the face and stammers that he doesn't believe in it—ask him again.

I came into Brazil on a long, roundabout way by land all the way from Mexico. I hit the Central American countries, then took a boat across the Panama Canal to Colombia. From there it was a downward swing (all by land—I couldn't afford a plane ticket) through Ecuador, Peru, Bolivia, Chile and all the way to the tip end of the continent near the South Pole and then up the coast of Argentina into Uruguay, over to Paraguay and at last to Brazil.

The very first Brazilian that befriended me was a Spiritist and I, in my colossal ignorance of things Brazilian, didn't even know it. He was a middle-aged Negro, the captain of a dingy paddle-wheeled boat that plied its way along the Paraná River. The last port of call, Presidente Epitácio, was also his home, and he invited me to have lunch and meet his family. My first shock (and this was in 1959, before Martin Luther King, Jr., and the hippies) was that his very charming and attractive wife was white. My second shock came after lunch when he opened a bottle of insipidly sweet peach brandy and poured the first drink into a small cup that was on a shelf in front of an odd statue that looked like a mermaid. "That's Yemanjá," he said. "She is my protector. She likes a nip every now and then." From across the room Pius XII glared out of a cheap colored print while Christ hung limply on a small bronze cross nearby. It was my first introduction to Yemanjá. It was not to be my last.

When I got to Rio de Janeiro I found it as big and exotic and as beautiful and dirty as I had expected it to be. The only disappointment was that the streets were not full of Carmen Mirandas; but they were full of the most beautiful people I had seen anywhere, either male or female. When it comes to physical good looks, the Cariocas of Rio have it over the inhabitants of any other city in Latin America. That, also, might have something to do with staying longer than I had planned.

On the very first night out in Rio, with some Brazilian friends of a friend, I came upon a circle of burning candles and a small clay statue of the devil. They were right there in the middle of busy Copacabana Avenue with its new cars, neon lights and all. I reached for the statue when one of the Brazilian young men grabbed my arm.

"Don't touch that!" he shouted. "It's a *despacho!*"

I pulled back in alarm, thinking the thing was a bomb ready to go off. "A what?" I asked.

"A *despacho*," said another. "You know, an offering to a spirit."

"To a spirit? Here in the middle of Avenida Copacabana?"

"Sure," the first young man said. "Someone must have gone to a spirit medium and asked for a favor. The medium told him to light these candles and place this statue right there and his wish would be granted." He paused. "It's a *despacho* for the devil. It's evil."

"Black magic?" They shook their heads in agreement. "But you surely don't believe in that stuff? You are all college graduates!"

"Of course we don't believe in it," said one; "but it's evil and you will get in trouble if you touch it."

"And," added another, "don't ever fool around with anything like that! It's dangerous!"

In the nights that followed I saw many of these offerings on the Rio de Janeiro street corners. Sometimes it was just a burning candle, other times it would be a bottle of cane alcohol and some rice. Once I saw a white couple slip into the darkened sands of Copacabana beach and in the light of the moon spread a tablecloth and set out food as if for a feast. They lined the cloth with candles, blessed themselves and moved quickly back into the twentieth-century hustle and bustle of Saturday night in Copacabana.

Drum and Candle

I had heard that even a starving man wouldn't touch the food placed for the spirits, and I've seen many a ragged man stop and stare at an offering and then go away leaving the plate untouched. I thought that, obviously, the food was sprinkled with poison, but since then I've found out that it's just ordinary food, cooked in an ordinary way. There are tales told of healthy men who steal the bottle of cane alcohol, drink from it and then wither away and die. They also tell of dogs who eat from the plates and then go howling off in agony. While I've never seen a dog eat any of this spirit food, I have seen several who have come up to such an offering, sniff at it and then back quickly away, leaving a steak or a roasted chicken to the gods.

I saw another spirit event take place (and it still goes on) every Monday evening in Rio de Janeiro. Monday is the Day of Souls—for some reason—and those wishing to pay homage to their dead, or to commune with their dead or to ask a special favor from their dead light candles and pray. The interesting fact is that these candles are always lit in front of a Catholic church! The strawberry-colored St. Teresa Church, located just before the tunnel to modern Copacabana, is a spectacle of flame, prayers and smoke. The devout (and I'm sure some not so devout) come just as the sun is setting, and the steps of the outdoor altar leading up to a statue of Our Lady is soon covered with burning tapers and kneeling, crouching figures. Those who come later find no room on the altar and so light their candles on the edges of the hill.

By 8 or 9 P.M. the sidewalk is covered with flickering candles, so is the gutter, the hillside and even several feet into the neon-lit tunnel itself. Melting wax runs across everything as the smoke rises slowly in the moist tropical night. The next day church employees chip away with crowbars at the hardened wax while dozens of poor women and children gather up huge hunks of it to take back to their shacks to melt down into candles that they can resell to the faithful on the following Monday. In desperation the church padres put up a huge sign saying "God values a single prayer more than an entire box of candles," but it's not done much good. For those that argue that this is a purely Christian manifestation, let them search the rubble on Tuesday morning and find the empty boxes that contained spirit incense, the cheap bead necklaces the spirits prefer and the small charred images of such non-Christian saints as the Old Black Slave and the Indian Seven Arrows.

This heavy dependence on spirits by the good citizens of Rio de Janeiro is not limited just to the poorer and/or darker classes but is a subject of concern in the upper and whiter classes as well. I recall a dinner party with several important Brazilian bankers where the subject (naturally) got around to long-term financing. At that time the Brazilian currency, called the cruzeiro, was as unstable as a drunken butterfly, and the longer leftist-leaning President João "Jango" Goulart stayed in power, the flightier the currency became. Nobody was investing in those days and money available went straight into dollar bills or Swiss bank accounts.

"I'm thinking of investing in such-and-such a company," one portly gentleman said after dinner.

"You're out of your mind!" exclaimed another. "That firm hasn't made any money for years and besides they had a series of labor problems that kept them closed almost two months this year."

"I know all that," the first man said, "but just today I learned that Joãozinho Goumeia has been asked to sit on the board of directors."

"Really?" several others chimed in, and two or three, muttering "how interesting," took out their notebooks and jotted the information down.

"Who is Joãozinho Goumeia?" I asked in all innocence.

The man nearest me coughed and said in a low voice: "Just one of the most important mediums in all Rio, that's who." Obviously, any corporation was worth investigating which had the spirits calling the shots.

Another time I was at a very luxurious home in a chic Rio section having a drink and waiting, with the other guests, for dinner to be served. Suddenly there was a series of loud crashes from the kitchen, and the lady of the house tried to look unconcerned as she hurried out of the living room. She was back seconds later and whispered something into her husband's ear.

"Oh, not again!" he said peevishly. Then to his guests, "It's our cook. She's been seized by a spirit and is whirling around the kitchen in a trance. I do hope you'll forgive the delay."

I was dying of curiosity but since everyone else there took it as a matter of course, I stayed seated and sipped my scotch. When dinner was finally served the cook, a huge black woman with large white teeth, was called out to be complimented. One of the men at the table said something about the delicious food "in spite of the interruption," and she smiled and said that her *guide* "has come very sudden" to give the "madame" of the house an urgent message. We all looked at our hostess, who was blushing above the neckline of her Dior gown.

"Not bad news, I hope," said one of the ladies nearby.

"No. It was my father. He just wanted to let me know that he was all right." The coffee and liqueurs were served in the library, and it was then that I learned that the hostess' father had been dead for about ten years but constantly kept coming back through the medium of the cook to reassure his daughter that he was feeling fine.

The physical aspects of these spirit beliefs were all around me in Rio. As in the States, where shops sell holy pictures, rosaries and first communion outfits, in Brazil there are shops that sell spirit merchandise. They are open to the public and anyone is free to come in and browse. Spiritism is not against the law in Brazil; what is against the law is practicing black magic and healing without a license, but more about that later.

These shops, while usually on side streets, are not necessarily in the poorer section of town. In Ipanema, where "The Girl from Ipanema" lived, there are three different spirit supply shops. One block away from the famed Copacabana Palace Hotel is another spirit shop. One block away from the Rio branch of New York's National City Bank is still another shop. Walk just two blocks from Rio's international airport and you'll find still another shop. The suburbs, where store rentals are lower, have even more.

All sorts of strange things are available in them. The first to catch the eye are the statues. Some of them, like Christ, St. Catherine, St. Peter and the Virgin Mary you can recognize but others are beyond anything ever seen in Catholic or Protestant Sunday School classes. There is the devil in various forms of dress (and undress), there is the mermaid Yemanjá, there is a double statue of two little men in medieval dress standing beside an altar, there is a young white man in a loincloth whose body is full of arrows, there is a man on a horse spearing the most ferocious dragon you ever saw, there is a squat and ugly toad and there is, among others, a North American Indian in full war paint.

Then there are racks of beads. Beads of all colors and all sorts of color combinations. Each spirit has its own color preference and if you are born under that particular *guide* you should wear his or her favorite color. Most of the beads are small and shiny. These come to Brazil from (of all places) Communist Czechoslovakia. Other beads, flecked with various colors and in the shape of cumbersome cocktail-party hot dogs, come from Africa. There are also trays full of special tin medals that are to be worn along with these beads. Mass-produced, they carry all sorts of designs from arrows to lightning bolts to pierced human hearts.

Then there are the boxes of incense and the cakes of soaps.

Has someone put the evil eye on you? Then burn this incense and wash with this special soap. A certain girl not paying any attention to your charms? Burn this incense and think about her. Your husband flirting with some neighborhood hussy? Switch his usual shower soap for this special one and he'll never look at her again. Are you unlucky? Burn this. Do you want money? Wash in this.

Then there are special candles to burn (red, green, blue, white, purple and black) and special perfumes to wear ("Happy Heart," "Homesickness," "Have a Safe Trip") as well as an infinite variety of dried leaves, dried flower petals, cactus thorns, petrified apples, candied orange peel, bats' wings, parrot feathers, various small animal furs (rat, sloth, cat) and such other delicatessen delights as dried cockroaches, dogs' jaws and pickled snakes.

Of course there are also tarot cards, books about the various saints and ethical practices, lithographs suitable for framing of Christian martyrs and local deities, the Holy Bible and *The Medium's Guide to Proper Reception.*

Do these things work? Brazilians keep on buying them and believing in them, so there must be *something* there.

I was no stranger to spirits before coming to Brazil, although I didn't realize it and probably wouldn't have admitted to it. I had read a great deal about ghosts in English castles and never missed a Frankenstein or werewolf movie when I was a kid. I had an intense interest in Haiti when I was in high school in Warren, Ohio, and read all I could find on the island for a term paper. I absorbed the descriptions of the voodoo ceremonies and after a while could actually hear the drums beating, smell the burning rum and hear the chanting of the priestesses. I was fascinated by tales of zombies, by the fact that lost objects were found through spirit voices and that the entire island was under the sway of a mysterious and brutal slave-introduced religion. I always wanted to go to Haiti, but I never made it.

Drum and Candle

It was about this time that I began to hear of the work being done by Dr. J. B. Rhine. I will confess that I tried his card test several times and failed several times. I did, however, believe in what he was doing and hoped that he was on the right track. As a pioneer he could not expect more than rudimentary success. It will be the scientists coming after him who will benefit from his basic research.

We never believed in ghosts at home. "They don't exist," I was told, and that was the end of it. My first experience with these non-existing things was when I was very young, maybe nine or ten years old. I was spending a few days with my grandmother and was upstairs while she was down in the living room. I started down the steps when I heard my grandmother say something to somebody. I stopped and a woman's voice answered. Then my grandmother spoke again but cut her sentence short and screamed. I froze on the staircase unable to move, knowing that Grandma and I were alone in the house and knowing that I had never heard that visitor's voice before. I waited for a while and then when all was quiet went down the steps. Grandma was sitting in a chair, looking pale, and her hands were trembling. Later she told my mother that she had been sweeping the carpet when she sensed that someone was in the doorway. She looked up and saw it was her sister Sib. She said, "Why Sib, what are you doing here?" and her sister answered, "I thought I'd just see how you were getting along." Then Grandma started to say something else when she realized that her sister Sib had been dead for years. That was when she screamed, and the apparition vanished. The rest of the family scoffed at the story ("Ghosts don't exist!"), and I didn't have the courage to tell my mother that I *too* had heard Aunt Sib's voice. I did not understand until much later that Great-aunt Sib had been long dead before I was born.

The next time that things that "don't exist" happened to me, I was fourteen and working after school in a neighborhood drugstore. There was an old man there named Mr. Reese. I don't know how old he was but at that time, for me, anyone over twenty-five was ancient. Mr. Reese was the stockman. It was his job to refill the shelves every day with the items that had been sold the previous day. He was a nice old man and treated me as an adult. Naturally, I greatly respected him. Then he took sick and was taken to the hospital. His doctor said it was nothing serious and I made plans to visit him when I had a free afternoon. I was on the bus, going to school one morning, when the horrible thought came to me: "Mr. Reese is dead!" I looked at my watch (I don't know why I did, but I did) and saw it was eight-ten. I worried all day about the old man and after school I went directly to the drugstore. One of the girls at the soda fountain told me, "Did you hear about Mr. Reese? He died this morning."

I paused and then asked very slowly, "What time did he die?"

"His doctor said it was around eight. Why?"

"Nothing," I replied and went down into the basement to cry behind the piled-up cartons.

I waited until I was in my late teens before trying any ESP experiments on myself. My grandmother had died (the one who talked to the ghost), and while I was brokenhearted I also wanted to get in touch with her. I was sure that if she came back and told me that there was something after all to this spirit business, then it had to be true. Grandma never lied. So I mailed a letter to the Rosicrucians and started receiving their lessons. In the privacy of my room I lit candles, mumbled archaic phrases and looked deep into a mirror trying to see my past reincarnations. Then one day a new lesson arrived in the mail and I tried it that night. It was to make the student completely relaxed so he could sleep better, or so they said. The instruction sheet explained that I was to take off my clothes (so as to have nothing binding my body) and lie down on the bed. Then I was to concentrate on the big toe of my right foot, and I was to concentrate on it completely until I felt it begin to tingle. When the tingling came I was to concentrate on the other toes of the right foot, and then with them all atingle, I was to do the same with the left foot, then joint by joint move up the body. I undressed and stretched out on the bed. I took a good look at my big toe to see what it looked like and shut my eyes. Much to my surprise it began to tingle very quickly. Then I mentally pushed the tingling to the other toes. Delighted with the results, I left the right foot tingling away and concentrated on the left. Soon it was in harmony with the right. Then, according to instructions I concentrated on the ankles, then the knees, then the hips, then started on the fingers, the wrists, the elbows and the shoulders. My entire body felt as if it was being pricked by millions of invisible straight pins. Happy that I was such an apt pupil, I started to concentrate on the face, and just then it happened. I felt a rushing of all those pin points straight into my scalp and when I opened my eyes I saw that I was floating above myself and looking down upon my own body! Terrified, I let out a yell and came out of the trance. The next day I wrote a letter to the Rosicrucians demanding just what it all meant. The answer said that what had happened to me was "very interesting for a beginning pupil" and no more. Disgusted with them and afraid of my own powers, I canceled the course. It was only years later, while reading books on psychic abilities, that I learned I had made an astral projection. That I had actually left my body and could have been able to travel anywhere in the world as a disembodied spirit. It was a frightening thing to do to a kid and I never quite forgave the Rosicrucians. Also, I never tried the experiment again because books told me that often people on these astral trips are seen and converse freely with other people. The Rosicrucians said you had to take off your clothes and I didn't want to be seen flying around the world bare-assed naked!

Because of all these things, I suppose that I arrived in Brazil

Drum and Candle

with a more open mind than most of the Americans passing through. I won't say that it was completely open, for, frankly, I just could not believe in transplanted African spirits, washing with soap to get the girl you wanted, or the power of the "evil eye." However, I did have an inquiring mind and wanted to look further into these things, but I didn't have much time to stay in Rio. I wanted to see the interior of Brazil and I wanted to see real live Indians and I wanted to see the Amazon River. I saw them all and more.

Stumbling along from town to town in my bastard Portuguese, I managed to arrive at the center of the Mato Grosso jungle and an Indian Protection Post in the Xingú River valley. There I met Claudio and Orlando Villasboas, two white city-born brothers who have dedicated their lives to protect Brazil's dying Indian tribes from complete white man annihilation. The Villasboas brothers are not missionaries, far from it. They like to booze and swear and have no qualms about "getting rid" of Indian killers. They welcomed me thinking I was a doctor bringing much-needed medicines. When they found out that I was only curious they were disappointed (with reason) but let me stay.

The Indian post was the center for supplies and communications with the outside world. There was a landing strip cut out of the jungle that the brothers kept strewn with empty oil drums. Only when these oil drums were removed could any planes land there. That way only official planes were welcome and tourist-chartered aircraft could only buzz harmlessly overhead. Their idea was to keep the Indian as far from the white man as possible, for "civilizing" these beautiful people only exposed them to such white man's curses as disease, hunger and abject poverty. The brothers, at that time, fought a running battle with land grabbers, poachers and missionaries. The Indians have nothing to gain from any of these people. Only doctors and nutritionists were welcome in the Villasboas

Drum and Candle

fiefdom, and also an occasional journalist to tell the world to stay away.

Orlando taught me many things about the Indians' spiritual side. Each tribe had a complicated set of gods and goddesses who dwelt in trees, under rocks, in the streams, in the bellies of fish, in the bodies of animals, in the clouds, in the mountains, etc. They believed in these spirits and were frightened of them. They had no conception of germs or disease and thought that each time a person fell ill it was because some evil spirit had entered his body. (Remember that it was only two hundred years ago that Pasteur linked germs with disease for the "enlightened and civilized" Western world!)

Each tribe had one man who could chase away these evil spirits. It was not a hereditary thing but more a matter of "being called." A youth who showed a propensity for slipping easily into a trance and who could speak with the spirits was groomed by the tribal doctor to take his place. These Indians do not read or write, so the young boy (often not even in his teens) had to live with the doctor and learn all his remedies by heart. He learned how to blow smoke over the sick (or enchanted) parts of the body. Smoke confused the spirits and cleansed the area. He learned how to suck out the evil by placing his mouth over the infected area. He learned how to chant and shake a gourd rattle to frighten off the spirit. He learned how to go into a trance to receive the evil spirit from the sick body into his own, and then, most importantly, he learned how to expel this same spirit from his own body.

He also was expected to look into the future, to tell who had put the evil eye on members of his tribe and to call down rain when it got so dry that there was nothing to eat except tree bark and locusts. He was expected to counsel the chief on matters of state, to perform the rites of marriage and death and to be an intermediary between his tribe and other tribes as well as with the white man.

While he learned a lot of purely show-business tricks he

also studied homeopathy. He knew which leaves were good for stomach-ache, which roots ground into powder could cure pains in the arms and legs and how to make a poultice of mud, beeswax and herbs to draw out poisons from scorpion and snake bites.

His was not an enviable job, for quite often he was forbidden to take a wife or have children, and while he had great power in the tribe, second only to the chief himself, he was not supposed to make a mistake. Failure to cure a patient, to bring down rain or to bring about a plague on an enemy tribe could result in banishment or even death. When an elderly doctor found his power waning he would turn everything over to his protégé. And there were times when the protégé, anxious to start on his own, would kill off his teacher and take over the tribe.

The Villasboas brothers taught me how to give injections, and for a while I worked in the palm-thatched hut that served as medical center and drug warehouse. The remedies were mostly manufacturers' free samples and almost all outdated. There were only a few hypodermic needles and very little alcohol to clean them in. (Once a monkey jumped into the pharmacy and before I could stop him smashed a full quart bottle of alcohol onto the floor. For us, it was a tragedy.)

A young Indian woman lay dying in a tribe some twenty miles away from the post. She had, Orlando thought, pneumonia and because she was too weak to come to the post he had gone there the week before and given her a shot of penicillin. He was occupied with other things that day and so sent me, armed with a hypodermic, a vial of alcohol, a dab of cotton and a dusty vial of penicillin, to give her an injection.

(Now before some purist cries out "how terrible" and berates the fact that neither Orlando nor I had any medical training and were completely unfit to minister to this woman, let me point out that this area is hundreds of miles from the nearest hospital, that the only way to have taken this woman to proper medical care would have been days and days of canoe traveling and that no Brazilian doctor wanted to give up his air-conditioned apartment and lucrative practice in Rio de Janeiro to take care of these people. If it hadn't been for Orlando and Claudio Villasboas these tribes would have been massacred and their land taken years ago. The Villasboas brothers (and I too in a way, I suppose) were merely doing the best they could in face of the indifference of millions of Brazilians who just didn't give a damn one way or another about their indigenous brothers.)

I walked the twenty miles through the jungle, following a twisting dirt path, and when I arrived at the village I was greeted by the chief and a few of the Indians who had gotten to know me at the outpost. I showed the chief the hypodermic and got him to understand that it was for the dying woman. He led the way to her hut.

She was probably in her late teens but already mother of two children. She lay in a string hammock not unlike a thick fish net, and the cords dug into her naked flesh. There was not much flesh there by that time, as the disease had wasted her away to flabby skin over bones. Her husband was there beside her and so were her two children. I wondered who was feeding the smallest one, for obviously no milk was coming out of those shriveled breasts. She was only half awake and she coughed once, spitting up a huge gob of green phlegm that was veined in blood. The ground around her hammock was dotted with these disgusting blobs. I thought I was going to throw up until I remembered that I was supposed to be the doctor and set a good example.

I smiled what I considered my bedside-manner smile and opened the box containing the hypodermic. As I was about to light the alcohol there was a commotion at the door of the hut. Everyone turned to look.

Drum and Candle

In strode an Indian I had never seen before. He was middle-aged and had red and black stripes across his face. On his arms he wore a band of yellow parrot feathers. Around his ankles he had braided palm fronds. That was all he was wearing.

He approached the hammock and looked at the woman. She saw him through half-opened eyes and started to moan. Calmly, but with firmness, he closed the hypo box and handed it back to me. I opened my mouth to protest when I felt the chief's steadying hand on my shoulder.

The tribal doctor barked an order and almost instantly two naked women began throwing ashes from the fire over the blobs of phlegm on the floor. Then another took a bundle of sticks and swept the area clean. Another order was barked and a gourd full of water was brought to the magician. He made some signs over the gourd and sprinkled the ground around the hammock, then the women swept it again and spread a layer of banana leaves over the clean floor. The man stepped onto this green carpet and sprinkled the remaining water onto the moaning woman. She jumped at the cold drops, probably the first fresh water she had had on her body in days. Then the magician/witch doctor/medical man opened a jaguar-skin pouch and took out a leaf that had been folded into a packet. From inside this packet he took some pink powder and placing it on the palm of his hand began to blow it over the woman. Soon she was covered in it. Then he began to chant and moan and beat his feet upon the banana leaves. Other voices behind me took up the melody of his chant and stamped their feet on the hardened ground. It was shortly after this that his body suddenly doubled up—as if it was hinged at his navel—and let out a long, low cry. He shivered as if freezingly cold and slowly righted himself. The chanting stopped. He turned and glared at the others and at me in particular but I saw only the whites of his eyes; the pupils had turned up into his head.

Drum and Candle

Again he reached into his bag and brought out a stone. It was just an ordinary dark stone about the size of a lime. He held the stone in the air, then passed it over the feverish woman and then under her as well. Then, with his eyes still gleaming white, he began to touch various parts of the patient with the stone. The woman uttered no cries and shut her eyes tight. Then he returned the stone to the bag, bent over the hammock and placed his mouth on her body. He sucked a spot on her leg, then moved his lips to her belly. From there he sucked the area over her heart, then dashed his head down to suck her wrist. Then he moved around the hammock and did the same with the other side of her body. He turned her over, brutally I thought, and placed his lips on her back, her buttocks, her upper legs and her ankles. Then once again the dying woman was roughly turned in the hammock and he put his mouth to hers. At this he fell back, clutched his neck and made sounds as if he was trying to vomit something stuck in his throat. Blind fingers searched the floor for his bag, and someone pushed it over to him. He grasped it, held it up to cover his mouth and made the most terrible retching sounds. Then he slumped onto the floor and stayed there for quite a while. He arose, weak and trembling, and left the hut saying not a word to anyone or even glancing at his patient.

The chief took me outside (never had fresh air seemed so delicious) and gave me a ripe papaya and a few manioc cakes to eat. I returned to the outpost just before sundown.

Orlando was not surprised when I told him what had happened. He seemed glad that the woman had a doctor looking after her and even happier that I didn't have to use the precious vial of penicillin. A few days later some Indians came from the village to get their ration of rice. Among them, carrying one child and hanging onto another, was the woman who was dying of pneumonia. She radiated health and was chattering happily with the other women. Her husband waved at me and smiled. The only thing I could do in my astounded state was smile stupidly in return.

2

From the Indians I returned to Rio via the Amazon River and the drought-stricken northeast, that part of Brazil that juts out into the Atlantic Ocean and was once, say some geologists, joined to the African continent. I collected stories and took pictures as I went along in hopes that someone would be interested in buying an article or two, for I was returning to Rio completely broke. The cheapest part of the trip had been with the Indians. There money is not valuable. With them a freshly killed deer is worth more than a diamond, a pound of sugar worth more than a pound of gold and a few white beads and some rifle shells keep the visitor in room and board for months.

I gathered my notes and my rather hazy photographs and timidly walked into the Rio bureau of *Time* magazine. The secretary, a stunning brunet beauty, told me the bureau chief was busy and I would have to wait. I could hear the clicking of his typewriter through his office door. It never seemed to stop. Finally she said I could go into the great man's den. He was seated at a desk that was piled high with newspapers, typing paper, books, cigarette butts and glossy photographs. He looked up at me and never stopped typing while asking me what I wanted.

"I'm a free-lance writer," I mumbled. He grunted and kept reeling out words. ". . . and I just got back from the Amazon and—"

He stopped, fingers twitching over the keyboard, and said: "The Amazon? Can you go back there tomorrow?"

The very next day I was on a plane and heading back to the jungle. What had happened was that on the very morning that I had gone so innocently into his office, he had received a twelve-page telegram from the editors of *Time* asking for a complete color takeout on the Amazon region. He knew nothing about the area and neither did any of the others on his staff. I had fallen out of heaven (or "the Green Hell") into his arms. He was not the kind of man to let go easily.

What had begun as a single idea to get enough money to return to the States suddenly became a full-time job. He was so pleased with my work on the Amazon story that he asked me to stay on for other stories.

Soon my life was completely absorbed by discovering and reporting Brazil in all its varied aspects. The bureau chief, George de Carvalho, was a tough master who seemed to be determined to fill all of Mr. Luce's magazines by himself every week.

Working for him was not easy. He demanded that each story be fully investigated with no loose ends that could bring doubts to the great minds that edited our stories up in New York. His was the "vacuum cleaner" approach to journalism, sucking up every possible shred of information until the story was complete. Often I would file thirty pages of research and *Time* would boil it down to two paragraphs in the magazine. It was frustrating, exciting, mad and it gave me the best journalistic education in the world. No college course could have taught me what I learned on the battlefield with Carvalho.

During this period I kept running into the strange religious beliefs of the Brazilians in almost every story. I would be interviewing a presidential candidate and note that he would be wearing a small gold fist on his watch strap. While doing a story on a local industry I would invariably see small shrines stuck in factory corners with candles illuminating Christian as well as pagan images. If I was doing research on an artist the spirit theme was always somewhere in at least one of his paintings.

I had to speak and read Portuguese for this work, of course, and I was amazed at the quantity of spirit news that was in Rio and São Paulo papers. Before *Time* I had read only the *Brazil Herald*, the English-language daily, and while it reported the goings on of Presbyterians and Catholics, it never mentioned the local spirit churches. Therefore it was a shock to me to read what time a session would be held at the tent of the Old Black Slave or find an item about an important medium who was to receive a special spirit on such-and-such a day or to discover a paid announcement from someone who thanked the goddess Yemanjá for a favor granted. Brazilian newspapers carried columns by Drew Pearson and Art Buchwald but often right beside them would be columns by Spirit Emmanuel or Guide Yansá. Readers followed the translated advice of Ann Landers or Dear Abby but they also listened to what Spirit Seven Arrows said about affairs of the heart as well. Even Li'l Abner had to share comic-strip honors with a character named Amigo da Onça, who was more often than not up to some deviltry with local devils.

Police pages are nice and bloody in Brazil. There is one daily about which people say if you twist it blood will drip. Editors look for gory photographs and spatter their stories with the number of knife wounds in a body, how the victim's screams woke the entire neighborhood or just who was in bed with whom when the murderer kicked in the apartment door. Headlines are often better than the stories themselves, like "Man shoots wife, slays neighbor and rapes his grandmother." One of my favorite headlines was over a story telling how a woman came home to find her husband in bed with a neighbor girl. She grabbed a kitchen knife and castrated him. The headline read "Wife cuts off problem at roots."

Drum and Candle

Spirits and strange beliefs brought many innocent people onto the crime pages. One woman killed her two children because she had attended a session and was told that her children were really demons in disguise and that the only way she would ever find happiness would be to rid herself of them. Another woman was horribly burned after being told by a spirit medium that she must walk through fire to be cleansed of the evil eye. A man committed murder because a spirit told him that his wife's cancer was brought about by a neighbor's curse.

While I worked for *Time* I had to investigate and report one of the most gruesome murders in Rio's history. A young married man, from a middle-class neighborhood and with a middle-class job, was having an affair with another woman. He told the woman that he didn't love his wife but could never leave her because of their small daughter, Tania. He, in reality, had no intention of ever leaving his wife but it was a good way to keep his mistress on a string. One afternoon the mistress waited outside a primary school and stopped six-year-old Tania as she was heading for home and put her into a taxi. The driver later told the police that he took the pair to a poor neighborhood on the outskirts of Rio and left them off at an open field. The child began to cry and the woman bought her some ice cream. They walked through the uncut grass as night began to fall. The child asked for her mother and started crying hysterically. The woman slapped her several times and knocked her to the ground. As little Tania lay in the weeds sobbing and exhausted, the woman prayed for guidance. She first prayed to the Virgin Mary and when she had no answer she began praying to the various spirit gods. In her madness and in the darkness of the abandoned field the spirits told her to kill the child, for Tania was the only obstacle between her and her lover. She took a sharp pair of scissors from her purse and plunged them over and over again into the small body.

The next day the corpse was discovered and when the husband confessed his love affair to the police they went to the mistress' home and arrested her. She immediately confessed. When I interviewed the murderess, through the bars of her cell, she was unemotional and calm. For her, she had only done what the spirits had commanded. She was sure that she would be freed and united with her lover.

The reaction of the public was amazing. As soon as the body had been found crowds converged on the murder site and declared Tania "a saint." They roped off a six-foot-square area and placed candles at each corner. They brought plaster statues and put them inside the ropes. They came with bottles and jugs of water and put them on the site. After chanting a few prayers they would take back their bottles and rub the water into an open wound, onto a crippled foot or even into thinning hair to cure baldness. Others openly sold this water for prices ranging from a few cents to several dollars a glass. The rumor that Tania had become a saint turned into a belief and along with this belief went the story that she was turning ordinary water into miraculous medicinal liquid. Police were called in, not to put a stop to this macabre spectacle, but to maintain order. With the passing of time the site became less and less frequented but even today you can find crosses, statues and bottles of water on the shrine of "St. Tania."

The stories were not without their lighter side as well. I remember one about a man named Djalma Tavares in the interior state of Mato Grosso. It seems that just about everything that could happen to one man during the course of a year happened to him.

First his only cow happened to give birth to a five-legged calf and a local circus offered to buy it, but before Djalma could close the deal a thief stole the calf. Furious, Djalma went into debt to buy barbed wire to put up a fence around the pasture. Before he could finish, the thief returned and stole the cow. The next night someone stole the barbed wire.

Djalma planted several acres in rice but when the rice refused to grow he dug an irrigation canal from a stream high up on a hill. The water flowed freely after that. Too freely, actually, for when the rains arrived they filled the canal, flooded the field and washed away the rice shoots.

One of Djalma's pride and joys was a huge mango tree in his back yard. Another of his joys was a chicken coop he had built himself and stocked with fifty laying hens. Lightning struck the mango tree and sent it crashing onto the coop. The chickens fled into the jungle.

His daughter Selma ran off with a stranger shortly afterward and when the stranger abandoned her she wrote asking her father to take her back. She said she was pregnant. Djalma assured her that one more mouth to feed really didn't matter. She had twins.

A bachelor uncle in another town died and Djalma received word from city officials that he had inherited his uncle's automobile. Djalma bought a one-way bus ticket and went to claim the car. The vehicle was his, officials told him, as soon as he paid the backlog of storage fees to the police garage. They had impounded the car years ago.

Well-meaning neighbors convinced Djalma that someone had put the "evil eye" on him and his property and told him that only a spirit ritual would put things right again. He visited a spirit session and was told to buy some candles, some incense and some special powders. He lit the incense inside his house and spread the powder from the front door to the back and then all around the house. Then he put the candles beside the powder and lit them all. He had purchased gunpowder by mistake and blew his home into a thousand pieces!

Once when I was on a paddle-wheel steamer on the Amazon, a group of people, in what could only be called steerage class, began a spirit session. Instead of drums they beat out the rhythm with their bare hands on the hollow deck. Candles came out of nowhere and the smell of jasmine and gardenia incense wafted up through the other smells of beans, urine and sweat. The captain, a short dark man with traces of Indian in his veins, didn't bother to go down and see what was going on. He could tell from the songs and the dull thumping on the floor. "It's for that baby," he said, and I recalled a pitifully thin child that had been taken on earlier that day. It looked like a skeleton and hardly moved. Even though the child was four years old the mother had to carry him in her arms.

"Is he dying?" I asked.

"Yes," was the reply, "but the passengers are trying to undo the curse that is killing him."

"Curse? But who would want to put a curse on a small child?"

"Who knows? A jealous lover maybe. Maybe a woman who can't have any children of her own. I don't know."

"You believe in that?" I asked.

He drew back and looked at me. "Of course not! After all, I am a civilized and educated man!" He walked into his cabin and slammed the door.

The next day, slightly before noon, the boat stopped at a small town. I watched the mother hand the sick child up from the lower deck to the arms of a Catholic sister who was waiting to receive it. The woman kissed the sister's ring and the white-garbed religious made the sign of the cross over the staring, mute boy. I wondered how the mother, in her uneducated backwater mind, could equate the two religions. I also wondered if the sister suspected the spirit cure of the previous night, but then I thought that probably she, being Brazilian herself, was quite used to exorcising demons of both creeds.

Brasília is called the twenty-first-century capital, yet rites that go back to the days of primitive Africa are practiced there every day. I accompanied the construction of Brasília from the time when it was just a few wooden shacks to hold the workers and everything—including steel girders and sacks of cement—had to be flown in because there were no roads running to the desolate spot. The growth of the city was rapid and workers labored around the clock to finish the major buildings in time for the inaugural date of April 21, 1960. I often saw President Juscelino Kubitschek, who considered Brasília his baby, arrive in a helicopter, climb girders to shake hands with the construction-crew men and then at midday open his own lunch pail, sit down and eat with the men. No wonder they slaved twenty-four hours a day for him.

On the eve of inauguration day I was in the new city with a team of *Time* and *Life* people as well as journalists and newsreel cameramen from all over the world. As far as the international press was concerned, Brasília was Brazil's hottest news item since Carmen Miranda, and they were all on hand to record its official birth.

I had been to three parties that evening and resolved to walk from the last one back to the unfinished house that was serving as the *Time-Life* "hotel." I was feeling no pain from the various cocktails and all those canapés and the night air felt good after I'd stuffed my tie into my trousers pocket and took off my jacket. The stars were winking and calling my attention until I saw the winking of candles behind the Planalto Palace. I heard soft chanting and the soft beat of one small drum. I knew immediately that a spirit ceremony was taking place behind the palace. I decided to investigate.

The Planalto Palace is a monstrous white marble and green glass edifice where the President gets his work done. In my opinion, it is the most imposing of all the buildings in Brasília. From it would come the presidential decrees, the conferences and the recommendations that would govern the majestic nation. Knowing what little I did about Spiritism, I felt it was only just that these people were there blessing the new building. The next day it was to be blessed by the Cardinal of Rio. I walked toward the flickering lights and the soft chanting when suddenly a huge black Cadillac came out of the shadows and straight toward me. The glare of its lights blinded me for a second and I jumped out of the way. But as I did, I got a quick look at the lone man sitting in the back seat. It was dark and the lights had confused my eyes, but I was sure that the person who was leaving this spirit session, the session asking the primitive gods to protect the futuristic palace, was none other than the President of the Republic himself!

Salvador, Bahia, is a lovely colonial city with winding cobblestone streets and buildings faced with multicolored tiles; it is studded with tall, swaying palm trees. It is also the home of the spirit religions of Brazil, and the first time I visited it I wanted to see a local ceremony.

I was the guest of a young American couple who had a lavish apartment in one of the best buildings in town. He was connected with some U.S. agency and she played at being a housewife. They both disliked Bahia, hated Brazil and only tolerated each other.

One Saturday evening I said I wanted to see a Candomblé ceremony. They immediately pooh-poohed the idea. They had been to one already and it was nothing but a lot of black people jumping up and down. I still said I wanted to see one. They wanted to go to a movie but I kept bringing up the subject of spirit sessions and they finally gave in. But we wouldn't stay long. I agreed.

We got into their small car and drove out of the city and into the hillside section of shantytown shacks and cement hovels. The streets were rough and unpaved, the sewers were open and foul and the sky was pitch-black yet covered in stars. We stopped several shabbily dressed people asking for a Candomblé session and each time got a stony stare. When we turned down one dark road we heard the sound of many voices and we slowly drove toward them.

Drum and Candle

The house was small, with a thatched roof and a huge mango tree in the front yard. It sat far back from the road atop a hill and we had to scramble up steps cut into the earth in order to reach it. The inside was filled with people. They were almost all black.

Several dozen small, two-pointed banners, cut from crepe paper of various colors, hung on strings that crisscrossed the roof beams. The walls had been painted white but were now a dirty gray and marred with hand prints and scars. There was an altar against the front wall that reached almost to the ceiling. It was divided into shelves and platforms that held some two dozen different plaster statues. I recognized the Virgin Mary, St. George slaying his ever present dragon, St. Peter, the two medieval soldiers who I had learned were St. Cosmas and St. Damian, the red devil I had seen for the first time on a Rio street corner, Jesus Christ, a silver snake coiled and ready to strike, St. Catherine, the Old Slave and my friend the mermaid Yemanjá. It was quite a collection of celestial dignitaries. There were vases of flowers between these statues, and on every level candles burned.

In any spirit session the sexes are divided, and so while I and the husband were shown to benches on one side of the room, his wife was motioned to sit on the other side. Several Negro women, barefoot and humbly dressed, slid over to make room for her.

I was so interested in the decorations that I didn't notice the three bare-chested men come in with their drums. They sat on a bench against the right-hand wall near the altar and began to make the drums "talk." The rhythm was straight out of Africa and so were the instruments. They were barrel-shaped, smaller on the bottom and wider at the top. They were each a different size and each painted with bright triangles, stripes and signs.

Then a huge black woman came out of a room behind the altar. She was dressed in white satin and white lace. Each of her many skirts had a wide hem of handmade lace that swirled around her bare feet as she walked across the beaten-earth floor. She welcomed the congregation, bowing low to the men, then the women and then the drummers. At this they began to beat even faster and after she twirled around a little and prostrated herself in front of the giant altar she beckoned to someone in the hidden room. Slowly about a dozen women, also dressed in pure-white satins and laces (but not in competition with the richness of the priestess herself!) came out of the room and formed a circle around her. She started a chant praising God the Father, and the women chimed in with shrill voices and began to revolve counterclockwise around her. The chant over, she began to praise Jesus, and the dancers changed pace and revolved in the other direction, singing and moving their hands as they went. Then came a hymn to the Virgin Mary, then another to St. George, then still another to St. Peter. Once these "Western" saints were out of the way, the next hymn of praise went to Oxalá, then one to Ogun, then one to Yemanjá and so on. The dancers never stopped, the drums never stopped, the tension kept increasing.

I glanced at the American husband and he was sitting with his arms crossed and scowling at the whole thing. His wife was tapping her foot to the drum beats. She caught my glance, made a face that she was bored with the whole thing and took a cigarette from her purse. As she was about to light it, the black woman next to her touched her lightly on the arm and, pointing to the tobacco, shook her head. The wife tossed the cigarette back into her handbag and noisily snapped it shut.

The pace of the drumming changed and became even more rapid. The dancers were going around and round like the tigers in *Little Black Sambo* and I half expected all of them to turn into butter.

Then one woman in the circle made a misstep and reeled

backward. A murmur, then an instant silence rose from the spectators. The woman, youngish and with a shining black skin, made a face and passed her hand over her eyes. She got back into the rhythm and made a couple more turns with the other dancers, then she stumbled again. The priestess reached out and caught her before she could fall. She was sweating profusely and her eyes were shut tight. She tried a few steps but her legs refused to obey her and she lurched into the woman in front of her. The others drew back, never stopping in their own rhythm, apparently unconcerned that one of their members was feeling ill.

Then she screamed, a high, shrill scream that broke the warm air inside the center and sent a shiver down my spine. She screamed again and began to strike out around her with her fists as if trying to drive off some invisible bird that was attacking her. Her entire body began to shake, shaking as if she had a terrible chill, and her hair, once carefully combed and hidden beneath a white kerchief, came undone and tumbled down around her shoulders.

The priestess put out her arms to protect her, but not to touch her, as she began to stagger and weave as if she was under a great weight. She tried to control her feet, tried to get back into the circle of dancers, but it was impossible. She twisted her body, tore at the air and kept up the horrible shuddering.

I kept my eyes glued to her until there was another shriek. Swiftly I searched the dancing group and saw one of the others, an old woman easily in her sixties, stagger and clutch at her face. She bent over at the waist, her kerchief coming undone and her frizzy gray hair almost touching her feet. Before I had time to marvel at such gymnastics in a woman her age, she threw herself on the floor and began to roll. The priestess, assisted by a young girl dressed in white who came quickly out of the back room, managed to stop the old woman's thrashings on the floor. She lay there gasping like a fish thrown up on the beach, then suddenly jumped up, her eyes closed and her fingers twisted into claws. The drumming and the shrill singing continued while the dancers somehow managed to move around the two who were deformed and staggering around to a music that only they could hear.

A third woman staggered and almost fell to the floor. A fourth stopped, stared wild-eyed at the spectators and began to laugh hysterically. Soon a fifth was rolling on the floor while a sixth had started shivering and pulling at her clothes.

"What a lot of crap this is!" the American beside me said and got up. "I'm going to have a cigarette." He turned his back on the altar and the dancers and walked up the aisle and out of the house. I didn't dare turn around to see the reaction of those around me.

One by one the dancers became possessed. One by one they took on the physical characteristics of the spirits that had entered their bodies. The one who had been seized by the spirit of the Old Black Slave ambled stiffly around the altar, bent over with age and leaning on an imaginary cane. A thin young woman, seized by the spirit of Oxóssi the hunter, crept through invisible grass looking for game with an invisible rifle. The woman that Yansá chose staggered in circles with her hand over one ear, for this spirit, like Van Gogh, chopped off one of her ears, as a present for her lover.

With the hysterical writhings and contortions, the insistent drumming and the shrieks and moans from the dancers, the atmosphere inside the small and stuffy house became almost unbearable. I felt a current of electricity pass around the room and more than once the hairs on my arms stood up. A man in front of me began to twitch and shiver. He tossed his head back and groaned loudly. His companion immediately pushed his head down between his knees and then crossed his arms over the back of his neck. This calmed him. I began to wish that I had gone with the American to have a cigarette, because I felt that any minute I too would start to shiver and groan. I tried to ignore the drum beats by staring at the altar. I shifted positions several times in order to prove to my body that I was still its boss. The last of the dancers were becoming possessed, and while most of them had been led away into the back room others were still writhing and trying to follow the insistent, primitive rhythm.

Then it happened. A shriek from the women's side broke my concentration. The men around me gasped and the women spectators called out in astonishment, for who else but my scoffing American female friend had risen and was scrambling over benches and eluding outstretched hands in order to get to the altar.

Her eyes were open but she couldn't see. Her fingers tore at the air and her head shook so much one of her earrings came free. She twisted her body and shouted something—I am sure it wasn't English—and pushed through the group of white-clad dancers.

The priestess made a lunge for her and grabbed her by the waist. She struggled and lashed out at the woman, who was soon joined by her young assistant. Together they managed to grab her hands and bring her to a halt. I could tell by the expression on the face of the priestess that she was not at all happy with this sudden seizure.

She barked an order and the three drummers immediately changed their pace. She barked another and someone brought her a lighted cigar. The woman took a deep pull on the cigar, filled her mouth with smoke and, still holding the hands of my friend, began blowing the smoke in her eyes, on each side of her head and over her heart.

The priestess let the American woman's hands free and she remained fixed, but her body still shook uncontrollably. Then the Negress blew smoke on her legs, her feet and her back. As if pulling off some disgusting pieces of filth, the priestess grabbed at the air around the American's body and threw invisible evils to the floor. She began to chant, and the drummers took up the new rhythm. She moved around and around the white woman, blowing smoke from the cigar and pulling away the evil. Then she faced the visitor, took her two hands in hers and jerked them as if she wanted to pull her arms out of their sockets. She did this three times, then embraced the woman and turned her toward the door.

It was then that my friend began to weep. She came out of her trance and started to sob. I jumped up but arms around me pulled me back onto the bench. Crying but making almost no noise, she walked slowly and alone up the aisle and out the door. The priestess looked at me, shook her head in the affirmative and smiled. Hands on my shoulders were released and I hurried outside to see what had happened.

On the way back to their air-conditioned, televisioned, deep-freezered twentieth-century apartment, the American woman, once she had stopped crying, tried to figure out what had happened to her. She remembered nothing except sitting there and letting the drum beats soak into her bones and then finding herself walking out of the house in tears. The few minutes she had been struggling and clawing and being worked on by the priestess she could not recall or explain. Her husband said she had been hypnotized. I told her that I too had felt the electricity in the room. Her husband repeated that it was just old-fashioned hypnotism, adding that he was surprised that either one of us "in this day and age" would think that it could be anything else.

To claim that I was unimpressed by this ceremony would be a bold-faced lie. Not only was I impressed, I was also bothered. What was it that made this skeptical, U.S.-educated white woman do those crazy things? She had been in a trance, there was no other word for it. But why? She did not believe in ghosts or disembodied spirits, and I rather doubt if she really believed in God or a life hereafter. Yet she had fought to approach the primitive altar with all those cheap, gaudy statues on it, had made herself ridiculous in her husband's eyes, had suffered the indignity of being thrown out of a pagan ceremony that had been invented by ignorant Africans and brought across to Brazil by terrified slaves. It made no sense.

And my reaction? Why had my arms been covered in goose pimples from time to time? Goose pimples are due to cold weather, and that humble house had been stifling hot. Why had I felt that electricity in the air and been afraid that if someone had lighted a match the whole place would have exploded? And why did I keep shifting my body on that hard bench in order to prove to myself that I too was not about to go under a spell? Was it all hocus-pocus? Was it just damned good theater? Was it hypnotism? Was it for real?

It was then that I decided to look into this Brazilian spirit business seriously.

3

Brazilian spiritism is not really Brazilian. . . . It all began generations ago in the jungles of Africa.

The continent may have been "dark," "unknown" and "forbidding" to Europeans when they first began to talk and write about it, but as we know now, it was also complex, well organized into tribal boundaries and had a culture all its own. Anyone studying the bronzes of Benin, for example, must admire the craftsmanship and culture of these supposed "savage" peoples.

Slavers brought "civilization" to Africa; the very nature of their profession broke up and destroyed African cultures and traditions. Instead of bringing tribal folklore, wit and philosophy to the New World, the slavers brought bodies. When they arrived in a village they often found it deserted, the temples destroyed to save them from white defilement and the gods broken and burned. The slavers were not interested in tradition; they wanted salable meat and muscles. Tribal priests and learned men were not taken captive as a rule, for they were usually old and not worth much on the white man's market. Traditions and knowledge that had, for generations on end, been passed from father to son were wiped out in a single raid.

Then too, these black people were pagans. They did not worship Christ or even know who He was. Therefore many enlightened slave owners considered these blacks as non-humans or some offshoot of the human race that was so far down on mankind's family tree that they were almost animals. (Catholic priests arriving in Mexico and Peru did not consider the pagan Indians human either.) There was no moral law saying that man could not buy horses and use them to plow his fields, therefore there was nothing morally wrong in buying these black animals to work the fields too.

Tribes were raided, destroyed, shackled and transported. Families were broken up, mothers separated from children, lovers sold to different traders, members of the same village shipped to different parts of the world. The cruelties of slave gathering and transporting were rivaled only by Hitler's oppressions in Europe two hundred years later.

It is to the disgrace of the Portuguese people that they began the international slave trade. They had explored the Guinea coast and had sailed around the Cape of Good Hope and they claimed the right to all the African continent. They were granted it. In 1493 Pope Alexander VI issued two papal bulls giving them what he didn't own: Africa.

The Portuguese began to build forts along the coast and depots where slaves could be held for shipment. The first fort was almost a castle, with walls thirty feet thick and high towers looking out over the sea and the jungle. Two moats, cut through solid rock, kept intruders away on land, and four hundred cannon were mounted to keep them away by sea. In the dungeons were manacles and space for one thousand slaves. So pleased was the Portuguese Emperor João II that he called the fort of Alminia "my Guinea castle" and added the title of "Lord of Guinea" to all his other titles.

Their main customers at that time were on the island of Haiti. Spaniards wishing to plant sugar and spices used local Indians as workers. At first they paid them in food and beads and then found it more economical to enslave them. The Indians, fragile and peaceable people, were not used to toiling for hours in the sun. Those who rebelled were killed. Tribes were uprooted and the Indians kept like cattle in corrals. Often a score of innocent Indians were burned alive in front of the other Indians in the hope that this punishment would convince the survivors to work harder.

A young priest, Bartolomé de Las Casas, was in Haiti at that time and was appalled by what he saw. He was afraid that the entire indigenous race on the island would be exterminated and he determined to save it. In 1517 he returned to Madrid and managed a private audience with Holy Roman Emperor Charles V (King Charles I). The priest explained the Indians' situation and asked that they be spared this work. The King, who had succeeded Ferdinand and Isabella, agreed that the plight of the Indian was grim but reminded the young cleric that the fields and the mines needed to be worked, and if the Indians were freed from his labor, who would take their place? Las Casas had the answer: Bring in Negro slaves. There were already a few on the island, they seemed "happy" and were hard workers. It would be an act of mercy to the Indians to import more Negroes, at least twelve for each colonist. After all, Las Casas had baptized many of these Indians and they were Christians now. The blacks were subhuman pagans.

Charles V agreed to the plan more from the knowledge that the Indians were worthless to him than from any piety toward them. He had heard that blacks were stronger and worked harder. The Indians were dying off and something would have to be done within a few years anyway. The King granted one of his favorite men at court the right to ship four thousand Negroes to the West Indies. This grant was the famous "Asiento," a legal document that was to be fought over and would cause the deaths of thousands of Englishmen, Frenchmen and Dutchmen as they fought to get legal control of the lucrative slave trade to the Spanish New World. The favored courtier, however, had no idea of the worth of this paper and certainly had no intention of leaving the comfortable palace to go off and capture a bunch of blacks and start traveling with them all over the Atlantic Ocean. So he sold the paper to some Italian merchants, who immediately placed an order for the slaves with the Portuguese. The famous slave trade had begun.

Haiti prospered, as did the other West Indian islands, because the imported Negroes really did work harder and produce more than the Indians. A colonist noted that "the work of one Negro was more than equal to the work of four Indians and that unless a Negro should happen to be hung he would never die, for as yet none have been known to perish from infirmity." By 1540 the original authorization of four thousand slaves had been forgotten, and ten thousand Negroes *a year* were being shipped to the West Indies. By the end of the century it was estimated that nine hundred thousand human beings had been shipped from Africa to the West Indies, Mexico and South America. The well-intentioned Las Casas, now a bishop, saw with horror where his idea had led. Instead of the Indians being left alone, they had been exterminated to make room for the imported Africans. Shortly before he died, he wrote "it is as unjust to enslave Negroes as Indians and for the same reasons."

Slaves came to Brazil for "the same reasons" they had been brought into Haiti: The Indians refused to work or else died off, leaving the plantations without unskilled labor. The Portuguese who had discovered and colonized Brazil were, above all, merchants. They let the Spaniards search for gold and fabulous cities (although they were jealous as hell of Spanish successes) as they concentrated upon sugar, spices, cotton and coffee. All of Europe waited for their products and paid whatever price was asked. The royal coffers in Lisbon swelled with gold coin and Brazil was considered as valuable as any crown jewel.

The first Africans came to Brazil about 1550. The need for slaves was on the farms near Salvador and Recife, the Brazilian northeast. They were rounded up in the area that today stretches from Senegal down to Angola. They were of good height and dark-skinned. Because of some intermixing from the Arab races to the north they were not all jet black like the so-called "true Negro" of the Congo and interior. They were mostly coastal Negroes dominated by the Yoruba culture, and it was this culture that was eventually replanted on the shores of Brazil.

The great linguistic and cultural achievements of the Yorubas were developed in the region today known as Southern Nigeria. Before the slavers came there were three million people organized into powerful states and kingdoms with their own cities, priesthoods, armies and political systems. It was a complex of Negro and Mohammedan ideas and beliefs, and the most powerful state to emerge from it was Benin.

It was described by the first white man ever to see it, in 1485, as "a magnificent empire of bronze." Later a Dutchman wrote that it was "a city larger than Amsterdam, with sumptuous palaces and wooden colonnades set with bronze plaques depicting battle scenes." The ruler was the *oba*, who was considered a god and the immediate reincarnation of his predecessor. The *oba* demanded human sacrifices and strict obedience to a pantheon of deities and spirits. These divinities were all-seeing and all-powerful. There was no way to escape them. Some were good and some were evil but they could all be called upon and reasoned with. These Yoruba spirits became, like the Greek gods, almost intimate members of the family. They were talked to, pleaded with and cajoled with special gifts. While they were all terrifying and powerful, they were also strangely "human."

Olorun was the highest of them all. He was their Zeus and their Jehovah. His name still turns up in Yoruba everyday conversations, as in *Olorun-shanu* ("Thank God!"), *Olorun yia busi* ("God bless you!") and *Ki Olorun kio sowa*

Drum and Candle

("May God keep us in perfect health until the morning"). He has other names as well, such as Alaye: Lord of Life, Elemi: the Spirit, etc. but they are as confusing to the Western reader as they must be to a Yoruba novice. This Olorun was unapproachable, at least directly. There was no cult in his honor because he was just too powerful. He had to be talked to through intermediaries, who were second-class divinities called Orishas. The Orishas were probably a carry-over from the Yoruba kings, who never lowered themselves to speak directly to their subjects. Only through their ministers and courtiers could the common man get a message across. (Which, after all, is not any different from the Olorun in the White House or the Olorun in Buckingham Palace.)

Like courtiers on earth, the Orishas were numerous and very self-important. It has been estimated that there were over six hundred of them, all with different names and all with the ability to get through to the big boss. But these spirits were more than just messengers, they were a force of nature, something from the supernatural. Every man, woman and child had his own particular Orisha who looked after him. It was a kind of personalized guardian angel. To find out which one was intercepting your messages and taking care of you, you asked the local priest. He knew, and often at a kind of baptismal ceremony the parents of a newborn child were told to which Orisha the child should pray. There might be seven members in the family and seven different spirits to placate. Just because your mother was in the line of Oyá didn't mean you would have that angel too. While it must have been confusing, it did give each family a lot of different holy days to celebrate, for the Yorubas, like the Brazilians, love any reason to stop the daily routine and have a party.

Now each Orisha had to be worshiped in a different way. They all liked to eat but they liked to eat different things. Some wanted bowls of rice, others a pot of beans and still others a shot of alcohol. They all liked beads and appreciated getting them often, but the novice had to know what color his particular Orisha preferred. Some divinities wanted a gift of perfume, some insisted upon cigars and others only accepted a black chicken.

Yoruba mythology is far more complicated than either the Greek or Roman but like our "classical" gods the African deities were fond of food, drink, battle and sex. And not always in that order.

When Olorun decided that he was just too busy to speak to the earthlings he had created, he took a handful of clay and created a masculine Orisha named Obatalá. Then he created a female Orisha and named her Odudua. Their Garden of Eden was on the island of Ifé, which has remained the religious center of the Yoruba spirit world until today. Obatalá represented the heavens, while his wife represented the earth. He protected the cities and temples and usually carried a spear. He was so pure he always wore white. His followers also wore white. Odudua, the typical "earth mother," was not quite as pure as her husband. She was more interested in procreating, and her amorous adventures helped populate the earth.

This black Adam and Eve (but with incredible powers that our first ancestors were never given) had a son named Aganjú and a daughter Yemanjá. They married each other (horrors! cry the Victorians) and had a son named Orungan. As if this was not bad enough, when the son got older he fell in love with his mother. Freud and Oedipus still being unknown, the boy waited until his father was away visiting someone up in heaven to tell his mother how he felt about her. She, naturally, was shocked by the whole idea, and when she saw the gleam of lust in his eye she tried to run away. It was useless and he knocked her to the ground and raped her.

Yemanjá was now so disgusted and ashamed with what had happened that she hurried into the jungle and tried to hide from the world, but her belly began to grow and grow. She fell onto her back and from her breasts came two streams of water, which quickly formed a great lake. Then her womb burst open and out came the hierarchy of Yoruba Orishas. There was Shango, the god of thunder; Olokun, god of the sea; Oyá, goddess of the river Niger; Orishakó, god of agriculture; Oshun, goddess of the river Oshun; Obá, goddess of the river Obá; Dada, god of vegetables; Okê, god of the hills and mountains; Ajê Shaluga, god of gold and wealth; Oshossi, god of the hunters; and (unfortunately) Ogun, the god of war. As if eleven children at one time was not quite enough, she also gave birth to the sun and the moon.

Yemanjá thus became the mother of everybody important and the most venerated woman in Yoruba theology, even surpassing her own mother Odudua. Her name comes from *Yeye*, meaning mother, and *Eja*, meaning fish. Thus she was the mother of the fish and the mother of the waters.

Shango was probably the most important of all her children. As the god of thunder all he had to do was open his mouth for the heavens to darken and the earth to shake. He was very masculine and had several wives. He was wealthy and cruel and lorded over his subjects with the fact that he was the firstborn son of Yemanjá. But he too could be brought down to size.

One day his grandfather Obatalá decided to visit his kingdom to see how the Orisha was getting along. Hearing that Shango had become a tyrant (and what politician wouldn't if he could bring on thunder each time he opened his mouth?), the god of the heavens transformed himself into an old man and limped through the jungles until he reached the limits of Shango's realm. No sooner had he arrived than he saw a horse standing in a cornfield. The horse's mouth was tied and Obatalá knew it was hungry. So he untied the rope and picked several ears of corn and fed the horse. Just then servants of Shango came running up to him. The horse had been stolen, they told the old man, and asked him what he was doing there. The god in disguise, not wanting to give himself away, replied that he was merely passing through. The servants accused him of having stolen the horse and began to beat him with wooden clubs. Then they took him and threw him into prison. The old man asked to see Shango but was only laughed at.

Then seven years of disgrace fell upon the kingdom of Shango. The crops withered, the lakes dried and the fish died. The women became sterile and, worst of all, Shango became impotent. Shango finally humbled himself enough to ask his priests what had happened to bring about such calamities. He was told that there was an old man in prison who had suffered great injustices. Quickly Shango had the prisoner brought before him and saw at once that it was his grandfather. Ashamed of his arrogance and his mistreatment, he ordered his servants to dress only in white, to make not a sound and to bring water and wash the old man. Humbled in front of his subjects, Shango became a deity worthy of respect once more. Also, his sexual prowess returned.

It was good that those powers returned when they did, for Shango had two very demanding wives to satisfy, his sisters Oshun and Oyá. Oshun was very pretty and very wise; she knew how to hold both her temper and her man. Oyá, to the contrary, was rather ordinary-looking and very jealous of her husband's other wife. One day Oyá asked Oshun how she managed to keep such a strong hold on Shango. "Very easy," said her sister. "He is like all mortal men and must be conquered through the stomach." Oyá didn't understand, so her sister said, "Come to my kitchen this evening and I will show you my secret."

When Oyá arrived Oshun was stirring a huge pot of soup in which floated many pieces of mushroom. She had her head wrapped in a white kerchief. "You see those pieces there?" she asked Oyá. "Those are pieces of my ear. I cut it off to put into the soup because Shango just loves soup made with female ears."

Oyá thanked her several times and rushed off to her own kitchen. She put water on to boil, scraped several vegetables and then chopped off one of her ears and threw it in the pot. When the soup was ready she carried it to Shango's table. Oshun was there serving him her soup as well. When Shango saw the human ear floating in the soup and saw the open wound and the blood streaming down Oyá's face he became disgusted and ordered Oyá to leave his house. Oyá grabbed for the white kerchief around Oshun's head and pulled it off. The goddess still had both her ears. Furious, Oyá threw herself onto her rival and started beating her. Shango bellowed and out came thunder and flame. The two women ran in terror and when they reached the jungle turned into two rivers that bear their names today. If you ever cross the river Niger never mention Oshun's name or the waters will rise up and pull you under. The same goes for the river Oshun. When these two rival spirits happen to descend at the same ceremony, there is always a battle and the priests must use force to separate them.

Ogun is the god of war and the god of metal. The Yorubas, having spears and shields of bronze, were able to conquer many backward tribes. Ogun also helped hunters aim their arrows and find herds of game, but he demanded a sacrifice of a living dog. Blacksmith shops in modern Nigeria often have dog skulls as testimony to their patron saint.

Orishakó is not just the god of agriculture. He is worshiped by the Yoruba women as the god of fertility. He is the one Orisha who has women rather than men as priests. The women have formed secret societies within the cult and remind some scholars of the girls who dedicated themselves to Aphrodite. He is, of course, also responsible for the harvests, and special services are said for him with every new moon.

When the harvest is in, there is a gigantic celebration with singing, dancing and processions.

Oshossi lives in the forest and protects hunters against wild animals, getting lost and dangerous rivers and swamps. He also helps the arrow find its mark.

Olokun, the Yoruba Neptune, once became very angry with the men on earth. He considered them ingrates for everything the sea had given them. He resolved to wash them into oblivion. He caused the waters to swell and rise up into the heavens. The rains came down in torrents day after day after day. Slowly the human race began to drown, and their bodies filled the great rivers as they were carried toward the bottom of the sea. Finally Obatalá had to intervene and send Olokun back to his watery palace. And this time there wasn't a Noah singled out to be saved, either!

The birth of twins is a mystery in most primitive religions and is received either with joy as a good omen or with despair as an act of evil. Sometimes the children are killed, more often one is killed so that the spirit may enter the surviving body to make it "complete." For the Yoruba a double birth meant that their ideas of a human life and a heavenly soul were correct and that the child born right after the twins would come into the world with supernatural powers. The birth of twins is a sign that fortune and happiness will come to the parents. Twins are treated equally, always. It would be an offense to favor one over the other. Naturally they have their own Orisha, the Ibeji twins. The image of this deity is two figures on one base and must be shared between the two children. Should one child die, the remaining one must venerate the image as his own brother and set out part of his food and drink for the statue.

Because disease and death are everywhere, the Orisha Sakpata must be constantly appeased. His devotees wear the finest jewels they can afford, paint their bodies with bright colors and sing happily during the ceremonies. No one wants to offend him, for he keeps disease away, especially smallpox and leprosy.

Two other beings were created somehow and somewhere after the main Orishas were delivered into the jungle world. They are Ifá and Exú. Ifá is a kind of high priest who hears the prayers and decides whether or not to send them on to the other Orishas to be delivered to the mighty Olorun. After all, with so many people praying around the world, Olorun hasn't time to listen to all those requests! (Ifá's high position, some say, is because he was created along with the Yoruba Adam and Eve and is their brother, but there is some doubt about this.) Exú helps in sending these messages and making contact with the other Orishas. He also is a guardian of temples, houses and villages. But there are times when he doesn't seem to take his work seriously and will deliberately mix up prayers and requests just to watch the confusion it causes man. Sometimes he will show up in the middle of a ceremony without being called and cause so much mischief that everything stops until the priest can send him away. Just because he acts likes a mischievous boy doesn't mean that you can scold him or punish him for his misdeeds, because he will become furious and bring all sorts of disgrace down upon you. Even death!

These were the gods and spirits that the Africans worshiped and feared before the white man came with his manacles and whips. These were the friends they had who kept them in good health, guaranteed them good crops, looked after their children, blessed their homes, gave them food and drink and cared for them after they were dead. They believed in them, they worshiped them and they needed them.

The powerful leaders of the Yoruba tribes were the first ones to sell their fellow men over to the slavers. Slavery between tribes, with blacks owning blacks, existed long before the Europeans turned it into big business. Nations plundered each other, putting strong men to work, turning pretty women

Drum and Candle

into servants and concubines and raising children for future trading much in the way we today raise cattle. Slavery did not begin with the white man but goes back to the time of the cave man. We humans have never had much compassion for anybody but ourselves.

The Yorubas were the masters of vast areas of Africa. Their language was spoken by tribes scattered for hundreds of miles along the coast and in the interior, into the Sudan and across the Sahara. They, like the Romans, had their military outposts and their political contacts. They knew what was going on and who had to be bribed to get certain things done. When the Portuguese arrived to put up their slave castle, the Yorubas were not anxious to have them there, but when such luxuries as rifles, bolts of cloth, beads, perfumes and gold were offered in payment for unwashed, uneducated enemies, the temptation was too great. The Yorubas agreed to supply the Portuguese with human beings. First they raided their farthest enemies, then their nearby friendly neighbors, and finally they began to kidnap and sell each other.

The Portuguese were driven out of Yoruba territory by the Dutch, who took over the slaving business only to be forced out by the Swedes, who were kicked out by the Danes, who were removed by a local tribe who were then captured by the English, who were expelled by the Dutch, who were later pushed into the sea by the English, who, although they kept the territory, had regular battles with the French and local native tribes. Everybody wanted to get into the act. And what a lucrative act it was!

One English slaver, Captain John Hawkins, managed to acquire three hundred Negroes "partly by sword and partly by other means" and traded them in Haiti and Cuba for hides, sugar, ginger and pearls. When Queen Elizabeth heard of the venture she damned it as being "detestable" and was sure that it would bring "vengeance from heaven upon the undertakers." But when Hawkins returned to London he showed Elizabeth his profit sheet from the single voyage. Her Majesty was so impressed with the money he made that she gave him another ship and went into partnership with him.

Another Englishman loaded his ship with secondhand furniture and traded it to a local chieftain for a cargo of slaves. His profits were enough for him to buy and outfit five new ships.

Even as late as 1858 a Southern trader made plans to go to Africa and buy twelve hundred slaves for merchandise worth $75,000. He calculated that he could sell each slave for $650 apiece, "which would leave a profit of $715,000 and still have the vessel on hand."

Slave-selling was a frightening procedure. Although sometimes entire shiploads were purchased as single lot, the European buyers usually bought their cargo man by man. A slave ship captain once described this process after being offered several hundred natives by a local king:

> . . . and our surgeon examined them well in all kinds, to see that they were sound in wind and limb, making them jump, stretch out their arms swiftly, looking in their mouths to judge their age; for the [suppliers] are so cunning that they shave them all close before we see them, so that let them be ever so old we can see no gray hairs on their heads or beards; and then having liquor'd them well and sleeked [them] with palm oil, 'tis no easy matter to know an old one from a middle-aged one, but by the teeth's decay.

He added that the women were separated from the men during the voyage to prevent "quarrels and wranglings" and that the crew always had to be on the lookout for the disease of yaws, which he compared to *Lues Venerea* or clap." He complained that the ship doctors had to examine the sex organs of both men and women, "which is a great slavery, but what can't be omitted."

Afterward the selected slaves were branded.

It is difficult for any modern reader to imagine what it

must have been like to be sold suddenly into slavery. It's difficult to put ourselves into the place of an ignorant black tribesman. To be suddenly uprooted by death and destruction from our families and friends, marched for days through the impossibly hot jungle shackled to the man in front and behind with iron collars that dig into our flesh and leg irons that wear away a little more of our skin with each step. Then to come out suddenly upon the sea. How many of us have never seen the sea! We were used to our own rivers and streams but here was an incredible expanse of water with waves crashing upon the shore and offering certain death to any of us who ventured into it.

Then to stand upon the shore, be told to jump up and down, to move our arms and legs and to have our sex organs examined by strangers and in front of all those other people. Then a sudden searing on our flesh that makes us faint more often than not. Then water thrown on us to revive us so we can walk to a small boat and be taken across those terrifying waves to be put deep inside a huge wooden ship, a ship bigger and more frightening than anything we have ever seen on any river before. A vessel that could only belong to the devil himself.

Payments for these slaves were made in trade goods. English slavers traded woolens and linens from Manchester and Yorkshire as well as calicoes from India and silks from China, along with English-made knives and swords, muskets and powder, brass tubs and iron bedsteads. Strangely enough, old bed sheets were very much in demand, as were glass beads, tall silk hats and bottles of whisky. Each section of the slave coast had its own preferences in trade goods. In some places a slave's value was reckoned in bars of iron. In Lower Guinea it was in so many "pieces" of cloth, gallons of rum or strings of beads. The area off Nigeria preferred sea shells called "cowries," which when strung together in lots of forty shells became a "toque." A slave's value was reckoned in terms of how many toques he was worth. No matter what was used for currency, it didn't take too many pounds, dollars or gold bars to fill a slave hold.

It was not easy to get the newly purchased cargo into these holds, for many Negroes believed that they were being sent away from their homeland to be eaten by whites across the sea. Hundreds of them threw themselves into the water before they could be put aboard the big ships; some refused to be saved and actually seemed to be glad to be devoured by sharks rather than be taken away from the African coast.

Statistics differ on exactly how many slaves were brought to Brazil before the practice was finally outlawed in 1888, because when abolition was declared all incriminating slavery documents were burned, but estimates place the total somewhere around 3,600,000. The West India Company delivered 15,430 slaves to Brazil between the years 1619 and 1623. The British Foreign Office reported that 37,000 Negroes were imported to Brazil in 1829 and another 50,000 in the first six months of 1830. The Brazilians had signed an international treaty in 1829 declaring they wouldn't bring in any more slaves, but no one had any intention of seeing it enforced. The British finally had to attack slave boats heading toward Brazil, and in 1849 a British squadron destroyed every slaver it found along the coast. As late as 1860 an English captain reported that he had been in Rio and saw in the harbor "several clipper-built, suspicious-looking vessels, all legs and wings, long-lined hulls . . . with impudent skysail-yards across. By the number of this kind of craft I would imagine that the Brazilians are still doing a large trade in human beings."

The Portuguese ships that carried future Brazilians toward the New World were no better or worse than those of the English, Dutch or French. The only concession the slaves received was that they were duly baptized by a Catholic priest as they were taken aboard. After being assured of a place in heaven they were assigned a berth in hell.

Ships that had been built for transporting cotton, silks and rum were converted into slavers. This meant that the hold, often no more than six feet in depth, was partitioned into platforms. The slaves were made to lie face up on the rough floor, and when it was completely packed a false deck was placed above them and a second layer of slaves was forced into the space. Often there was not more than twenty inches of room over their heads, which meant that while they could breathe they could not sit up or move around for the entire voyage. They urinated and defecated where they lay, and their food was passed to them in flat tins. Once a week, if the sailors had time, the slaves were allowed to come up on deck and the filth of their holds was washed clean. This practice was abandoned after a while because the slaves often rebelled and tried to kill their captors at washing time.

Mutinous slaves were killed as an example to others. So were sickly or diseased slaves. Once when an English patrol ship, toward the end of the slavers' history, approached a Portuguese slaver bound for Rio, the captain ordered his men to slit the throats of all 920 slaves and throw their bodies overboard. Often drunken sailors would enter the women's hold and rape the female slaves. On other occasions sailors with homosexual tendencies would single out healthy young male slaves for their fun and frolics. Any who refused were butchered.

A doctor aboard one of these slave ships wrote to his wife: "The slaves sing, but not for their amusement. They sing songs of sorrow. Their sickness, fear of being beaten, their hunger and the memory of their country, etc. are the usual subjects."

The slaves sang, and when they sang they prayed. They prayed to all the gods and spirits they had left behind.

Crowded in the hold, almost dead from disease, starvation

and the lash, they knew there was no escape, for under them and all around them was the terrifying sea. They remembered Yemanjá, the goddess who had created other Orishas, the goddess who was the mother of the fish and the mother of the waters. They begged her to take care of them. They sang and beseeched her not to let them drown. When a storm came up they sang to Yemanjá, asking her to calm the waters, for they were terrified and ill. They asked her protection constantly. There was no use asking the god of the rocks, or the god of agriculture or the protector of cities. They were out over the water and the water belonged to Mother Yemanjá. They cried her name aloud and whispered fervent thanks when the waters under them calmed.

Then they arrived on Brazilian soil. They were more dead than alive but they *were* alive. Yemanjá had listened to them and had delivered them from the terrors of the sea. She was magnificent. She was all-powerful. In Africa she was only the mother of the various Orishas, but now that they had arrived she was as great as the Creator himself. They had called to her and she had answered. She had saved their lives and given them a chance to start anew. She was to be venerated.

4

Yemanjá had arrived, and the others followed immediately.

The slaves were sheltered on Brazilian soil, examined and sold. In the beginning almost all of them came to the northeast plantations around Salvador and Recife. They found, to their great relief, that they were not going to be eaten by the white man, but were to work instead in his cotton patches, his sugar-cane fields and his houses.

The early Portuguese settling Brazil did exactly what the Spaniards did in Haiti and Cuba. They enslaved the Indians, who died off rapidly or fled into the interior. On an island it was easy to catch a runaway Indian, but in gigantic Brazil it was almost impossible. The colonists knew that their own countrymen were selling blacks around the world and it was to the crown's advantage to import as many as they could. Brazil was not, as had been hoped, full of golden cities like those the Spaniards found in Mexico and Peru. What it did have was a good climate and excellent soil. It meant that Brazil could, with planning, supply all of Europe with spices and sugar. It also meant that a lot of work would be needed.

The Portuguese were not afraid of work. Unlike the Spaniards, they were not averse to rolling up their sleeves and pitching in. Their tiny nation had managed to discover new continents, claim vast colonies and become international leaders in commerce exactly because they were willing to work. No one ever gave the Portuguese anything; in fact, people kept trying to take what they already had.

In order to set up an agricultural empire on the new continent the colonists needed a work force. There were too few of them even to attempt doing the work alone without slave labor. There were no tractors, harvesting machines and cotton gins in those days. The only machine was the human machine, and the Portuguese already had a monopoly on it right on the coast of Nigeria.

The Portuguese have another trait that helped them get ahead in the New World: thriftiness. They know how to make money and they also know how not to spend it. Modern Brazil is full of Portuguese immigrants who run little coffee stalls and snack shops, bakeries, restaurants and grocery stores. Many of these businesses stay open seven days a week with the entire family working a sixteen-hour day with as little outside help as possible. They live on the premises, if possible, and make their own clothes. After ten or fifteen years of this they go back to Portugal, buy a farm or a town house and live a life of ease. Brazilians criticize them but do nothing to emulate them.

With this basic national trait of thrift it was only natural that the Portuguese masters treated their slaves well. What was the use of spending all that money on a slave and then mistreating it so badly that it died? Why deny the slaves decent food if this food kept them healthy and good workers? Why beat them and make them resentful when a happy slave was a better worker?

This is not to say that slaves were not beaten and at times killed by the Portuguese, because they were, but it was usually to punish a man for a wrongdoing rather than just to keep him miserable. If a slave was tortured it was done for a definite reason and in front of the others to keep them in line. Seldom did a Portuguese master slaughter groups of slaves just because he was angry or set one free for the sport of later hunting him down, as the Spaniards did. A slave cost money, he was a valuable piece of property.

The early colonists were family men. They had been taught to respect their fathers and grandfathers and to honor the idea of a family unit. A family, for a Portuguese, is the center of his world. Mama's table loaded with food, Papa's pipe and favorite chair, visiting Aunt Maria's house on Saturday, going to Mass with all the cousins on Sunday. This love of family made the great navigators return home, and as home was also the nation of Portugal, "home" meant both the parental dwelling and the Emperor's palace.

But being a family man in Brazil was not easy, because very few married men volunteered to come to the new colony. Their wives didn't want to leave their families. So single men and widowers came first. They marked out their tracts of land, built houses and bought slaves; but there was something missing . . . a wife.

Had they been British or Dutch the newcomers would 1) have arrived with their own women and 2) never have thought of taking a native or a Negro girl into wedlock. But the Portuguese had very little racial prejudice and soon every bachelor household had a dark-skinned mistress and several light-skinned babies playing around the door.

The Portuguese settlers had every inclination to begin a "melting pot" in Brazil, for they were the most racially mixed people of Europe. Miscegenation did not start in Brazil. It started long before, between the Portuguese and the Moor, the African, and the Negro.

Portugal is just a day or two across the waters to Africa's northwest coast. It was overrun with Romans and their slaves and overrun again by the Visigoths and their slaves. In the year A.D. 711 the Moslems grabbed the land and Arabs and Berbers built upon it, organized it and populated it. The Arabs were dark-skinned and romantic. Their passion was religion and voluptuous dark-eyed women. Examples of their lavish architecture can be seen scattered all over the tiny nation, and the traces of the Arabic language are more than noticeable even in modern spoken Portuguese. For six hundred years everything African dominated the land, so that when Christian soldiers finally managed to expulse the Moors in 1383, the people were so mixed that it was hard to tell who was who without a program. Six hundred years of cultural domination is a long, long time in anybody's history and not easily erased in a generation or two. Brazil was discovered only 117 years after the Arab *political* influence in Portugal had been destroyed, certainly not time enough for the Arab *cultural* impact to have been wiped out and replaced by the culture of pure-blooded whites and devout followers of Holy Rome. When the first African slaves were brought to Brazil, Portugal had been free of the Arabs for only some 167 years or a mere six generations. There was not the mass-media communication then that we have today, and very little of their Arabian heritage (and six hundred years is a heritage!) had been "re-educated" out of the Portuguese people. True, the Catholic Church had crushed the Moslem religion and forbidden it to be practiced anywhere in the country, but many of the most magnificent Catholic houses of worship were nothing but reconverted Moslem mosques. Arab dress was no longer worn but styles are always changing anyway. The Spaniards had also suffered under the Moslem invasion and had (with typical severity) purged their language of any Arabic influences, chopping out old words and replacing them with new ones. The victorious Christians spoke a Romance dialect and simply melded it with the Mozarabic language that was spoken by everyone during the Moorish domination. Thus the "Portuguese" language was born.

The young sugar and cotton planters were, therefore, more than ready to establish interracial marriages and households. Colonizers of other nationalities would never have gone so far with these so-called "inferior races" and probably would

Drum and Candle

have passed laws against any interracial affairs and marriages. Brazil's top sociologist, Gilberto Freyre, defines this instant miscegenation beautifully:

> For this they had been prepared by the intimate terms of social and sexual intercourse on which they had lived with the colored races that had invaded their own peninsula or were close neighbors to it, one of which, the Mohammedan faith, was technically more highly skilled and possessed an intellectual and artistic culture superior to that of the blond Christians. . . . Long contact with the Saracens had left (with them) the idealized figure of the "enchanted" Moorish woman, a charming type, brown-skinned, black-eyed, enveloped in sexual mysticism. . . . The brown-skinned woman was in fact preferred by the Portuguese for purposes of love, at least for purposes of physical love.

While Pizarro or Cortez may have taken a few Inca or Aztec girls to bed, they formed no long alliances with any nor did they found families. Spanish noblewomen came from Madrid to wed the brave conquistadores, and a rigid European-above-all caste system was created that still shows up in Mexican and Peruvian high society. The Portuguese who came to Brazil didn't give a damn about a woman's title or the color of her skin. If she could cook, keep his house clean and perform in bed he was satisfied.

The slave women were also satisfied. Many of them, torn from their past, dumped in the hold of a ship like sacks of merchandise and certain that they were to be eaten by their white masters, were pleasantly surprised to find themselves in positions of power and influence. It was well worth sleeping with the master if he allowed them to walk around unchained, if he gave them beautiful clothes and the command of his kitchen. Those who had envied wives of their tribal chief now considered themselves queens as they strolled with their mulatto babies and were waited upon by other slaves.

Drum and Candle

They were looked up to by the African men as well, for more than once a word from a slave wife would make a master put down his whip. More than once slave quarters were made more comfortable, better food was handed out and days of rest declared because the black wife of the white master asked him to help her people.

As generations passed and more white women emigrated from Portugal or were born and wed in Brazil, the sight of a white plantation owner with a black wife became less common. But the women were there anyway, as lovers, maids, cooks, advisers and, most importantly, nursemaids.

Never has any one profession done so much to influence an entire nation's personality as the profession of nursemaid. After the first, early years, when better houses were built and white (or almost white) wives had scores of servants, the children had their own nursemaids. Quite often the nursemaid was a wet nurse as well, for the imported white wives were young and sickly and didn't have the milk to feed their own children. A healthy slave woman, her breasts full of milk, was an indispensable part of every household.

The nurse fed the child, talked to it, cared for it and worried about it. The child, seeing more of this black woman than his own mother, grew to love her. He could sit and listen to her tell tales for hours. He was fascinated with the stories she invented about the spirits of the forest and the sea. He liked to visit the houses where the slaves lived, for they were always pleased to see him and welcomed him (as the young master) and let him eat from their cooking pots and roasting pans. If he had no brothers and sisters his own age he would play with slave children and think nothing of it, for a child only sees differences when adults start pointing them out.

As he grew older the child also learned what kind of leaf to pick to cure his stomach-ache, what kind of stone to carry in his pocket to bring him luck and how to make something happen by burying a frog or lighting a candle. He learned all these things often without his parents' being the wiser, because they only talked to him about plantation affairs, relatives coming to visit and catechism.

And he could not have helped but notice something else as well: The slaves had their own set of gods.

They often didn't show these gods to the master and they were careful to hide them from any Catholic priest, but with each new generation of Brazilian-born slaves and each new shipload of African brothers the gods of old took on more and more meaning.

Probably the most important thing that kept these gods alive was the fact that the traditional jungle spirits were *all* the slaves had. They did not own the land they tilled, they did not own the houses they lived in and, very often, they did not own the children they had borne. The white man and the wealthy half-breed master (and there were many of them later on) owned everything. The only things the slaves could rightfully call their own were these old country gods and spirits.

The second reason that the gods were so powerful was that they held the slaves together as a group. Families of slaves were broken up and shipped around the new colonies. Importers made sure that members of the same tribe were not sold in the same area. Those united by bonds of the same tribal language were carefully separated and not allowed to work or live together. All slaves were expected to speak to their masters and take orders in Portuguese. This was done to avoid groupings and diminish the chances of rebellion. What it did was to give the slaves something even more powerful to cling to: a firmly established religion.

The Portuguese didn't really care what their slaves believed in as long as they produced. The whites, as Catholics, were devout, yes, but they were not fanatics on the subject of religion the way the Spanish were. Their brand of Catholicism

was easygoing even at home, and now that they were so
far from Lisbon cardinals and Roman popes they became
even more casual in their worship. God existed, oh most
definitely, and he had sent Jesus to save men's souls, oh yes,
and the Virgin Mary was right up there at the top of the
list, but somehow in the lazy tropical climate of Brazil the
devil seemed far away, the pomp and awe-inspiring richness
of cathedral Mass was becoming a pleasant memory and the
Inquisition at home had been more concerned with converting
the Jews than frightening those already born as Christians.

So the slaves would hold their own services. They were
allowed a couple of drums (what harm did drums do?)
and permitted the use of an old shed or allowed to build
their own small church. As long as the sessions didn't end up
in fist fights and bodily damage to a slave, the master couldn't
have cared less.

In fact, in the beginning, he was even encouraged to let
his slaves blow off ancestral steam. An eighteenth-century
priest (and a Jesuit at that!) advised the white owners: "Let
[you] not be shocked when [your slaves] create their own
kings and sing and dance for hours, in a respectable manner,
on certain days of the year, nor if they amuse themselves
decently one afternoon, after having in the morning" he was
careful to point out, "observed the feasts of our Lady of the
Rosary, of St. Benedict, and of the patron saint of the plantation chapel. . . ."

The masters were glad for this advice because it made their
religious duties to their slaves that much easier. They did
have duties, legal duties set down by the Church of Lisbon,
that concerned their black workers' souls. Slaves were baptized upon being put aboard the ship for Brazil and often
branded with a small royal crown on their breasts to show
that they were then officially Christians. Upon arriving at a
plantation the slaves were expected to be treated as the

Christians they were and it was the master's obligation to teach them certain prayers and read from the lives of the saints. The Negroes were also expected to learn (even if they didn't understand) how to behave at Mass. After being in a master's possession for two years, the African newcomer was supposed to be given an examination by the Church to see if he had really become repentant of his pagan ways. The lack of ordained priests (then as now) made this law nothing but words on paper.

But the Portuguese was a Catholic and he did like to have his family and slaves around him on feast days, baptismals and Church holy days. There would be much pomp and Latin chanting as the smoke from the incense wafted around the various images of Our Lady, St. Peter and Christ on the cross. The slaves, given the day off on these important days, washed and put on their best clothes and attended the chanting and the praying eagerly. They were allowed into the family chapel and allowed to pray to the beautifully painted statues of white men and women. They admired the priest's fancy clothes and his gold cross. They tapped their feet to the chanting and shouted aloud when the Host was elevated. After the ceremony there would be tables loaded with fine foods, and they would be allowed to sing and dance for the master and his guests. A good time was had by all, and if this was what it meant to be a Christian, why, they had no objection at all.

At times a do-gooder Catholic priest would visit the plantation and insist on seeing the slave quarters. He would be appalled that there was an altar decorated with "magic" stones, pieces of "magic" wood and crude carved images of African spirits. He would demand to know why there was not a cross above the altar and an image of Our Lady as well as another image of St. Somebody who was the patron of that particular plantation. The white master would then have his slave artisans turn out a cross, a statue of the Virgin and another of the patron saint. He told the slaves to make sure they worshiped those images as well.

The slaves were delighted. They figured they could use all the help they could get, and if calling on their African spirits came to no avail, then maybe the master's spirits would turn the trick. In the world of ghosts and demons you can never have too many friends, and so the Negroes accepted the Catholic Orishas as well.

They were accepted and revered and within the passing of a few years they became interchangeable and identical. When vast quantities of Yoruba slaves arrived in the middle eighteenth century they found a religion waiting for them that was not only acceptable but encouraged. They were taken to areas all over the new colony and with them went their common language and their common beliefs.

Thus Olorun, who had been so powerful in Africa, was transformed into Jehovah and God the Father. But he lost something in translation. Even in the old days he refused to talk directly to his people and remained aloof and alone. The Negroes saw that the Christians had no image of him and said most of their prayers to his son and his son's mother. So Olorun was bypassed and almost forgotten, and his son Obatalá came into prominence. Obatalá had also been known among the Yorubas as Orixalá, and Brazilian-born slaves shortened his name to Oxalá. (The *x* in Portuguese is pronounced like a double *s*: Thus the god's name comes out Oh-ssha-lah.) In Africa Oxalá was the "god of purity" as well as the direct descendant of the Creator. It was an easy (and logical) step to meld him in with Jesus Christ.

Odudua, who was Oxalá's wife, fared not at all well in the New World. She was female and important in Africa, but it had been her daughter Yemanjá who had saved the slaves from a watery grave. They figured that they owed their very lives to Yemanjá and that she would be quite upset if they honored any other woman above her. So Odudua was forgotten and Yemanjá became identified with the Virgin Mary.

Shango, the most powerful of Yemanjá's explosively conceived children, had the spelling of his name changed to Xangó and became one and the same with both St. John the Baptist and St. Jerome. Xangó was the controller of thunder and the elements and both John and Jerome had mastered life in the harsh desert. St. Jerome had even lived with a lion, said the Catholic priests, and any saint man enough to do that must certainly be old womanizer and lightning-striker Xangó.

Xangó's wives Oshun and Oyá were also in the white man's list of saints, the slaves were happy to learn. The master referred to them as St. Barbara and St. Catherine. The master had some other female images that he called Mary Magdalene, St. Anne and St. Joan of Arc. The slaves took them onto their altars and promptly confused them all.

Ogun, who was the African god of war as well as iron, readily fit the image of St. George, who was killing a horrible dragon with an iron spear.

Oshossi, who had been a minor Orisha of hunters and the aimer of arrows, began to spell his name Oxóssi and was easily identified with St. Sebastian. Sebastian had been an esteemed officer in the Roman army and when he converted to Christianity the emperor ordered him executed. On the master's statue he was tied to a tree and filled with arrows. A natural for Oxóssi if there ever was one.

The Ibeji twins were also found in the minor hierarchy of Catholic saints. There they were, with white faces and called St. Cosmas and St. Damian.

Sakpata became Omulu in Brazil but was still protector against terrible diseases. He was matched up with St. Lazarus. Naturally.

Top messenger Ifá and his helper Exú were melded into just one spirit. Because he was mischievous and could even cause death and evil, he was melded with the white man's Satan. The Africans needed somebody from the nether world, and Satan was the perfect choice. Besides, his red body, long tail and horns made him much more a figure out of tribal folklore than Lisbon drawing rooms.

Now when the Catholic padres came snooping around they would see that the slaves were venerating the Christian spirits. Now when a visiting bishop asked about the spiritual condition of a plantation's blacks the master could take him into the slave temple and point out Jesus, Mary, St. George and the entire Roman Catholic heavenly host. If the bishop questioned the drum beating and the dancing in front of these holy images the master could only shrug his shoulders and reply that it was the natural Negro sense of rhythm. There was little the bishop could do but bless the happy Christians and go away, content that the houses in his domain were free from paganism. If the bishop was not content, and demanded that the rituals be stopped, the master would give him a weak promise to "do something about it." The master, by this time, was Brazilian-born and, having grown up among these slaves, knew what they were doing and often *believed* in these jungle spirits himself. Had he not grown up hearing about them from his black nurses? Hadn't he himself seen miraculous cures and inexplicable trances? Hadn't the priestess herself blessed his children when the padre had gone away after the baptism? Hadn't he seen the power of the evil eye make one of his slave's enemies shrivel up and die? And didn't he, at that very moment the bishop was lecturing him, have a tiny magic wooden fist attached to the gold cross and chain around his neck? He didn't want to stop these practices, for he was afraid of what would happen to him if he did. Not from the slaves themselves, but from the phalanx of spirits they would bring crashing down upon him.

It was at this time that black matriarchy and the power of the nursemaid came fully into force. In the jungles the men had been in charge of the spirit sessions and women played almost no part at all in the mysteries. But now in Brazil the men were working in the fields all day and the women had more time to organize ceremonies, prepare the special spirit foods and take care of the primitive temples. The women also had special access to the main household. They gained the confidence of the white family and were allowed more liberty than the men. Female cooks got what they wanted by special meals for the master. Maids ran errands for their mistresses and were entrusted with secrets. The white daughters, cooped up inside the main house, often had no one to confide in but their slave servants. If they said that they wanted to marry a certain gentleman on another plantation, the black maid would promise to ask the spirits to intervene. Lovesick daughters would often slip out at midnight with their maids and carefully follow instructions as to toad burying, cross planting or candle burning. The female servants prepared potions, powders and special perfumes that were supposed to bring about a new love, keep an errant husband at home or assure the safe birth of a child.

Witchcraft and sorcery began to go hand in hand with High Mass and the Rosary. African amulets were worn under dresses. Small packets of magic herbs were slept on under pillows. Special foods were cooked and eaten at certain hours. Bedrooms and often entire houses were cleansed of evil spirits.

Childbirth was the terror of Brazilian colonial wives. The women were expected to be constantly bearing new heirs into the family, and because of early marriages and lack of proper medicines many of the wives were forever weak and ailing. There were no doctors to consult or hospitals to be delivered in. They had to remain on their isolated plantations and depend upon the care of their female slaves. The slave women prescribed mandrake root to assure pregnancy and to undo evil eyes. They carefully collected small stones and after hiding them inside the altar to be blessed during Mass, they tied them into a small bag that their pregnant mistress could wear around her neck. They warned the future mother not to pass under a ladder or the child would not grow. Should the pregnant wife think that her husband was deceiving her with another woman, the maid would capture a toad and put it in a pot under the woman's bed. The toad was kept alive on cow's milk. Coffee, that old Brazilian staple, was also an old witchcraft remedy. An erring husband? Let him drink a cup of very black coffee with much sugar and a drop of menstrual blood from a mulatto woman.

When the child was born a female servant of confidence would burn the umbilical cord in a fire or throw it into a river so that rats would not eat it and the baby grow up to be a thief. The child would sleep in a room illuminated by several oil lamps and never be allowed to sleep in the dark until after it had been baptized, so that no witch or werewolf could come in and suck its blood in the darkness.

The plantation white men were equally under the spell of those black sorceresses. They needed them to bless the seeds to assure an abundant crop. They needed them to chant and keep evil spirits away when a prize cow or horse was about to foal. They also depended upon them to catch the eye of the pretty girl at the neighboring farm and to give them a magic potion when their sexual powers began to wane.

The children of the household were warned about playing too close to the edge of the ocean and being eaten alive by "the old man of the sea." They were admonished about getting lost in the forest because it was inhabited by one-legged demons, by headless horses and by a devil with long, hairy hands. These spirits would often come right into children's bedrooms while they were sleeping and smear their faces with a "ghost oatmeal" that, invisible to the eye, must nevertheless be washed off the first thing in the morning. And if a bath wasn't taken at least once a week, warned their Negro nursemaids, a devil with a pock-marked face would eat them alive.

No wonder the master and his family let the slaves have their own religion and keep their African services. Not to do so could mean the ruin of them all!

5

When Brazil finally freed her slaves, in 1888, the African rituals and saints were firmly marked on the national character. Belief, or at least the half fear of not believing, had been in the land for almost 350 years! Whites, mulattoes and blacks had grown up—fifteen generations of Brazilians—hearing of Yemanjá's powers, what Ogun was capable of doing and the dread of going against Exú. Fifteen generations of Brazilians had listened to their nurses tell of the demons in the jungles and the devils in the seas. Fifteen generations grew up hearing tales of death by the evil eye, of illnesses cured by spirit consul and of marriages saved by spirit intervention. No Brazilian then or now gives a second thought to the pulsing of drums from a slum section or a spirit church. No modern Brazilian even questions the right of spirit believers to buy their ground snakeskins and colored plaster images in shops located next to supermarkets and air-conditioned banks. No Brazilian is ever surprised to hear of someone who went to doctor after doctor until finally he went to a spirit session and walked away cured. Today, only eighty years have passed since slavery was abolished in Brazil. Many children of slaves, now gray and tottering, are still alive to remind their grandchildren and great-grandchildren what it was like to wear chains and how the spirits helped their parents to endure it.

When Princess Isabel, the Emperor's daughter, signed the

paper that set all slaves free, she also signed the nation's economic death warrant. Huge coffee, sugar and cotton plantations could no longer continue operating. What they produced wasn't able to meet the new salaries they had to pay their former slaves. Big houses were boarded up or invaded by homeless blacks. Large farms were chopped up and parceled out to sons and heirs in the hopes that they could manage alone. One by one the farms were abandoned and the land sold off. The cities swelled and when the nation became a republic, by tossing out the royal family, the political leaders became so embroiled in urban squabbles that the rural area was left to go to pot.

Blacks, freed now but with no place to go and nobody to work for, formed their own groups. Some of them even rebelled against their plight and had to be quelled with soldiers and rifle bullets. Others just took a piece of land and started working it for enough to support their families. Any education they had been getting at more enlightened plantations before their emancipation was cut off. Black children were not forced to go to school. Indeed, there were no schools for them, and youngsters grew up as illiterate as the mules that helped them to plow. In their poverty, their ignorance and their isolation they still had one thing: their spirit religion.

It has spread across the country from the harsh pampas of Rio Grande do Sul to the dense Amazon jungles, from chic Rio de Janeiro to the most backward farm settlement, from predominantly white Santa Catarina to predominantly black Salvador, Bahia. Because the land and the people vary, the religion has also varied with the political and economic areas it covers. It has four distinct movements in today's modern Brazil: Candomblé of Bahia and the northeast; Spiritism of Rio and the more advanced urban centers; Umbanda in the urban centers not influenced by Bahia, and Quimbanda, a form of black magic that is practiced clandestinely everywhere.

Drum and Candle

The names themselves are confusing enough, and there is, in spite of their common ancestry, a notable difference between them all. It took me quite a while to see the difference and then to understand it, but then I'm still not too sure about the differences between the Episcopalians and the Presbyterians either.

My first encounter with Candomblé had been the time the doubting American wife threw herself into a trance. It had set me wondering and possibly even considering that maybe we "moderns" were losing touch with the world of nature. Most delvers into ESP and spirit manifestations claim that we are born with special faculties to sense, if not actually see, the "unknown," that children actually talk to spirits and are able to receive messages from the spirit world more easily than adults. But the adults either don't want to know what the child is listening to or else put it down to imagination or the need for a playmate. We all know of a child who keeps company with an invisible friend, playing with him and carrying on long and involved conversations. This friend (from the spirit world?) is almost always driven away by the child's parents, who are, after all, modern adults who don't believe in ghosts.

There have been ghosts in every civilization and cultural age and they have influenced the folklore, the religion and even the politics of group after group, century after century. What are elves and leprechauns if not spirits? What about Hamlet's father? Shakespeare was not writing a comedy but a tragic historical drama. What about the demons that possessed the abbess and her nuns at Loudun? What about Joan's visions with detailed battle plans that defeated the mighty English? What about the countless tales of sudden warnings that a disaster was about to occur, that a parent was ill or that a loved one had died? And what about Christ himself, who after being killed and entombed appeared once more to His disciples and this time walked right through a closed door? Ah, the Christian anti-ghost brigade says in unison, but Christ was the Son of God! But do we moderns not consider God as a *spirit* rather than a *physical being*? And do we not firmly believe in the Father, the Son and the Holy *Ghost*?

Keeping this in mind—and trying to keep an open mind— I returned again and again to Salvador, Bahia, and began to investigate the cult of Candomblé.

It is the oldest of all the Brazilian spirit religions and is in a straight line from the beliefs the Yoruba slaves brought to the New World 450 years ago. It has suffered slight modifications but has remained faithful to the gods that roamed the African jungles.

There was quite a large colony of free Negroes in Bahia by the beginning of the nineteenth century. A few of them had managed to purchase their freedom but the majority had been freed when a master died or had closed down his plantation and moved to the city. Many women slaves had been given their freedom for personal services rendered their master or mistress, for it was often with freedom in mind that a servant brewed a magic potion or searched for toads at midnight. If the hex worked, she bargained, she wanted her liberty. Portuguese and Brazilian masters were notorious for their extramarital activity with their more comely female slaves and often gave a dusky bedmate her liberty when they suspected that the wife was getting wise. Others freed their faithful nursemaids when they reached the age of twenty-one. Most masters who had a child by a slave woman usually gave both the woman and the baby their freedom, for the idea of having one's own son sold to somebody else was not a pleasant prospect. These freed Negroes came from the northeast farm and manor houses and settled in Salvador, Bahia. Salvador was a bustling commercial city with shops, small factories and an active port. It had been the headquarters of the royal family when Napoleon made them flee from Portugal to Brazil and had been the nation's capital. It was full of buildings and lofts where people could live and work, and the surrounding hills were ideal for small homes and a few chickens. It was a traditional city, not trying to modernize itself in the way of Rio and other towns to the south. Therefore, it was a perfect place for traditional slave religion.

No one is quite sure why the cult began to call itself Candomblé, but the probable reason is that the Negroes on the coffee plantations had a community dance they called *candombé*. To have a *candombé* meant to invite folks from miles around to a celebration. In the beginning the freeborn Negroes tried to keep the priests and the police away from their meetings and figured little suspicion would be aroused over a common community dance party.

In the beginning the Candomblés were held far from the center of town, often in a secluded grove or a hut. It was thought necessary to keep the ritual away from the lights of the city but near enough for everyone to reach. Finally, in 1830, three black freedwomen, brought as slaves from the African coasts, bought an abandoned millhouse and set up Brazil's first permanent Candomblé. (To avoid confusion, the word "Candomblé" is used not only as the name of the cult but to designate the place of worship as well.) This church became known as the Candomblé do Engenho Velho ("The Old Mill"), and the three high priestesses were known by their African names of Iyá Dêtá, Iyá Kalá and Iyá Nassô. (*Iyá* in the Nagô dialect, the main language spoken by the Yoruba slaves, means "mother.") They presided over their congregation with the force and assurance of three black queens, and it must have been quite a sight to see them dressed in their full white skirts and blouses, wrists and ankles covered in gold bracelets, while they whirled and chanted in the lamplight to the sound of three talking drums.

While they didn't make Candomblé legal (the padres tried more than once to shut them down), they did make it permanent and gave the freed black a place where he could worship his own gods now that he was no longer able to attend services at a plantation. The Old Mill also gave the blacks a sense of having something of their own, and they contributed money to it, attended every session and told of the miracles that had been performed there when the spirits arrived.

The high priestesses set up their Candomblé with the absolute powers invested in themselves. They were in complete charge and their assistant dancers, known as "Daughters of the Saint," were second in command. They obeyed no outside religious or political authority where matters of ritual and procedure were concerned. And being women they were determined that only other women could take their places. Men could serve as drummers or secondary assistants but could never hold complete power. Their ideas have held, in Salvador, up until today.

One by one the African priestesses died off and were finally replaced by Daughter of the Saint Marcelina, who had worked her way up into the hierarchy over the years. She ruled the Old Mill until her death, upon which two Daughters disputed for first place. As only one could be the high priestess, the loser walked out in a huff, taking half the congregation with her, and founded her own Candomblé in a building she purchased from a Frenchman named Gantois. Salvador now had two cult centers, and as the years went on, other Daughters broke off and formed their own Candomblés, until today there are an estimated seven hundred different temples in and around the city of Salvador.

It is not every building that can become a Candomblé center, and almost all of them are built to specifications. A piece of land that has room for a house in the center and lots of space around it is the most preferred. If there is a stream running through the property, all the better. The plan of the house is laid out so that there is a large room for the dancers and the drummers. It should be at least sixty square feet and have enough space so that the dancers when they become possessed by their spirit guides don't fall into each other or onto the congregation. There should be a front door with a path leading directly through the spectator area to the dance floor. Benches are placed on the right for the women and on the left for the men. There should also be a window on each side of the congregation to facilitate the arriving of the spirits and the driving out of the unwanted ones. Another door to the side of the dance floor leading outside is also useful for these spiritual arrivals and departures. At the rear of this main room, another door opens onto a corridor with several small rooms branching off it. These are the rooms destined for various gods, and it is to these small, sparsely furnished cubicles that the Daughters are taken when the spirit has possessed them. The walls are usually painted white and the floor is usually of beaten earth. There are some wooden and even cement floors in the newer centers, but old-timers claim that the Daughters should dance with bare feet upon bare ground.

The roofing and the exterior of the house are not important, but what is built outside most definitely is. There are certain spirits that simply are not wanted in the house at all and they must be placated by having small huts of their own. Exú, the devil, has the most lavish hut of all, and before any ceremony is started inside he is given food and drink outside so that he won't come barging in and disturb the ritual once it gets under way. Spirits of the dead, called Eguns, also have their outside huts, for while they are respected, they are not welcome when the African gods arrive. These spirits are given food and drink, but served in broken dishes and cups to remind them that they have broken their bodily chains and must not mingle with live humans any longer.

(It seems a good idea to point out here that Candomblé is *not* a cult that calls upon the dead. Their interest is strictly in maintaining contact with their African spirit guides. It is true that they have added such Brazilian spirits as the Old Black Slave, the Mother Jurema and the Indian known as Seven Arrows, but these are not individual personalities that have passed away but representatives of those slaves, freedmen and Indians who have incorporated all these dead souls into one spirit. A Candomblé is not interested in making contact with the dead. Believers seek advice from the heavenly deities, and want their dead to rest in peace.)

These high priestesses, called *Mãe de Santos* or "Mother of Saints," are usually women in their middle forties or older who have come up through the ranks to their present position of power and importance. They must all begin as simple Daughters of Saints and dedicate their lives to their religion. This is not a dedication like a Catholic nun's, however; rather, they must always be present for any important ceremony, they must know all the rituals, the varied drumbeats, the songs to the gods and must always be willing to take on more and more work for the benefit of the temple and the congregation itself. Unless an ordained Mother breaks off and starts her own group, she must wait until the present Mother dies, and even then she cannot be sure that leadership will be hers, for often, in the sealed testament, the departed Mother has chosen another more to her favor. The fight upward is slow and arduous and only the strongest and most dedicated ever make it. Once they do arrive, they have a direct and open line for conversing with the spirits. The spirits obey *them* and respect their temples and come when these women call them. For this reason these high priestesses are feared and obeyed; they become the flesh-and-blood representatives of all the gods of heaven and the demons of hell. Every now and then one of these powerful women will die and the entire city will be plunged into mourning as her funeral cortege winds through the narrow streets stopping traffic and closing down commerce.

Once in Salvador and just by chance, I was introduced to a middle-aged Negro woman who ran a small pension. I saw that she wore the small clenched fist, or *figa*, of most Candomblé adepts and that her "line" or "guide" or "patron saint," as you will, was Oxóssi. I began to talk about Candomblé and ask questions. Somehow I must have asked the right questions, for she took me for someone truly interested and not just one more tourist. She asked me if I cared to go with the family that night and watch her daughter "be sold on the market."

"Sold?" I asked, sure that I hadn't understood her regional-accented Portuguese.

"Sold!" the woman laughed.

"Like a piece of meat?" I questioned.

"No, like a slave of an Orisha!"

Of course, I agreed to go and met the entire family that evening after dinner and loaded them all into a taxicab. It was to be quite a party, the mother told me, and the family had been looking forward to it for a long time. "In the beginning," said the husband, "I didn't want our Eunice to become a Daughter of the Saint, but with both her and her mother pressuring me, what could I do?" He shrugged and looked at his large, happy wife. She was dressed in a pink and shiny dress, had her hair neatly curled and was wearing lots of lipstick and powder. Her other children, three boys and two girls, were all under fifteen years of age and were equally combed, washed and shining.

"Has Eunice (pronounced You-knee-sea) been a Daughter of the Saint for long?" I asked.

"Oh no," said one of the children, "she is still a novice."

"But she will be one soon, won't she, Mama?" put in another of the kids.

Mama shook her head in the affirmative and smiled. "I am so happy for her! She has really worked for this honor. It's an honor for the family too, you know."

I admitted that I knew it was an honor but also admitted that I would like to know what had gone on before this night. Mama was eager to bring me up to date.

"In the beginning when she said she wanted to become a Daughter she went to our Candomblé center and had a long talk with the Mother. She told her that it wasn't easy. That it wasn't just one more childish game—Eunice is only sixteen—and that it was a very serious step. But our little girl had made up her mind and that was all there was to it." The taxi slowed down in order not to hit a blind beggar who had decided to cross the street alone and unaided. "The first thing she did was to find out who her Orisha was. We always suspected it was Yemanjá but weren't sure. I had hoped it was Oxóssi, like me, but the búzios said it was really Yemanjá."

"Búzios?" I interrupted.

"You know, those shells that they throw and then read what is there by the way they land." I figured she was talking about the cowrie shells that are on sale in the Salvador market, and I shook my head that I understood. "Anyway, after we knew who her guide was we had to start buying material and making clothes. Yemanjá only wears blue and Eunice only wanted the best so I had a cousin of mine buy the very best he could find in that big store there on Rio de Janeiro's bay."

"Big store? You mean Sears?"

"That's it," she beamed with pride. "Eunice's cloth all came from Sears!" There was a general murmur of approval from the rest of the family as the mother continued. "Well, we had to make skirts and slips and blouses and head scarves and aprons and everything. You can't buy it already made, you know, it must be done by hand. Then we had to buy beads to make necklaces for her costume. Yemanjá is the goddess of the waters, so naturally blue is her favorite color."

"Naturally," I commented. "The beads also came from Sears?"

"Heavens, no! The Mother had some for sale that came directly from Africa. They were more expensive than local beads, but they were authentic."

"I went with Eunice to the market," put in the oldest girl, "and we bought a beautiful feather fan, a silver fish and a pretty silver half-moon with a star on its tip. She'll be wearing them tonight, you'll see."

"Everything cost a lot of money," said Mama, "but it was worth it." The father only coughed and held tighter to one of the children on his lap.

"After she had all those things ready she moved into the Candomblé and stayed there for almost a month. None of us were allowed to visit her or to do anything except send her money and food. Because she was preparing for Yemanjá the only thing I could fix for her to eat was fried or baked fish and fresh papaya. We really miss her at home, because she was always helping me with the pension, doing dishes and washing clothes. I had to hire a woman to come in and do the work. It's an extra expense but Eunice is happy." Again the father only coughed.

"You haven't seen her since she went in?"

"Last week we saw her, for the first time. It was at the ritual where she received her name. She looked thin, poor thing, but she looked so pretty in her clothes. Didn't Eunice look pretty in those clothes, children?" They noisily agreed that their sister was by far the prettiest of all the novices at the center.

Between the time Eunice had gone in and the time she made her first public appearance, she had been subjected to fasts, rituals and blood sacrifices that had come straight from darkest Africa. It was hardly the thing a modern teen-age girl who had a boy friend, wore lipstick and watched tele-

Drum and Candle

vision would have understood, yet obviously Eunice was no worse for the experience.

At 3 A.M. on the morning following her arrival, Eunice was stripped, taken outdoors and washed in a bath of special herbs according to the demands of her saint. Then she was dried with special leaves and told to put on her new clothes, not the very fancy ones, but others that she had made for everyday wear, in her case pure blue with long sleeves and multiple skirts to the ground.

Then the lessons began. She was taught how to sing, beat the drums and dance for the various spirit guides. Each guide has his own song and knows which way he likes the drums to be beaten best, and Eunice had to know all this too. After this, which took days and nights of study, she learned how to read the message in the cowrie shells. Then came lessons in the Nagô language, because the saints speak and understand Nagô. Very few of them ever bothered to learn Portuguese. Then came lessons in how to sacrifice properly an animal or a fowl to the gods. She couldn't just chop its head off or slit its throat. There are special positions, special tools and special blood-collecting rituals that must be rigorously obeyed. She had to study herbs and be able to brew special teas and potions. She had to learn which guide preferred to eat steak and which wanted chicken and to memorize the recipes of at least seventeen various spirit gourmet menus. Then came the process of committing to memory all the rituals used in the many ceremonies.

While all this mental work was going on, a special ceremony was conducted halfway through the course. Eunice was placed in the center of the huge dance room and her guide was shouted to come and possess her. The drums beat and the Mother danced, chanted, prayed and demanded until finally the girl began to tremble. Her face contorted and her fingers lost their control as she tore at her hair and vestments. Then it happened. Yemanjá, the mother of the waters, the holy mother of us all, the Virgin Mary, came charging out of heaven and into the body of the helpless girl. Eunice felt nothing, but those at the closed-door ceremony saw her lose her balance with the impact and heard a strangled moan as the spirit took her and "rode" her for the first time.

The Mother was delighted with her future Daughter and after embracing her seven times sat her down on a stool and removed the girl's head scarf. Eunice's hair fell to her shoulders, but when the Mother had finished with her the hair was lying on the floor. She had taken a special pair of scissors and then a straight razor and with the cutting and scraping Eunice became completely bald. This done, an assistant scraped away the hair under the girl's arms. (Sometimes the hair around the sex organ is removed as well.) The bald dome was then washed with holy water that had been mixed with the blood of previously sacrificed animals. Then the Mother took another blade and cut a circle into Eunice's scalp about the size of a quarter. Blood ran down her face but as she was still being ridden by her saint, she felt nothing. Quickly, the Mother washed the wound with anesthetic and cauterizing herbs and powders. A white duck (female, of course) was brought in and blessed. Then with a deft stroke of the knife the Mother severed the bird's neck and blood spurted in gasping heartbeats onto Eunice's head, face, arms and feet. Then a bleating white goat (again female) was dragged into the room. With terrified eyes it watched the whirling dancers and watched as the Mother's knife came closer. It gave one scream and, in triumph, the Mother hoisted its kicking body over the seated girl and the blood gushed from the animal's severed jugular vein.

For two or three hours afterward Eunice sat in her trance, her dress bathed in human, bird and animal blood. The gore began to dry on her eyes and lips and flies buzzed around the puddle on the floor. Then they washed her and perfumed her and helped her to change into another set of clean clothes.

Drum and Candle

Once more she was led back to the stool in the center of the room, but this time, instead of with blood, she was daubed with spots of white paint. The Mother dotted her bald head, face, neck, shoulders and arms. This ritual symbolizes the deep scars and skin mutilations that African tribes used (and use) to decorate and identify themselves. Eunice was lucky that the scars were only symbolic.

Now Eunice was taken to the room set aside for her saint and virtually locked into solitary confinement for thirty days. She was only let out long enough to be washed by the Mother with special waters. The rest of the time she studied the herbs and the rituals, ate fish and papaya and was forbidden to see or even to speak to anyone. When she wanted something she had to clap her hands and try to make the attendant understand through sign language. She was also forbidden sexual relations during that time, and though that didn't bother Eunice, it must be very trying to married Daughters' husbands.

Before the month was over an emissary of the Candomblé called on Eunice's mother and father and presented a bill for the food, the lodging and the sacrificed animals. She also gave them a list of items needed for their daughter's "name-giving" ceremony, telling them when it was and inviting them to appear.

"Father and I were very nervous that night," Mama said, "because we hadn't seen Eunice for such a long time and didn't know what to expect at the ceremony. But everything went just beautifully. The Mother had everything arranged so well. It was a *lovely* ceremony!" (I was reminded of my own mother describing my sister's wedding and realized that proud mothers are all alike.)

Eunice had been brought out with the other novices, who were dressed in their appropriate colors. One girl was to receive the name of Oxóssi and was dressed in green and white.

Drum and Candle

Another, to be named in the line of Obaluayê, was in scarlet, while the girl destined for Ogun was in deep blue.

First the devil Exú had to be fed, and after blessing a dish of corn-meal flour and several bottles of local rum, the center's assistants carried them far outside the house and threw them into the darkness. Let the devil find the food and booze and stay away from the dancers!

Then the drums started to "talk" and the Mother began to call down the spirits. Eunice and the other girls danced to the music, sang their newly learned chants and waited to be possessed. One by one the dancers faltered, stumbled and began to shiver, and one by one they became ridden by their guide. When it became Eunice's turn she shut her eyes, bent double, cried out as if in terrible pain and then slowly straightened up again. As she did, she opened her mouth and screamed the name of the saint whom she had received. "Yeeemaaannnjáááá!" The crowd of spectators burst into applause.

Each initiate, after receiving her proper spirit, was then taken back to the room where she had lived in harsh loneliness and dressed in all the fancy regalia that identified her guide. They donned the long skirts of colored silks and satins, draped themselves with beads, amulets and bright scarves. They put on their wrist and ankle bracelets and took up the symbols of their proper Orisha. Ogun's "horse" (the girl "ridden" by Ogun) carried a small silver sword, Oxóssi's a miniature shotgun and Obaluayê's three silver arrows. Eunice, as Yemanjá, carried the fan, the silver fish and the half-moon that she and her sister had purchased in the market place.

"I felt like crying," Mama said. "Eunice looked so beautiful!"

"You did cry," put in one of the children. "Remember? I gave you a handkerchief."

With all the Daughters dressed in their regalia and presented to the world for the first time, the congregation rose and applauded. The Mother sang a special song of gratitude and the audience was all smiles and congratulations. The girls threw themselves onto the floor in front of the Mother (like a new priest does before his bishop) and were blessed, told to rise and then publicly embraced by the high priestess. The dancing and singing continued far into the night.

The next day Eunice and the other girls were allowed out on the streets of Salvador. They visited their parents and asked for their blessings. They also visited other Candomblés, asking for blessings there as well.

Now all this had happened before that evening when I entered the Candomblé house with Eunice's parents. The building was like most of the others I had visited, with the exception of a colored photograph of the late President Kennedy. (Kennedy, for some reason, became a special friend of the African spirits after he was assassinated.) The room was already crowded with people and the father led me up to the dance floor, where Eunice, standing with head shaven and scarred, but in all her blue satins and blue beads, was waiting with the other girls. She waved at her father and smiled doubtfully at me. Her smallest brother called her name and she waved to him. In spite of the ordeal and the bald head, she was still an attractive sixteen-year-old girl.

The Mother (a formidable old woman with deep lines around eyes that I am sure must shine in the dark) called for silence and began to extol the virtues of the first Daughter. Then she asked for bids. A man called out a ridiculously low price and everyone laughed. The Mother, obviously enjoying herself, scowled at him and reminded him that these were all first-class slaves of the gods and would give lifelong protection to their owner. Because of this they were expensive and should be bid upon accordingly. Another man called out one price, then a woman shouted what she would pay. Someone made a smart remark and everyone laughed, including the Mother and all the Daughters. Finally the right price was reached and the slave was led off the floor by the purchaser, who had paid cash on the spot to the Mother. It was a loud and lively impersonation of an old-time slave market, but both the price and the purchaser had been agreed on beforehand. Usually the buyer is a member of the family and the money goes into the Candomblé coffers. Eunice was "sold" to her father for a sum that was almost $250 and I wondered how this humble man with all those children to support had managed to get this much money to pay the Mother. (Afterward I learned that most families of novice Daughters go into debt for years to pay for the ceremonies.)

Afterward came the market. The girls had been busy for a week baking special cakes and puddings, roasting chickens and making jugs of a fermented rice flour drink. They spread their wares on the floor and sitting behind them on a stool began to shout and barter with the public.

They managed to sell everything for exorbitant prices, and the noise and laughter was heard for blocks away.

When Eunice had sold everything (I bought a baked fish, although I didn't know what I was going to do with it) she chatted with her parents and other invited friends and asked me questions about Rio de Janeiro and New York. She wondered if there was a Candomblé in Harlem. When I told her that I doubted it, she said, "But all those Negroes! Don't they believe in anything?"

I replied that they believed in Christ.

"But so do we," she said and pointed to a plaster statue of Jesus on the altar, which was also laden with a host of other saints and spirit figures. "Don't they believe in the others that go with him? Don't they have Ogun and Oxóssi?" I told her that they did not. "And Yemanjá?" Again I shook my head. "Not even Yemanjá . . ." her voice trailed off, and she seemed sad for the first time that day. "They have so many other things and they don't have Yemanjá. What a pity."

"Don't worry about the Americans, honey," said her father

Drum and Candle

as he put a protective arm around her shoulder. "When Yemanjá wants to be worshiped up there, she'll let them know. They probably just aren't ready for her yet, that's all."

In the taxi going back to town the conversation was about the market and who bought this and who said that. The family was delighted with the whole thing in spite of all the money it had cost them.

"I suppose Eunice will be coming tomorrow," I said. "You'll be glad to have her back, won't you?"

"Oh, but she can't come home yet," said Mama. "She still has one more ceremony to go through before it's all over."

"You mean after everything else has been done there is still one *more* ritual?"

"Oh yes, this Friday she and the other girls will shave their heads again, paint those white spots on their faces and put on their beautiful clothes. Then the Mother will take them to hear Mass at Our Lord of Bonfin Church. When that's over, then Eunice will be an official Daughter."

The others shook their heads in agreement and chattered on about something else while I sat stupefied with the fact that after all the paganism and African mumbo jumbo the final and crowning ceremony could only take place inside a Roman Catholic church!

6

To investigate Candomblé and to understand it, I had to research the history and conditions of primitive Africa. To see what makes Spiritism so big in Brazil I had to delve into the history of France.

It all began with a table which said "There is no death."

In the middle 1700s the idea of *animal magnetism* was discussed and debated by scientists and educated laymen. The idea, which was said to have been originated by Paracelsus, was that there was a force or invisible fluid that radiated from all things, animate and inanimate, and that these fluids reacted to each other. How else to explain the fact that one piece of metal could be attached to another without bolts or meltings? How else, if not by invisible fluids that readily mixed, did a lady's hairpin jump off the table and hold onto another piece of metal? And what about the fact that if you ran a comb through your hair and then held the comb over a scrap of paper the paper would jump onto the comb?

French drawing rooms of that period were often more scientific-minded than many university classrooms, and these problems were discussed and debated over demitasses and petit fours. More talk opened other avenues. If a simple hairpin had these powers, then what must the human being have? Obviously the human body was bathed in a mystical fluid as well. This fluid (if the hairpin or the comb reacted

Drum and Candle

so violently) must also react violently when it comes into contact with other fluids. When two lovers embrace the fluids must be harmonious and cause that special feeling that only a lover's kiss can bring. When two people fall in love "at first sight" it could only mean that their fluids are attracted to one another immediately. Of course this also works in the opposite manner. Enemies must be enemies because their fluids don't meld. People who take an instant dislike to one another or immediately distrust each other are not going on intuition but on instant fluid repellence. A dog doesn't like a cat. Why? Their fluids. Sugar and vinegar? Their fluids. The priest and the sinner? Their fluids. The mystic searched for a magnetic formula as avidly as did the scientist. In London a humble Irishman named Valentine Greatrakes awoke from a dream telling him he could cure the sick merely by laying his hands on them. He ignored the dream but it continued night after night. Finally he experimented on his wife, who had suffered long and loud with stomach complaints. Her pains went away immediately. His fame grew and he was invited to cure the royal family. Naturally, a bishop was called in to see if it was the work of the devil or not, and after weeks of observation he had to admit that Greatrakes was "of sound moral character and honest in that which he did." Through the simple laying on of his hands Greatrakes "drove the pains to the extremities of the limbs. Many times the effect was very rapid and as if by magic. If the pains did not immediately give way, he repeated his rubbings, and always drove them from the nobler parts to the less noble, and finally into the limbs." The bishop testified that he had seen Greatrakes "cure dizziness, very bad diseases of the ears and eyes, old ulcers, goiter, epilepsy, glandular swellings, schirrhous indurations and cancerous swellings."

The news of this early medium (and we'll go into that term later) was carried to all the drawing rooms of France and profoundly influenced the thinking of one Franz Anton

Drum and Candle

Mesmer. He claimed that the forces Greatrakes had caused to flow from his hands were influences directly from the planets, and that these interplanetary forces acted upon the magnetic fluids of the body. Diseases were nothing more than foreign forces acting upon normal fluids. To remove a disease all you had to do was rid the body fluid of these uninvited outside forces. Mesmer himself was a medical doctor and abandoned pills and poultices for magnets and a tub full of "matter."

He would work with a group of patients and have them sit in rows around a vast tub. He would tie one end of an iron rod to their waists and put the other end of the rod into the liquid "matter" in the tub. Then he asked his patients to link thumbs with the person to the left and to the right, thus forming a chain around the vat. Sometimes a pianoforte was played and at other times a sweet-voiced soprano sang. It was "to diffuse magnetism" into the air.

The patients were also directly "magnetized" by Mesmer himself, who waved a finger or a wand in front of their faces, above or behind their heads or on the diseased parts of their bodies. With some he would stare into their eyes; others felt his hands massaging their solar plexus.

The Société Royale de Médecine ordered an investigation of Mesmer and his cures, and from the report of one session, it's easy to see why learned doctors scoffed at the man and why clerics of the era called his treatments witchcraft.

> Some [at the start of the cure] are calm, tranquil, and experience no effect. Others cough and spit, feel pains, heat or perspiration. Others, again, are convulsed.
>
> As soon as one begins to be convulsed, it is remarkable that the others are immediately affected.
>
> The commissioners have observed some of these convulsions last more than three hours. They are often accompanied with expectorations of a violent character, often streaked with blood. The convulsions are marked with involuntary motions of the

Drum and Candle

throat, limbs and sometimes the whole body; by dimness of the eyes, shrieks, sobs, laughter and the wildest hysteria. These states are often followed by languor and depression. The smallest noise appears to aggravate the symptoms, and often to occasion shudderings and terrible cries. It was noticeable that a sudden change in the air or time of the music had a great influence on the patients, and soothed or accelerated the convulsions, stimulating them to ecstasy, or moving them to floods of tears.

Nothing is more astonishing than the spectacle of these convulsions.

The patients pronounced themselves cured.

The commission, after seeing and writing the above, pronounced that it was all in the patients' minds and "magnetism did not exist."

Mesmer felt disgraced and his science of mesmerism became passé in the important drawing rooms of Paris. Of course, the scientists of the day refused to investigate further or take seriously anything the man was connected with.

In other countries, notably Germany and Sweden, Mesmer's ideas were studied and put into practice. The Germans took the notion of magnetism and coupled it with their own ideas of spirit intervention. They had never really believed in this business of fluids, but they did believe that evil spirits were the cause of illness and that those who were able to heal did so because good spirits controlled the "mediums'" hands and chased away the bad spirits.

The Swedes were enthused about one of their own countrymen, Emanuel Swedenborg, who went into trances that lasted for days and told of conversing directly with God and visiting the planets Venus and Mars and the moon. Much of what he wrote is scoffed at today ("The inhabitants of the moon are small, like children of six or seven years old; at the same time they have the strength of men like ourselves. Their voice . . . proceeds from the belly, because the moon is in quite a different atmosphere from the other planets.") but much had a basis of fact. Swedenborg was no ordinary religious visionary, for before being admitted to the world of spirits he had been one of the most distinguished scientists in Europe. He had designed an airplane and a submarine, had written books on algebra, chemistry and physics and had so studied human anatomy, "looking for the seat of the soul," that he made the discovery that the motion of the brain synchronizes with that of the lungs and not with that of the heart. His thesis on the formation of the planets is astonishingly close to the theories of modern nuclear physicists.

Yet at fifty-five he abandoned the world of man and entered the world of the spirits. He went on long journeys, he said, and was given the answers to everything he asked. He was not a mystic in fear and trembling of what he was experiencing, but a sharply observant, clinical reporter of his brand of facts.

His writings fused both the French idea of magnetism and the German one of spirits. The spirits were those of the dead—he called them angels—and they were constantly trying to contact man. "When angels speak spiritually with me from heaven, they speak just as intelligently as the man by my side. But if they turn away from man, he hears nothing more whatever, even if they speak close to his ear. It is also remarkable that several angels can speak to a man; they send down a spirit inclined to man and he thus hears them united."

What about the practical side of the spirits? What about the healers and what Mesmer was up to? What about body fluids? Swedenborg had the answer.

> The sphere proceeding from God, which surrounds man and constitutes his strength, while it thereby operates on his neighbor and on the whole creation, is a sphere of peace and innocence; for the Lord is peace and innocence. Then only is man conse-

quently able to make his influence effectual on his fellow man, when peace and innocence rule in his heart, and he himself is in union with heaven. This spiritual union is connected . . . through the touch and the laying on of hands. . . . The body communicates with others which are about it through the body, and the spiritual influence diffuses itself chiefly through the hands; because these are the most outward or *ultimum* of man. . . . The whole soul and the whole body are contained in the hands as a medium of influence. Thus Our Lord healed the sick by laying on of hands, on which account so many were healed by the touch; and thence from the remotest times the consecration of priests and of all holy things was effected by laying on of hands. According to the etymology of the word, hands denote power. Man believes that his thoughts and his will proceed from within him, whereas all this flows into him.

The ladies in their Parisian salons chatted about these new theories but neither investigated nor read Swedenborg's numerous tomes. They had always believed in spirits, and that funny old Swede just assured them they had been right all along. That was when table rapping became the fad.

To make a table "talk" all they did was sit around a heavy table, place their hands palms down on the table top and ask it questions. They would start saying the letters of the alphabet, and when they came to a certain letter the table would rap on the floor. Then they would start again and get another letter, and so on until a word had been formed and finally an entire sentence. It was all great fun and the silly table would tell Madame X where her lost brooch could be found or Mademoiselle Y whom she would marry. When they asked the table who was sending the messages the answer would often be rapped back that it was the spirit of some great and long-dead poet, religious or king. The ladies laughed at the pretensions of the humble table and entertained their guests for hours with the game. Soon even Napoleon III was holding these amusing table-rapping sessions.

They were amusing to everyone except one man: Allan Kardek. He was at first skeptical, then appalled at the manifestations, then intrigued enough to devote the rest of his life to researching the reasons "why" of table talking and spiritism.

Kardek's real name was Hippolyte Léon Denizard Rivail. "Kardek" was the nom de plume that he used when he wrote. He did not take the name—it was given to him by the spirits!

Kardek (and we might as well start calling him that from now on to avoid confusion) was born on October 3, 1804, in Lyon, France. His father was a local judge and his mother a housewife. There was nothing in either of their lives even to hint that their son would start believing in ghosts. They were good, middle-class, solid Roman Catholic citizens. And being such, they wanted their son to have a good education, and seemed to have the necessary money to send him to Switzerland and the academy of the then famed Dr. Jean-Henri Pestalozzi. Pestalozzi had made a name for himself as a teacher, a writer and a humanitarian. He knew a little bit about a lot of things and, more importantly, could teach what he knew. Young Kardek liked the man immediately and became his disciple. He learned the rudiments of medicine (based largely on herbs in those days), learned to speak, read and write both Latin and Greek and learned to investigate things rather than take them for granted. He studied, wrote, traveled and read widely. Under the guidance of his tutor he became a medical doctor at the age of twenty-six.

He moved to Paris and set up a "technical institute" along the lines of Pestalozzi's teachings, but he had unwisely chosen one of his mother's brothers as partner, and the man gambled everything away. Kardek had to make his living and repay his debts by translations, teachings and an occasional patient. He kept on studying and piling up diplomas and citations from such diverse institutions as the Society for Elementary Instruction, the Historic Institute and the Society for the

Incentive of National Industry. Between 1824 and 1849 he published ten different books on ten different subjects. He was profound, witty and talented.

These traits brought him to the attention of Parisian society, and he heard the brittle laughter as people discussed table rappings and spirit writings. Kardek had never seen any of these take place before, and even though he had studied spiritualist pamphlets and read up on hypnotism, he was convinced that it was all a fad. Then one evening he was invited to the salon of Madame Plainemaison. It was in May of 1855 and Kardek was already fifty-one years old and well-known for his scientific mind. They sat around a table, "a heavy table with a stout base and difficult for even two men to carry," and placed their hands on it palms down. Madame Plainemaison asked them all to be silent, to clear their minds of everything material and to concentrate on God. They waited several minutes like this when the table, much to the learned doctor's amazement, began to sway. "Who is there?" called out Madame Plainemaison. "If you are a spirit from the dead rap twice." The heavy base rapped twice on the uncarpeted floor. "If you are a good spirit rap once. If you are a bad spirit rap twice." The table rapped once.

Then began a series of questions which were followed by the slow reciting of the alphabet. When the right letter was reached the table would rap. Kardek heard words, then messages slowly being spelled out. He left the session confused and troubled. If these rappings were the work of spirits, he reasoned to himself as he walked home that night, then shouldn't they be taken seriously? Shouldn't they be investigated and reported upon as in any other science? And if it was found that there really were spirits and they could communicate with the living—and he must have stopped short on the pavement—if there really were spirits, then didn't their existence put an entirely new aspect on *all* the sciences? He asked to be invited back to Madame Plainemaison's salon several times and managed to be invited to other houses to watch other tables in operation. It took him one full year to come to the conclusion that there was "something beyond the control of mere man" that made these tables act the way they did. When he came to that conclusion the religion of spiritism was born.

He began to organize his studies and to hire others to help him in his research. While he would be at one session his aides were at another asking the same questions and recording the answers for later comparison. The use of tables as spirit receptacles became uncomfortable, and one evening he was told, "Go get a small basket in the next room, stick a pencil through the base of the basket and place it onto a piece of paper. Then place your fingers on the edge of the basket and let the pencil write." He did this and the spirit began to write the answers on the paper. It was much faster and even more amazing than the table-rapping method. After that, he experimented and found that just leaning a pencil on his closed fist was enough to make the words appear.

He also noticed that it wasn't everyone who tried who was able to make the pencil write or the table tap. He reasoned that only certain people were "given this special power and are called *mediums*, that is, a way or intermediate between the spirits and man."

It was about this time that he decided to write his first paper on the subject, and one night a spirit message came through to him. "You have been on French soil before and your present spirit was in the body of a great teacher and Druid named Allan Kardek. It would be best if you would use this name when you sign your papers." And so Allan Kardek he became.

"One of the first results of my observations," he wrote, "was to realize that, as souls of men, the spirits did not have complete wisdom or science, that their knowledge was limited to their degree of advancement and that their opinions had the value of personal opinions only. This fact, which I recognized from the beginning, preserved me from the dangers of believing in their infallibility, and also from forming premature theories on the messages received from one or the other spirits."

The spirits were, after all, only dead human beings who managed somehow to get through from the "hereafter" to the present. If they knew nothing of chemistry while they were on earth it was useless to think they had all the answers to chemistry after they were dead. If they could not speak French during their lifetime, no wonder dead Germans, Chinese or Americans did not appear to the French. The idea of the spirits was to get a message across, and their only method was through language.

Kardek also found out that the mental attitude of the medium had a lot to do with what kind of spirits answered. If the session was serious and on a high cultural level then the spirits of people who had been well educated and cultured would answer, but if the medium was a rather simple person who took the whole thing as a joke then the spirit he would get would also be inclined to confuse things and fool around.

"It was up to the observer to form a complex whole, coordinating and correlating one document with another as they were obtained. I proceeded with the spirits as I would with men, considering each one, from the smallest to the greatest, as elements of instruction and not as predestined revealers. To observe, compare and judge: that was my unchangeable rule."

In 1857 he published his first book, *The Book of Spirits*. It was the result of two years of intense study and of the research of ten different medium assistants, and had 1018 questions and answers. Kardek divided his book into four parts. The first was "Primary Causes" and contained answers to questions about the proof of God, universal space, the formation of the planets and human beings, about Adam and

Eve, the diversity of the human races, life and death, intelligence and instinct. The second part, titled "The Spirit World or the Spirits," talked about origins of spirits, perispirits, the different classes of spirits, the progression of spirits, the intervention and the mission of the spirits in the mortal world, the reasons why we don't recall our past lives and what is meant by clairvoyance. The third part of the book deals with moral laws and gives spirit comments on such subjects as the laws of nature, work, reproduction, destruction, progress, equality, freedom, justice, love and charity. The fourth part offers "Hopes and Consolations" and tells of rewards both on earth and in the hereafter.

To say that this book, and the ones that followed, like *The Book of Mediums* and *The Gospels According to Spiritism*, created an overnight sensation in France would be a gross exaggeration. They were commented upon, glanced through and lightly discussed. A small group of adepts was formed and Kardek managed to put out a monthly called *Revue Spirite*, but his ideas and discoveries were too much for the intellectuals of Paris, who, after all, were good Catholics and who had, after all, their own medicines and hardly needed spirit doctors with so many brilliant French doctors around. In Britain Kardek's ideas were taken up by one Miss Anna Blackwell, and she coined the word "Spiritism" to differentiate his ideas from those of the French "Spiritualism." Allan Kardek and his followers today are "Spiritists" and *not* "Spiritualists."

But if these direct questions and answers between Kardek and his spirits did not catch hold in France or Europe, where did they finally dig in? In Brazil, that's where.

Even before the abolition of slavery, enlightened Brazilian city dwellers were looking for a better connection with the spirit world. They knew about Candomblé from their nurses and their travels, of course, but they were also white, educated and far removed from Yoruba culture traits. It was possible to believe that there were unseen forces controlling man's destiny and even curing his ills, but that these forces were guided to earth by such characters as Yemanjá, Ogun and Exú just could not be accepted. These superstitious beliefs were all right for the blacks living up in muggy Africanlike Bahia but definitely not suitable for the enlightened whites in modern Rio de Janeiro.

The whites of Rio and the Emperor's court had searched for a more "civilized" way of believing in spirits. In spite of their educations and their comfortable daily lives, they still had enough of their Portuguese Moorish beliefs in them to want to believe in something else besides themselves and what the Catholic Church had to offer. Many had been raised by black nurses who filled their heads with spirits and hexes. They knew that something existed beyond their own earthly world. Just what that "something" was was open to debate.

By 1818 a group of Neospiritualists were practicing in the Emperor's palace in Rio. They were led by José Bonifácio de Andrada e Silva, who was Dom Pedro I, Minister of Foreign Affairs. De Andrada was later to be known in Brazilian history books as "the Patriarch of Independence." The aspect of Spiritualism this group adhered to was the idea of homeopathy as developed by Samuel Hahnemann in Leipzig. Hahnemann, a German physician, had discovered that the symptoms produced by quinine on the healthy body were similar to those of the deranged mental state it was used to cure. He investigated and came to the conclusion that many diseases are cured, or should at least be treated, by those drugs which produce symptoms similar to these diseases in the healthy. He called this the "law of similars" and his basic tenet "homeopathy." De Andrada kept up a correspondence with Hahnemann (in spite of the fact that he was finally barred from practice by other German doctors) and took immediately to his idea that to cure one must work through God and make the soul react and search for its own cure. The Brazilians liked this idea of soul/spirit reaction and by 1840 homeopathy was actively being practiced in Rio.

Two doctors were the leaders of the group: Dr. Martins and Dr. Mure. They were Spiritualists and mystics believing that the power of God should be applied to everyday life. They spent much of their time curing the poor free of charge. Brazilians abound with charity for their fellow men, and the two doctors practiced their beliefs on anyone who was willing to be cured. They would hand out tiny vials of liquid, boxes of small pills, and tell the patients to take one every hour and to pray to God to help them get well. In addition, they would also practice the "laying on of hands" on the sick. Stretching their hands over the patient, but never touching him, they would pray for a cure. While Hahnemann had privately stated that the "laying on of hands" could be used along with the proper medicines, he probably had no intention of having the hands play such important roles as the mystical-seeking Brazilians gave them. The homeopath's motto was "God, Christ and Charity" and he devoutly believed in all three.

The year 1848 was a big year for Spiritualists. In the United States two young girls, Margaret and Kate Fox, became frightened at the various knocking and rapping sounds that haunted their frame home in Hydesville, New York. The girls were sure it was the ghost of a man who had supposedly been murdered in that house. Huddled in bed with their mother one night, they became brave enough to ask the maker of the invisible noises some questions. They asked the sound to tap out the ages of the two children. The rappings began and went to fifteen for Margaret and then after a long pause to twelve for Kate. Then, as the mother recalled, "three more emphatic raps were given, corresponding to the age of the little one that died. . . . Then I asked: 'Is this a human being that answers my questions? . . .' There was no rap. . . . 'Is it a spirit? If it is, make two raps.' The sounds were given as soon as the request was made."

Drum and Candle

The Fox women soon worked out a code with the mysterious noisemaker and their friends dropped in to ask it questions. They gave each letter of the alphabet a certain number, as well as a number for yes and no. As they had guessed, the rapper turned out to be the spirit of the murdered man. What was more, he told them, his body had been buried in the cellar. He told them that he had come to the house as a peddler and that the owner had killed him, burying his body and his box of wares. When the cellar was dug up, sure enough, there were pieces of bone, hanks of hair and a small tin peddler's box. The girls were declared by the local press to be mediums and their fame spread across the nation and got into the foreign papers as well. In 1855 the sisters gave in to public pressure and to rid themselves of teams of investigators confessed that most of their mediumistic talents had been a hoax and that they had discovered how to make the rappings by cracking their knee joints. People who did not believe in spirits (or who were afraid to believe in them) were delighted with the "confession," but in 1904—some forty-nine years later—the basement of the house where the Fox sisters had lived was thoroughly excavated and a complete man's skeleton was found.

The year 1848 was just as big for Brazilian Spiritualists as well. The news of the Fox sisters was in all the Rio papers, and Dr. Mure (of the homeopathy group) had returned to his native France and reported via letter what was going on in Parisian salons in the way of table rappings. His assistants back in Brazil put some of the techniques to work, and in 1853 they reported that they were in active communications with the "dead" and founded the first spirit group in the country. This group consisted mainly of medical doctors and included such important political and cultural figures as the Viscount of Uberaba and the Marquis of Olinda. The African spirits had been brought to Brazil by the very lowest members of the social strata, but Spiritualism came in by way of the royal palace.

In 1858 an event occurred that revolutionized the Brazilian religious scene forever: A member of the nobility returned from Europe with a copy of Kardek's *The Book of Spirits* in his suitcase.

If there was ever a fertile field just waiting for such high-powered seeds as Kardek's Spiritism it was Brazil. The book was translated and sold in shops everywhere. Brazilian and Portuguese mediums took to it, worked with it and wrote their own commentaries and reported their own case histories. Newspapers ran accounts of Spiritist meetings and in 1869 the first Brazilian Spiritist magazine appeared in print. Its editor was L. O. Teles de Menezes and he called his highly successful publication *The Echo from Beyond the Grave*.

With books, magazines and newspaper articles in their own language, the Brazilians who had always wanted something a little higher than Candomblé converted eagerly to Spiritism. Here was a credo that combined what their black nurses had taught them, what their priests had hinted to them and what their doctors had suspected. And it seemed to be tailored to their exact specifications. There were no drums and raw-rum drinking. Uneducated blacks were unable to grasp it. It could be carried out in a decently decorated home instead of some isolated hut, and it had come from France. This last was very important, because the Brazilians were (and still are to some extent today) devout Francophiles. French was their second language. Their sons were sent to French universities. French furniture filled their tropical living rooms and bedrooms and French novelists were preferred over local writers any day in the week. Italian culture did not go beyond the Vatican, lasagna and *Rigoletto*. German culture had science and Wagner. English culture had the royal family and morality. And American culture . . . the Americans *had* no culture!

Just what did Kardek have to say that appealed so much to

the Brazilians? Just what did he uncover in his question-and-answer game with the beings of the spirit world? What did the spirits have to say that the Bible and Candomblé had not already said?

The most important tenet: "There is no death."

What there is, the spirits told Kardek and his researchers, is a body and a soul. The soul enters the body at the moment of conception and enters with all its past experience from other lives and other eras. When the child is born it is as much a shock for the spirit as it is for the flesh, and it takes time for the spirit to readjust to another worldly existence. Only when the child is able to talk and carry on a conversation does the spirit also start remembering his past. But he doesn't remember everything. Kardek learned that one lifetime was bad enough on earth with all the cares, frustrations and tragedies that go into it, and to make the spirit remember all the frustrations and tragedies of his other lives would be too much to bear. God is not that cruel.

The child loves his parents because the spirit usually is allowed to choose the family he wants to be born into. Often a spirit will choose a family group where there are other spirits of his past lives. That way there is immediate affection and tenderness. Should a child be rebellious and dislike his parents and his brothers and sisters, it's because his spirit is being punished in this life for something it did in the past life. That one child can be bright and the other stupid comes about because the spirits that entered the bodies are of a different level of maturity in the spirit world. Having the same mother and father only means that their flesh is the same, and the flesh has nothing to do with the spirit.

As the child grows older and enters the adult world, he will often have strong friends and equally strong enemies. The friends are spirits he knew and admired in his past lives and the enemies are those with whom he didn't get along in his other incarnations. (Of course, the human mind doesn't know this at the time, but what about that expression "kindred spirits"?)

Poverty-stricken Brazilians wanted to know why they were so poor and others were so rich. The spirits had the answer: They had probably been rich in their past lives and had abused their fellow men with their wealth. This life was an expiation for the others. Or else the spirit had evolved to such a non-materialistic stage in his other lives that he naturally chose one more poor body to continue his path of righteousness. (It must have been comforting to hear that your poor soul was closer to heaven now than that of the millionaire in the fancy mansion.)

If there is no death, what happens when a person dies? The answer: The soul leaves the body and, enriched with one more lifetime, returns to the spirit world (hopefully) one notch higher than he was before. Since body death is a slow process, the spirit begins to prepare itself for its trip back to the other world. When the body breathes its last the spirit rises up and stretches its arms and legs and is glad to be rid of the cumbersome flesh it had been chained to. Sometimes the spirit will hang around the house for a couple of days getting used to the sensation of freedom and then return to the other spirits. In the case of suicide, accidental death or something unexpected like murder, the spirit is forced roughly out of the body. It has not expected this sudden change and often is not ready for it at all. It may wander around the area where its body was killed (i.e. haunting) or return to the family group without knowing that its body has been left behind. It may stay in the earthly sphere for days, weeks or even years after its body death, only rejoining the other spirits when it is convinced that it is no longer physical or when a human being takes pity on it and prays that it go back to the spirits and find happiness. No matter what the circumstances, death is always confusing to the spirit for a while, and it usually takes a couple of days before it abandons the body forever.

The spirits told Kardek that "they cannot work miracles" and that once a body is without a spirit it stays moldering in the grave. Flesh is merely the covering that the soul uses in this world. It does not go with him to the spirit world nor is there ever a chance of it being resurrected.

Okay, you ask, but what about apparitions of the dead person that appear with features recognizable to their families, friends and even total strangers? Simple question! The spirit, while inhabiting a body of flesh, is enveloped in a semimaterial body of its own called the perispirit. This semimaterial body is a fluid (shades of magnetism, Mesmer and Swedenborg!) and contains a certain amount of matter and electricity. During a lifetime this semimaterial takes on the form of the material in order that both may function together. When the perispirit is broken from the material body the spirit that remains resembles the body it inhabited. It does not lose its lifetime of features until it returns for good to the spirit world. Thus a man killed in an automobile accident could easily be seen weeks or years later at the place of the tragedy if his soul had not conformed to the idea of bodily death. And because spirits are really people without bodies, they can be just as stubborn or stupid or vindictive as people with bodies. If they decide that they are going to "get" their murderer, hang around the bedrooms they used when they were alive or guard a treasure they worked hard to get and then buried, they will do it. There is no long finger of God that comes down to earth and flicks them back into the spirit realm. On the contrary, God lets them have their own way, for it is only under their own intelligence that they (we!) ever reach complete perfection. If a spirit decides to drag its feet, then it is its own affair. God has given it all the chances to improve itself, but He has other things to do besides convincing every stubborn spirit to go back home.

The first time I visited a Spiritist session, I was not prepared for what I saw. I knew that there was a difference between

Spiritism and Candomblé, but I thought it would just be white folks jumping around instead of black. For the umpteenth time in my life, I was wrong about Brazilian religions.

I had gone to São Paulo for something else, not spirit research, but had heard about a "temple" that was supposed to have over a thousand members and ran a day nursery, an old folks' home and a small hospital. Naturally, I didn't believe it.

The city of São Paulo was another thing I wouldn't have believed if anyone had told me about it without my seeing it. It sits some two hours' highway ride from the Atlantic coast on a high plateau. It sprawls for miles in all directions, has towering skyscrapers planted one after another down all its main arteries, has buzzing pedestrian crowds and impossible automobile jams. There are huge air-conditioned movie houses, big brassy night clubs, block-wide department stores and restaurants serving dishes from all over the world. The people earn more money than those in Rio because there is more commerce and industry. They dress better and seem to be living better. At first the city reminded me of Chicago and Cleveland rolled into one. It is the biggest city in Brazil and will, within a matter of a few years, be bigger than Buenos Aires, which is South America's largest city. São Paulo is also one of South America's most unknown cities. It is also the dynamic center of the Spiritist movement. It's difficult to reconcile spirits with concrete, neon lights and a subway system. But there it is.

The temple was a modern three-story, cement-block building painted white with blue shutters. There was a bronze plaque on the door giving the name of the group and adding that they were affiliated with the São Paulo Spirit Federation. The days and hours of the weekly sessions were also engraved in bronze. I joined the group of people who were sitting in a huge room with chairs facing a large round table. On the walls were pencil drawings, enormous framed drawings, of people I didn't recognize. Later I found that they were all spirit drawings of certain saints, guides and founders of the Spiritist movement. Allan Kardek was there right beside Joan of Arc. These drawings had been made by a medium of the congregation who had been under the spell of a spirit artist. The medium was in a trance while the spirit drew the portraits. There was a huge color lithograph of Jesus Christ with halo and beard right in dead center of the wall we were facing. There were no statues, no drums and no African deities. On every wall, between every portrait was a small sign asking for "Absolute Silence, Please."

I was told that the session would start at 9 P.M., and just as my watch hand moved around to the exact hour a hidden phonograph began playing Schubert's "Ave Maria." The few whispers heard in the crowd before the music died out completely. A door opened under the portrait of Christ and a group of men and women came filing out. They were ordinary-looking Brazilians, and while a few may have had some Negro blood in them they were mostly white. They were also dressed in white. The men wore white jackets, trousers and shoes and had a blue cross sewn over the pocket of the jacket. They would have been mistaken for hospital interns back in the States. The women wore starched white dresslike uniforms and white shoes. All they lacked was the little white cap to make them look like hospital nurses. They took their places at the round table, half of them turning their backs to the audience.

Then one man rose and welcomed the congregation. He asked that we all put any evil or ill-feeling out of our thoughts while we were there that evening. He said that evil could only perturb the good that they would try to do. He did not guarantee that anything at all would be done, it all depended upon the force of the spirits and the receptivity of the patients. He asked scoffers and disbelievers in God and Jesus Christ to leave the premises. No one moved and he seemed satisfied. Then he asked everyone to think silently on God the Father and to bring pure thoughts into the room for the next five minutes. He sat down and there was five full minutes of absolute silence. I used the time to slip sly glances at the people around me. They were all decently dressed and middle-class-looking. Like those around the table, most of them were white. There were no children.

The man rose again and asked us to bow our heads in prayer. For at least five minutes he begged God and Jesus to look in on the night's session and to permit the workers to carry out God's will of mercy and charity. Then he took a large pitcher of water and prayed over it for a while, then pulled back his right hand and stretched out his fingers. After a minute or so he seemed satisfied and poured each of his assistants a glass of this water. He had "magnetized" the water, charging it with the electricity of his own body and thus preparing it to receive still other discarded electrical shocks as the night went on.

Then came a sermon. As a kid back in Ohio I used to squirm through the preacher's sermon, counting the minutes on my Mickey Mouse watch. I did the same then and noted that the man indoctrinated the crowd for twenty-five full minutes. Most of what he had to say was concerned with the fact that we had been entrusted to help our fellow man and that most of us weren't doing anything of the sort. He preached against apathy, against cigarettes, against alcohol and against those who expect a reward every time they do good for another.

I picked up my ears when he lambasted those in the congregation who thought that joining a Spiritist church would lead them to salvation. "There is no personal salvation," he thundered. "Today you reap what you sowed yesterday, and in the next life you will reap what you have sown today. There are no miracles, only divine justice!" The crowd listened without batting an eye, but I wondered how far any Ohio preacher would get with such a defeatist doctrine.

Then he changed course again. "There are those here tonight who do not have faith in the power of healing. They prefer to take manufactured pills and injections of acids into their systems rather than let the spirits put their bodies into order. Pills and injections do have their place in today's world, yes, but for those who have faith all that is needed is the laying of the hands. It says right here"—and he picked up a copy of the Bible that I hadn't noticed before and flipped it open to a red satin marker. "It says right here in Mark, sixteenth chapter, eighteenth verse, 'they shall lay hands on the sick and they shall recover.' Then in Matthew X, eighth verse, it is commanded, 'heal the sick, cleanse the lepers, raise the dead, cast out devils: freely ye have received, freely give.' And didn't Christ himself place His hands on the ill and make them well? Didn't He show that He could bring back Lazarus simply by the raising of His hands?" In spite of the "silence, please" signs, there was a murmur of agreement. "Then don't doubt tonight that Christ can repeat what He has done before. For He is with us and we are His receptacles."

He sat down after that and clasped hands with the nurse to his right and the intern to his left. The others at the table did the same until they had formed a "current" link. Then he prayed again asking for spirit help in what they were about to do. The silence when he finished weighed heavily on the room, and the strains of "Ave Maria" kept playing over and over again. I stared at the pictures on the wall, wondered where I was going to have dinner and glanced at my watch several times when suddenly one of the nurses began to shake. The hands that were linked with hers clasped tighter and she stiffened and began to perspire heavily. Those nearest to her in the circle also shook from the effects of her "seizure," and she hung like a rag doll for a few moments before raising her head and with her eyes closed saying, "Good evening." The voice was low and husky, almost masculine.

"Good evening," said the leader of the group. "Welcome to our session. I hope you have had a pleasant trip." The woman muttered something and the man asked, "Is this your first time here? What is your name?"

The nurse's mouth opened several times, as if she was trying to force a fishbone lodged in her throat. Finally the sounds came out. "Tomás Antonio da Silva."

"Welcome, Sr. da Silva," said the leader. "Do you have a message for us?"

The congregation leaned closer.

"Message?" stammered the husky voice in the feminine throat. "Message? No, I have nothing to tell you. I just don't know . . ." the voice trailed off.

"You don't know what, Sr. da Silva?" There was no reply. "You don't know where you are? Is that it? You are wondering where you are?"

The nurse shook her head in the affirmative. Finally she sighed, "I am so tired, so very tired. I seem to have been traveling for such a long time."

"And you still don't know where you are going or where you have been. Isn't that it?"

"I was not going anywhere," whined the husky voice. "I was at home and in bed. I was very ill." He moaned and the sweat poured down the woman's face. "I was very ill. I hadn't been able to work for days and days. My wife was so worried. So were my children. Then they went away and left me alone." Here there was almost a sob.

"They left you alone? Who left you alone?" the leader's voice insisted.

"Marta, my wife, and Carlos and João, my two sons. They said that the doctor was coming and they turned out the light and left me alone. They went away." The voice rose almost hysterically then. "Are they here? Where are they? They promised to bring the doctor! I can't stand any more of this pain!" The nurse's body shook and she tried to rise but was pulled down again into her chair by the assistants at her side. She sobbed.

"Tomás," the leader called softly. "Tomás da Silva, listen to me. Can you hear me? Will you listen to me?"

The sobs died down and the nurse turned her tear-streaked face toward the leader. She nodded and said weakly, "I can hear you."

"Tomás, what I am going to tell you may come as a shock, but you are to face it and to listen carefully." The leader's voice was almost a whisper but it was firm. "Tomás, before you entered this life and this body and took this name you were a spirit. You know that?"

The nurse shook her head violently.

"Yes, you were!" said the leader. "You were a spirit! We all were spirits before we came here and we will all return to being spirits after we leave here. It is as natural as the sun in the daytime and the moon at night." The man's voice began to protest. "You have trodden this path before, Tomás," said the leader. "You have trodden this path before, only you don't recall it. You are here tonight because you are tired of wandering on this earth. You are tired of seeking that which no longer exists."

"Yes," spoke the voice. "I am tired, I am so tired."

"Tomás, listen carefully. The body of Tomás da Silva no longer exists. The body that you inhabited under that name has been cast off and buried. Tomás da Silva is decaying flesh of the past. You are free of him now." The voice from the nurse began to howl like an injured animal, but the leader cut it off sharply. "No! Don't lament the fact that you no longer are unencumbered by that sickly, earth-bound body. The sufferings you endured are over. The aches and pains, the hunger and the thirst are all over. You have served your time; now you are ready to return to the spirit world. Do you understand? You are ready to return to the spirit world."

All eyes were on the nurse. She seemed to relax and a smile flickered momentarily on her tear-wet lips. "Tomás is dead?" she said at last.

"The physical body is dead. His spiritual body has been freed. For some reason you were unaware of what had happened. No! Don't try to question it or even understand it. Just return with the other spirits. You will soon begin to recall the way back there. You have made the trip several times before. You can rest there. You have deserved your rest."

The nurse began to smile and with her eyes still shut tight began to twist her head as if she was looking around the room, as if she was looking around at the world for the last time. Then she shook, violently, and collapsed face down onto the table. She breathed deeply in a sigh that echoed in the vast room. Then she opened her eyes, shook her head as if to clear it and looked as embarrassed as if she had been caught sleeping during the service.

The leader released his hands and broke the current. "There are many spirits walking the earth who do not know that they have died," he said. "They are unhappy and can make those who are still living also unhappy. The spirit we have just oriented to his proper place for some reason did not know that his fleshly body had been cast off. He thought that he was still inhabiting that body and that the ones he had loved had abandoned him. Why he did not witness his own funeral and his own burial I cannot say. Obviously the family moved away from the house after the body had died, and the spirit, probably shocked by the physical pains, failed to perceive this. He has gone now, gone back to the world from whence he came. He will rest and be happy and await his next chance to be born again."

They all joined hands again and after several minutes five of them were shaking and trembling as the nurse had done before. The leader kept watch on them and when he was satisfied that the others were not going to be "possessed" he broke the chain and rose from the table. Those who were in the normal state helped the others to their feet. The women who had received a spirit were placed on one side of the room,

Drum and Candle

the men on the other. Their eyes were glazed and perspiration shone on their foreheads and upper lips, but there was none of the hysteria, screaming, cigar chomping and rum swilling that I had seen at the Candomblé.

The leader took a piece of paper that had been on the table and read a list of names. At the calling of each name a member of the congregation rose and walked toward the entranced mediums. A white-garbed assistant whispered into each one's ear and received a whispered reply. Then the assistant pointed out which medium the person was to consult. They lined up, Indian fashion, in front of each medium and patiently awaited their turn for consultation.

There was a silence in the great room that was eerie yet as charged with electricity as the noise in the Candomblé hut had been. One woman spoke softly to an intern medium and pointed to several places on her back. I figured that she must be having trouble with her spine or maybe her kidneys. The medium made a sign for her to turn around. He stretched out his arms and opened his hands, separating the fingers. He placed his hands at the level of the woman's shoulders and slowly moved the outstretched hands down to the kidney area. Then, holding his hands there for a few seconds—but never actually touching her body—he brought his arms down to his side, clenched his fists, then moved his arms sideward and rapidly opened his hands as if to fling something from his fingertips. Then he closed his hands, extended his arms to her shoulders and repeated the action four or five times. When he had finished, he spoke softly to her, and the next person in line was treated. Other mediums were being consulted and going through similar "laying on of hands" movements. A few patients were sitting in chairs and one man was lying on the floor.

What they were doing (I found out later) was sending healthy magnetic rays from their fingertips into the magnetic fluid of the patient. We all have an aura or fluid body around our physical bodies, say the Spiritists, and this fluid gets unbalanced right along with the physical organs. A good medium can spot immediately a diseased-fluid body. The aura of health is bluish-white. The aura of illness is gray. Around this liquid body form is a second aura that is colored by thoughts and desires. Our thoughts influence us as much or more than they influence others, and evil thoughts can bring about physical illness. If this second aura is blue it shows sublimation to a spirit. An orange color means ambition and pride. Red is violent passions, fury and sensuality. Deep red is love, and a pink love is even better. Green means treachery, artifice and rudeness. Dark green is jealousy, while light green means tranquillity and politeness. Gray means depression, sadness and egoism. Dark gray is hypocrisy and lying. Light gray is fear, doubt and irresolution. Black (of course) is hate, revenge and evil. Now around this aura is a current of electric particles that runs clockwise. It is separated by a blank space from another chain of electric particles that encloses all these auras in a counterclockwise movement. These magnetic particles come from other planets, from the stars, from the waters in the earth, the stones and the sun. When everything is running perfectly then the human body is healthy, but when something begins to interfere with either of the electrical currents —be it outside currents or mental currents from inside—then an imbalance occurs and the physical body becomes ill.

The laying on of the hands, then, is nothing more than the medium sending jolts of good electrical particles into the different auras to push out the particles that are in conflict with the others. The force of "good" electricity eliminates the weak force of "evil" electricity, putting everything back into balance once more. Thus diseases are nothing more than particles gone haywire, and the only cure is to put them back into their proper order by removing those particles that are not functioning correctly. If everything can be reduced to atoms, including the human body, reason the Brazilian Spiritists, then what is more logical than repairing damaged atoms and "curing" atom-caused diseases?

A medium, to be able to send charges of good electricity from her fingertips, must be in good physical and moral health herself. "You cannot give what you do not have" is a Spiritist maxim, and a medium is expected to live an exemplary life. There must not be an excess of sexual activity (although they do not frown upon married mediums and encourage large families), there must not be any alcohol drinking or cigarette smoking and there must be, if possible, a complete abstinence from meat. Fish is okay, steaks and chops are out.

Often a medium is in good health but after several sessions begins to absorb some of the unhealthy rays from her ailing patients; then she becomes ill as well. The only way she can be cured is to have another medium chase away the imbalancing particles. Some foolish or uneducated mediums have been known to die from an overdose of a patient's malfunctioning charges, and organized spirit groups abhor the free-lance medium and advise their congregations to stay away from them.

They also advise the public not to pay for any treatment, for they contend that what they do is a gift from God. Therefore it is a present that no human can compensate for and for which no money should ever be taken. The big centers (and the little ones too) keep clinics, orphanages, old folks' homes, homeopathic shops and all the rest open strictly by the contributions of the faithful. You can attend a session and donate whatever you wish. You can be cured on the spot and not pay a thing. It's all up to you.

Many of these doctors and nurses at the sessions are in fact licensed physicians who have taken the required university medical courses, have been granted a license and have switched to Spiritism because they believe that it is more effective than regular medicine. Many of them are expert neurologists, chiropractors and pediatricians. When they deem it necessary they will write prescriptions that are accepted in pharmacies all over Brazil, and compound herbal remedies. The more advanced know that certain penicillins and modern drugs are effective, and they use them as a compliment to their cure of the laying on of hands.

While Brazil is supposedly a Catholic nation and therefore full of the usual Catholic charitable institutions, there are actually more Spiritist orphanages, hospitals, old folks' homes, libraries and shelters than Catholic. There are more Catholic schools than Spiritist in Brazil, but the Catholics get state and federal monies while the Spiritists get no government grants at all. There is a 300-bed hospital in Pôrto Alegre. There is a "transitory shelter" in São Paulo that serves 1250 meals daily. An orphanage in Rio de Janeiro takes care of 1000 lonely children. Santos has a "spiritual" first-aid station. A hotel in Poços de Caldas lets Spiritists stay a few days at this fashionable mineral water spa and gives poorer members bus tickets to visit their families or seek jobs in bigger cities. A library in Belo Horizonte has all of Kardek's volumes as well as the latest best sellers for Spiritist readers. A garage outside Campinas gives discounts on gasoline and repair services to those professing to be Spiritists. "Spiritism without charity," writes one Spiritist author, "is inconceivable: It just is not Spiritism."

The woman is Brazilian, Catholic and educated. She is the widow of a highly successful Rio de Janeiro lawyer. Her sister is married to an American newsman. Her daughter is married to an American foreign correspondent. She suffered from terrible arthritic pains. Doctors told her there was nothing she could do because the medicines she needed hadn't been invented yet. She listened to them all, suffered silently and then one day went into the interior and consulted a man named Arigó. He told her what her trouble was—she didn't get a chance to explain her symptoms. He scrawled

Drum and Candle

out a long prescription calling for some of the latest medicines and some that were so old that druggists had to search dusty shelves to find a remaining dosage. She drank a special brew and spread her hands with a special salve. The pains went away and have never come back.

A teen-age boy walked with a decided limp because one of his legs was three inches shorter than the other. Doctors in São Paulo had told his parents that there was an operation that could make the two legs the same length but they didn't want to try it because the boy had a heart condition and they didn't want him dying on their surgery table. The only thing they recommended was his wearing a thick-soled boot to even up his body. The boy fell in love with the prettiest girl in his small town and although she liked him, her father refused to have a cripple for a son-in-law. That was when he went to see Arigó. The boy was asked to lie on a small camp bed and to prop his good leg up on a box. Then Arigó took a large knife and a kitchen meat saw and cut a three-inch chunk out of the boy's good foreleg. Then he rejoined the two pieces, passed his hand over the wound, and the boy (who had not been under anesthetic or drugged at all) rose and walked out of the humble house. The story has a happy ending: He married the girl.

I had heard a lot about Arigó. Most of it was straight out of some science-fiction comic book. An uneducated man who operated on people without anesthetic, who used a common kitchen knife instead of a scalpel, who never spilled blood and who patched up his wounds simply by wetting his finger and drawing it over the incision . . . and there was never any scar. Fantastic, unbelievable, could never happen, all public relations stuff, I don't believe it . . . it's true . . . it's true . . . it's true!

José Arigó's real name is José Pedro de Freitas, but he has been nicknamed Arigó, which means "country bumpkin" or "simple individual." His friends call him that because he, in spite of his fame and incredible powers, has remained an honest, good-natured farm boy who loves his small home town, his wife and his children. He wouldn't hurt a fly, yet when he is under the spell of "Dr. Fritz" he slashes, stabs, twists and gouges with incredible, aggressive speed. Thousands come to him each year from all over Brazil, Uruguay, Paraguay and Argentina. He has been studied by a team of U.S. university medical specialists, and Pope Pius XII sent him a silver box inscribed with his personal thanks for mysterious services rendered.

There is no operation he doesn't undertake, from tumors, lipomas, cataracts and colostomies to cancers. His tools are an everyday paring knife, nail scissors and a pair of tweezers. These are usually kept in a rusty tin can. The patients assist every move, never sense pain and walk away feeling only slightly tired. How does he do it? With a spirit.

Arigó was born in the town of Congonhas do Campo. It is a traditional town of Catholic churches, colonial buildings and narrow-minded people. His father was a landowner and a local politician. His uncle was once mayor of the town. Arigó was just like every other local kid.

When he started to school he could only go half a day because he was needed to work his father's fields. Every now and then he would look up from his labors and be startled by a moving light. "It was a bright, round light, so brilliant that it nearly blinded me," and with this light there was usually a voice "speaking to me in a strange language." He dismissed the lights and the voices and blamed them on the tropical sun. Once he mentioned them at home and was told that "a good Catholic boy doesn't experience such things."

Growing up for him was easy and bucolic, and he waited until he was twenty-six before asking a local girl to marry him. Once he had a wife he realized he also had responsibilities and got a job in an iron-ore mine that was eight miles away. He had to get up at three in the morning in order to be there by six, and after wielding a pick and shovel for eight hours he had to walk all the way back home again. The money he made didn't pay the bills and his wife had to take up sewing for extra income. When he tried to get a raise for himself and the others and arrange for better working conditions the company fired him and called him a Communist. Nobody would hire him after that and he had to live on his wife's meager earnings. Seeing his children actually going hungry day after day, he asked his father for a loan and opened a small restaurant and bar. Because the town has some interesting colonial statues there are always tourists there. The tourists began frequenting his restaurant and he was able to repay his father and buy a house in town.

It was about this time that Arigó was in his father's barn and discovered a small crucifix hidden amid some corncobs. Nobody on the farm knew to whom it belonged, so he took it home with him. When he arrived in front of his house there was a little old man, a complete stranger, who asked Arigó for some food. He gave him food and the next night the same little old man was back asking for dinner again. Once again, Arigó fed him. For several nights running the little old man appeared and each time he was given a meal. Arigó asked no questions and the man volunteered no answers, but Arigó's wife complained that the man was coming almost at her bedtime. Arigó asked him if he couldn't come earlier.

The man shook his head. "I cannot come earlier, but if you would like, you can bring me the food at this hour every evening in the cemetery."

Arigo had no intention of going into a cemetery at that hour and told the stranger so. "Very well," said the man, "then take my dinner every day at this hour to the front of the church. You are a good man and have a good heart. It was I who left the crucifix for you to find among the corncobs. I left it for you to use when you cure the sick.

Drum and Candle

You must hold it in your hand and make a prayer. Yours is a great mission. . . ." Then the old man walked away into the darkness of the night.

To anyone else hearing such a story, the old man would have been put down as some nut and his free meal ticket torn up, but Arigó immediately went looking for someone to cure. Crucifix in hand, he went and knocked at a neighbor's door. A woman who had complained for years of sharp pains in her shoulders opened it. Imagine her surprise to see Arigó, nervously pushing a cross toward her and shouting, "You are cured! Your aches have all gone away!" She shut the door in a hurry and told her husband that the neighbor had gone mad. Next day, however, she came to see Arigó to thank him for chasing away her illness. That night had been the first night in years that she slept without waking up in pain. And the pains never came back.

In a small town, and especially in mystical Brazil, the word that Arigó could heal circulated rapidly. A man came to his door, dragging two worthless legs on crutches. Arigó swallowed deeply, said a quick prayer and then bravely commanded: "Throw away those crutches. You can walk!" The man let one crutch fall and then the other, and, as much to his amazement as Arigó's, he turned around and walked out of the house.

Arigó continued helping others and setting aside time from his regular job to heal those who came to him, but it became more and more difficult, for he began to have fainting spells and often blacked out for hours at a time. Local doctors examined him but could find nothing wrong. Then one night he heard a voice beside him. He awake and saw a short, fat and bald man in a white suit. Arigó thought he was still dreaming and put on the bedroom light. The man was still there. "I am Dr. Fritz," said the vision in German-accented Portuguese. "You will cure many. . . ."

He said nothing of this to his wife or his friends, sure he

was suffering from some mental block because of those fainting spells, but night after night the fat little spirit returned to his bedside. When he finally described him to his wife ("an enormous belly and a heavy German face") she thought the house was under the evil eye and called a priest to exorcise the demon. It did no good; the spirit kept returning every night.

It was then that a friend, a state senator, showed up in Arigó's home town. He had come for a political rally and afterward he, Arigó and some of the boys spent the night eating and drinking. He told Arigó that he was suffering from a lung tumor and that doctors neither in Rio nor New York were able to operate on it. But the senator was a good drinking companion and it wasn't until three in the morning that Arigó brought him back to his hotel. Then Arigó went home. Or so he thought.

The senator tells a different story. "Arigó took me to my room and stayed chatting while I brushed my teeth and put on my pajamas. Then he slowly began to disappear and in his place stood a fat, bald little man in a white doctor's uniform. Right behind him were three others, also in white and with non-Brazilian faces. The fat one announced that he was going to operate on my tumor. I told him he was crazy and thought I was drunk. Then I collapsed onto the bed and lost consciousness."

The senator awoke a few hours later and went to fetch Arigó back to the hotel room. He told him what had happened. Arigó at first took it as a joke, then when he saw that his friend was serious he became irritated. "You drink too much whisky and then invent stories that I am a Spiritist. I am a strict Catholic and don't want to hear anything about spirits. My family would be very upset to hear you say this!"

But the senator showed him his pajama tops. They had been slashed down the back. "You operated on me last night, Arigó my pal. I was not that drunk."

"But I wasn't that drunk either!" he protested. "I know nothing about operations. I would never think of doing such a thing." He searched the bed sheets and the torn jacket. "If this happened where is the blood? Huh? Where is the blood and where is the scar on your back? Stop with your fooling around, my friend. You just had too much alcohol, that's all."

The senator returned to Rio that afternoon and went immediately to his regular doctor. The physician took X rays and examined the man's back. Then he said, "The operation you must have had in the States was perfectly successful. The tumor has completely disappeared from your lung. They did a beautiful plastic job on the incision scar."

The senator told everyone of his operation, including the Brazilian press. Arigó got a lot of publicity, but still thought that his friend had been drunk.

Then it happened again, and this time in front of dozens of witnesses. There was an old lady in his town who was dying. The priest had given her extreme unction and her family had placed her on her deathbed and surrounded it with candles. The room was full of neighbors, all there to pay their last respects, when Arigó arrived to pay his as well. He stood beside the bed and studied the old woman's face. His eyes were moist with tears. Suddenly those eyes became hard and brittle and without saying a word he rushed out of the bedroom and into the kitchen. He was back almost immediately, carrying a large knife. He pushed the people away from the bedside and ordered them to "stand back" in a harsh, German-accented voice. Before anyone could stop him he plunged the knife into the old woman's abdomen.

As the crowd stood aghast he worked at lightning speed, opening the stomach wall, cutting and removing a growth. Then he joined the incision simply by pressing it together, edge to edge. The operation over, he blinked several times and was amazed to see the knife in his hand. The old woman, within a few minutes, rose from her bed and began to walk around the room. No one there could believe their eyes, yet "something" had happened. The woman was now far from dying and the tumor was there for all to see, and yet there was not a sign of a scar on her belly. The priest who had administered extreme unction asked him what he had done. Arigó shook his head. "I don't know, Father. I fainted, I think. I have had fainting spells lately, and when I came to they told me the old woman had been operated on. I don't remember anything. That's all I know."

After that Arigó and his miraculous operations became legend. Buses were charted from points all over the nation for pilgrimages to his home. He operated on every type of patient and was investigated by doctors from the larger cities. One medical man even took a film of Arigó in action showing him operating on a giant cyst and stopping the hemorrhaging by merely saying, "Let there be no blood, Lord."

Testimonies from hundreds of patients have filled Brazilian magazine articles and books about this spirit healer. He has been persecuted by the Catholic Church, which has called him a "heretic" and accused him of being in "league with the devil." Police, acting under orders of local padres and bishops, have invaded his home several times looking for reasons to stop his practice. Once someone (whispers say it was a group of local doctors) hired a thug to beat him up. He was condemned to two and a half years in prison by a municipal court for practicing medicine without a license but was pardoned by then President Juscelino Kubitschek, who (say the whisperers) had asked Arigó to operate successfully on one of his daughters.

Even his spirit medium, "Dr. Fritz," has been interviewed by the press and by visiting medical men. An investigating team from Berlin watched Arigó in action and conversed with Dr. Fritz in perfect German all during the operation. Dr. Fritz identified himself as a German surgeon who was killed in the

First World War and said that he is often aided in these operations by Dr. Gilbert Pierre, a Frenchman who specialized in ophthalmology when he was alive, and by a Japanese specialist named Takahasi, who does the tumors. They work with the spirit of Friar Fabiano de Cristo, who when he lived was famed for his charity, and who sterilizes the instruments and anesthetizes the patients with a paranormal "green light." Often spectators to Arigó's operations (and there have been literally thousands of witnesses) have heard Dr. Fritz's voice call out for "more green light" and those sitting near the operating table have lost consciousness immediately.

Catholic persecution and outright ostracism made Arigó abandon Mass and convert completely to Spiritism. It was a difficult thing for him to do, because of his traditional upbringing, but it was a natural consequence of his association with Dr. Fritz. Arigó refuses to accept money for his operations (and one grateful husband offered him $50,000 when his wife was cured of a "hopeless" cancer) but does accept contributions for his spirit center and hospital called Jesus Nazarene.

It was at this hospital that I arrived one morning, accompanied by an American newsman who was a "materialist and I don't believe in ghosts and spirits" kind of person. Hardheaded, he had filed stories from Paris, Moscow and Vietnam. I was asked to help him interview Arigó and translate for him. (When I worked for *Time* and wanted to do the story of Arigó they turned it down, saying that they had no place for witch doctors on the medicine page.)

The ground around the small clinic was covered with people, most of them poorly dressed and almost all of them with lumps on their faces and arms, bandages around their heads or patches over their eyes. There were those who walked with crutches and others in crude wheelchairs. There were also three women in a brand-new Cadillac who covered their faces with their purses when we passed by.

Drum and Candle

I managed to squirm my way through the crowd and got to the front door with the Ace Foreign Correspondent in tow. A very charming girl stopped me at the door, and when I explained who I was and why I was there, she let us pass. We walked a few steps and then right into the operating room. It wasn't like any operating room I had ever seen before. Granted, the walls were painted white, but that was the only concession to normality. It was about forty-five feet square and had a wooden bed against the left wall. There was a straw mattress and a pillow on the bed. A large window let in plenty of sunlight and a Coleman lantern hung overhead for illumination at night. There was an old door in the middle of the room, upon wooden carpenter's horses. Beside it was a small table with a tin can. Inside the can there were several kitchen knives, a scalpel, a pair of tweezers and a pair of scissors. There were also some twenty people standing or crouched around the walls.

Arigó came striding into the room and smiled at us. The Ace Foreign Correspondent wanted to be introduced immediately, but I held him back. In Brazil you have to "sense" the right time for doing things.

The famed healer, dressed in a pair of dark trousers and a light blue sport shirt, seemed heavier than in his photos. He was dark-complexioned, almost Italian, with dark, short-cropped hair and a short bristle mustache. He needed a shave and also looked as if he could use some sleep. I had heard that he was working from daybreak to way past midnight every day and managed to get a few hours' sleep only when his wife insisted that he stop for the night.

He walked to the group of patients and stared at each of them in turn. He merely glanced at me and the newspaper man, but he stopped and pointed to a woman beside me. "You don't need an operation," he said quickly. His Portuguese came out heavily accented in German. If it hadn't been for that, I would never have known that he was at that moment possessed by the spirit of Dr. Fritz.

"But doctor," the woman began, "you don't know what my problem is."

"Your problem is your spinal column! You can't sleep at night and often half your body seems to be numb. Here"—and he wrote rapidly on a pad of paper, tore off the page and handed it to the woman—"take these medicines. And stop drinking so much coffee! The caffeine only aggravates your condition!" Then he moved on to the next person.

"You! In the yellow shirt!" A man stepped from the rear of the crowd. "Come over here!" He followed Arigó to the horizontal door and climbed onto it when he was so ordered.

"My God!" whispered Ace Correspondent, "that piece of junk is his operating table!" Somebody behind us said, "Shhh!"

Arigó grabbed the man's arm and turned it over, palm up. We could all see a lump the size of a lime under the skin of his upper arm. Arigó reached for a scalpel from the tin can, but instead of making an incision, he merely rubbed the blade over the skin. The tissues parted—but without shedding a drop of blood—and Arigó squeezed with his fingers. There was a slight "pop" as the fatty tissue (lipoma) came out whole. Then he passed a piece of ordinary cotton over the wound and told the man to go home. The man stared at the place where the tumor had been and broke into a big smile. We all just stared. No scar, no pain, no more tumor. He started to say something to Arigó, but the healer just pointed rudely toward the door. The man left smiling and incredulous.

A woman went through the same sort of thing, only this time the tumor was in the middle of her back. We saw it all, and she immediately left the room with no scars or pain.

Ace Foreign Correspondent turned to me and whispered, "Must be some kind of a trick. I remember once seeing a medicine man in Indonesia . . ." But Arigó had chosen a

Drum and Candle

teen-age boy from the group and was leading him toward the operating table/door. He had to lead him, I noticed, for the boy was blind.

He helped him onto the table and told him not to be afraid. The boy said he wasn't afraid. "Fine," said Dr. Fritz, "you just relax."

Then Arigó grabbed a kitchen knife and jabbed it straight into the boy's right eye. With brusque and even violent movements, he pried the eye out of the socket until it was resting in his hand. A little bit of blood came out of the empty hole but Dr. Fritz mumbled something and the blood stopped. He reached for a scalpel and gouged at something on the back of the eyeball and then stuffed it back into the socket. The boy did not cry out, did not try to push Arigó's hands away. He just sat there quietly and let himself be attacked. Then the other eye was pried loose and hung for a moment onto his cheek while Dr. Fritz sliced away at the rear of the eyeball. Then it too was shoved back in place. Then he patted the boy on the arm and told him to leave.

The boy got off the table and stood uneasily for a minute or two. Then he shut his eyes with all his might and opened them again. He gazed around the room in wonderment. Then he put his hands up to his face and looked at them, each in turn. A woman who had been in a far corner began to cry, came and put her arms around him. He also began to cry as he looked into his mother's face for the first time in his life.

I felt tears running down my own cheeks, and not wanting to appear ridiculous in front of Ace Foreign Correspondent, I turned to him ready with some sophisticated, sarcastic remark, but he wasn't there. He was hanging out a side window throwing up the scrambled eggs and coffee he had had for breakfast.

7

Copacabana. On one side of the avenue, tall, modern apartment buildings. On the beach thousands of flickering candles. On the avenue the latest automobiles, on the beach drums and animal sacrifices. On the avenue well-dressed Cariocas celebrating New Year's Eve, on the beach white-clad adepts celebrating the day of Yemanjá.

Auld Lang Syne and Sarava Umbanda. Château Neuf de Pape and *cachaça* rum. Humming air conditioners and sand crunched under bare feet. Chanel Number Five and Good Luck incense. Twinkling Christmas trees and spark-shooting bonfires. Diamond brooches and cheap bead necklaces. Father Time and Oxalá. Christianity and paganism. Today and yesterday.

Copacabana beach is probably one of the best-known pleasure spots in the world. It has figured in countless films and dozens of books and on countless postcards. It attracts thousands of tourists every year and millions of Brazilians all year. It plays host to stars of Rio's International Film Festival and to famous singers of Rio's International Song Festival and has been visited by such world-renowned figures as Queen Elizabeth II, Franklin Delano Roosevelt, Brigitte Bardot, the Shah of Iran, Yuri Gagarin, Neil Armstrong, the King of Belgium, the Emperor of Ethiopia and Cardinal Montini just before he became Pope Paul IV.

Yet every night it is visited by humble believers of Umbanda

Drum and Candle

who place candles on the sand and pray to a host of gods and spirits. And every December 31 it becomes the stage for the biggest, most colorful and strangest religious ceremony in the world.

The people begin to congregate on the beach just before sundown. They come from all over the city and in buses and trucks from outlying towns as well. The big groups are congregations from various Umbanda "tents" or temples. Smaller groups may be friends or members of one family. Individuals also appear and claim their plot of sand.

The congregations bring huge allegorical gifts to the sea goddess. They may spend the better part of a year building a lightweight boat, decorating it with paper flowers and streamers and filling it with things the goddess likes, such as mirrors, hair ribbons, perfumes, combs and bottles of whisky. Another group may have a tall altar built on wheels that is covered in white crepe-paper flowers and ornamented with statues of all the important Umbanda and Christian saints. Another may bring an expensive double bed with white satin sheets and pillowcases and strew the white satin spread with gifts for the goddess.

Usually the best clothes are saved (or made especially) for this New Year's Eve festivity. The women will wear white full skirts that stop just short above their dancing bare feet. The men usually wear white trousers and sport shirts. Depending on the financial situation of each temple or individual there will be bead necklaces, costume jewelry and feathers. Sometimes there is enough money for the male leader or Father of the Saint to wear a billowing white satin cape. Sometimes the female leader or Mother of the Saint will wear a blouse of the finest Portuguese lace and her skirts will be of Hong Kong silk. The children, and there are always small girls and boys in these rituals, are usually dressed in white. It's not that white is their favorite color (for Brazilians love to dress in all the

Drum and Candle

colors of the rainbow), but it is Yemanjá's favorite color when she is in Rio, and after all, the party is for her.

The large groups spread their area with flowers, gifts and burning candles, while the family groups and individuals dig a small hole in the sand and place their offerings and candles in it. The idea is that if you offer a present to Yemanjá and she accepts it, then your wish will come true. If your want a material thing, like a new car, a fancy hat or a trip to Paris, then you light an even number of candles. If you want an immaterial thing, like a lover returned, your health restored or your mother-in-law to go away, then you light an odd number of candles.

How do you know if the goddess has accepted your gift or not? Because she comes up out of the sea and takes it, that's how!

By eleven-thirty the beach is completely covered with burning candles, dancing people and curious onlookers. The drums beat, throats are strained in chanted praise of Yemanjá and flashbulbs from tourists' cameras illuminate a black face or a frightened goat. The sound of sand being squashed under bare feet, the sound of laughter from playing children, the sound of crackling bonfires.

From the avenue, just a few feet from all this primitive spiritism, comes the sound of automobiles, the sound of Frank Sinatra's latest record, the sound of popping champagne corks, the sound of chapel bells calling the faithful to midnight Mass.

By eleven forty-five the tension begins to mount. You can taste the electricity in the air. The beach is so full that you find it difficult to take even a few steps. Those who have watches keep glancing at them to check the time. The drums beat faster and the singers stretch their vocal chords to the utmost as they beseech Yemanjá to make her appearance.

By eleven fifty-five the drums are so rapid that you wish you had worn earplugs. The groups are dancing in a frenzy and several women have become possessed by their spirits. The crowd has pushed to the very edge of the sea. There are people in bathing trunks and others in sparkling evening gowns. There are black faces and white faces, young faces and old faces, rich faces and poor faces. The faces all have one thing in common: an intense strained look as they wait for the first stroke of midnight. Hands are filled with flowers, mostly white gladiolas on long green stems, but others have bouquets of roses, carnations and even orchids.

Midnight. Suddenly the air around you explodes. Fireworks shoot out from the tall apartment buildings along the avenue, church bells ring and automobile horns screech. The crowd surges toward the water, but the amazing thing is that the water also comes surging up onto the crowd. Waves unseen before rise up and pound the shore. Waves grab at bare feet, at pants legs, at gown hemlines. Waves engulf the swimmers who have dived into them, their arms covered in flowers and their hands full of presents. Flowers, hundreds of them, arch from the blackness of the crowd into the blackness of the sea. The air is filled with their rushing perfumes. They hit the water and are immediately carried away.

Those who have built their altars and lit their candles away from the edge of the water watch in fascination and fear as the waves come swirling up to extinguish the candles and carry off their gifts. You feel the force of the water as it rushes back into the sea and you feel the mirrors, combs, bottles of rum and champagne as they bump against your ankles. Somewhere nearby a chicken squawks and its white body, neck twisted and gasping, is thrown to the goddess. A man breaks into tears as he sees his flower offering returned to him. A woman kneels into the waves and the water rises above the shoulders of her Paris-inspired *tailleur*. A goat bleats in terror, then is silent. Its body will be found in a few days miles away from the beach.

At twelve-ten the waves have diminished considerably (or

is it just your imagination?) and the groups have gone back to their dancing and drum beating. The fancy altars, the gift-laden boats, the satin sheets are all gone. They have been pushed into the water and the goddess has been pleased.

The curious start to leave, heading back to their parties in air-conditioned nightclubs and apartments. They carry their silver slippers in their hands, the hems of their gowns raised high so as not to drag them on the damp sand. The devout stay to watch the ritual dancing and to consult the possessed. An ancient Negress is smoking a stubby pipe, her hair matted over her face and her eyes glazed. She grabs the man who is talking to her and pulls him first to her left shoulder and then to her right. She blows smoke in his face and snatches at some evil that only she can see covering his body. He asks a question and she gives a loud, insane laugh. Then she whispers something into his ear. He breaks into a smile and seems relieved. She embraces him again, pulling him first to the left shoulder and then to the right. Then she makes the sign of the cross. He steps aside and another believer seeks her spirit-given advice.

Of course, you don't believe any of this, even though it is colorful and different, but you stand in a circle where another old crone is being consulted. A white girl, dressed in a fancy party gown, listens intently as the woman speaks. Right behind her is another white girl, obviously a friend and obviously not believing anything that is going on. She makes a face to her boy friend in the crowd and laughs at something he has shouted. The woman gives the first girl her blessing and she steps aside. The friend, still grinning, approaches the woman and jokingly asks for a blessing. Suddenly the girl stops. Her arms and legs begin to shake as if she had turned terribly cold on this hot night. Her elbows and hands twist into the air. Her neck bends forward and then snaps back, throwing her neatly combed hair into confusion. She shakes so violently that she begins to stagger. She cries out, her eyes two orbs of terror, as she tries to control her bobbing head. The pins and ribbons fall from her hair. She sinks onto one knee, the pink chiffon gown embedded in the coarse sand. She clutches at her throat and only manages to send the pearls of her necklace scattering in the darkness. She goes down on one elbow, her other arm reaching out, pleading, toward the old woman. The Negress watches her gyrations with disdain. She lets her collapse onto the sand before she makes a few hand passes in the air over the girl's body. The unbeliever becomes quiet immediately. Her shaking and hoarse, guttural cries cease. The woman stands with her legs apart, the smoke from her pipe hiding the glint in her eyes. The girl manages to rise to her knees before the old woman helps her to her feet. Her hair is a mess, her dress is torn and her face is marred with tears and sand. She walks unsteadily toward her boy friend, who puts a protective arm around her and leads her away. "What happened?" he questions. "I don't know," she replies. "I just don't know."

The religion of Umbanda. The religion that has Rio de Janeiro in its grasp. The religion that calls upon the African gods but is far different from Candomblé. The religion that uses the spirits to heal but is far different from Spiritism. Umbanda: the unique, powerful, hybrid religion of an estimated two and a half million Brazilians.

Umbanda is not as simple to define as Candomblé, nor does it have the historical background of Spiritism. Dozens of books have been published on it in Brazil and none of them seem to agree on anything but the basic points. It is more modern than the African rituals of Bahia and more organized than the Spiritism of the larger cities. On the spiritual level it is higher than Candomblé but lower than Kardekism. It is often called macumba by those not in the know, but the word "macumba" really means a place or meeting house for African practices. It denounces black magic, yet considers Quimbanda as a natural branch even though evil spells are

Quimbanda's basic creed. It has all of the familiar African spirits and dozens of local Brazilian ones, but it has none of the spirits that inhabit Kardek's world. It lights candles and beats drums, yet Jesus and the Virgin Mary play very active roles. Does it all sound confusing? Well, it is.

Umbanda, claim the high priest practitioners and professors, is a religion that uses African spirits because they are a way of identifying with the common man. It uses Christian saints for the same reason. It does not use the spirits of dead human beings, because these spirits don't know anything. They cannot give anything to the earth-bound man that the earth-bound man doesn't already know. The oracles of Umbanda are "spirits which never existed in human form." Should anyone ridicule these deities they ask the skeptic to remember that Jesus was never really a "man" but an "embodied spirit." They remind bishops and priests that Christians believe in such "non-human spirits" as God the Father, the angel Gabriel, heavenly cherubs, angels of all species, demons and the devil. One Umbanda writer, after listing such entities as Jehovah, djins, elves, vampires, gnomes, sylphs, nymphs, divs and witches, asks, "Why should all languages give a name to these beings if they don't exist? They must exist or else the world has been classifying Nothings!"

Umbanda is accused of classifying Nothings by the Brazilian Catholic Church and the Spiritists as well. The Umbandistas have divided the spirit world (*their* spirit world!) into seven different Lines. Each Line groups together certain spirits who have the same affinities. Like truckers, musicians, actors or carpenters, they move around in their own union. A believer is born into a certain Line or else moves into another, more suitable Line through worldly experience. Each Line has a "four-star general" who commands seven "divisions." Each division has a three-star general who commands seven "battalions." Each battalion has a two-star general who commands seven "subdivisions." With all those leaders, divisions,

Drum and Candle

troops and regulations, it's no wonder it is confusing. And, of course, each four-star general has his or her favorite food, preferred color, favorite day of the week, special number, special chant, special magic symbol, preferred perfume, incense, herb and way of being greeted.

In command of Line 1 is Oxalá, who is also known as Jesus Christ. Line 2 is under the strict authority of Yemanjá, who is called the Virgin Mary. Line 3 is Ogun/St. George. Line 4 Oxóssi/St. Sebastian. Line 5 is headed by Xangó/St. James, 6 by Oxun/St. Catherine and 7 by Omulu/St. Lazarus.

To give a complete rundown on all the four-star generals and their various divisions would take up too much time and only add to the confusion. Pedro McGregor (a Brazilian in spite of the name and one of the nation's most expert spirit mediums) has published an excellent book on the religion,* and his rundown of the seven Lines takes up four full pages. His paragraph on Line 1 is an example of the complexity of Umbanda:

The First Line: Oxalá/Jesus Christ
Oxalá-Alufan is the "three-star general" who is second in command. He only "comes down" to take a medium under control every seven-times-seven years. Next in line is Oxalá-Guian, who "comes down" every seven years. Oxalá-Dacun and the remainder of this rank "come down" each year. St. Anthony, St. Cosme [sic] and St. Damion [sic], known as Ibejis, St. Catherine and St. Francis of Assisi, are among these leaders of the Phalanxes in the First Line. The color used by the *Filhos* or *Filhas de Santo*, the children of this saint, those mediums whose Orixá or spirit guide belongs to the Oxalá-Line, wear white in religious ceremonies, sport white beads with three red ones among them, make their offerings of white bread, vegetables and light wines. Oxalá's favorite food, however, is *canjica*, made of corn. His day is Sunday, though special incantations have to be made on a Friday. The fetich is a golden ring; the metal, gold.

* *The Moon and Two Mountains,* Souvenir Press, London.

Drum and Candle

Yemanjá is just as complicated, only she prefers milky blue beads, likes green corn to eat and is in charge of the mermaids, the ondines and St. Mary Magdalene. The other female four-star general is Oxun, who is St. Catherine. She is also, somehow, connected with the Greek Aphrodite! She prefers fish to eat, blue and yellow beads to wear and to be called upon on Friday.

Umbanda has only been around for the past fifty years or so. It was a natural—and needed—result of the lower- and middle-class urban citizen needing something to believe in that was more sophisticated than African ritual and more understandable than French-implanted Spiritism. Kardek's works were far too complicated for the majority of the poor and almost unintelligible to the millions of uneducated. His Spiritist findings are purely mental and to be understood must be studied and discussed. His various planes, his theories of death and reincarnation did find a place with the upper classes and better-educated, but when they tried to explain it all to the mass of illiterates it just did not come across.

The blacks and mulattoes wanted to believe and did believe that there was another spirit world, that this earthly prison was only a passing phase toward better things. They had heard enough ghost stories, seen enough physical cures and experienced enough extrasensory events to know that the basis of what Kardek reported was true. But he and his spirits had made everything so difficult!

And his practitioners in Brazil had also made it boring! What was the use attending a Spiritist session where there were no drums, no dancing, no excitement, no incense and no loud possessions of the mediums? And when the spirits did come down, who were they? Doctors, padres, professors and the like—not people that the Negro lower classes could identify with. They missed the lusty Xangô and his two jealous wives. They remembered their parents talking about Yemanjá. And where were the Ibeji twins in Kardek's organized white spirit world? What had happened to Oxóssi and his hunting equipment? Where were all those spirits that came down when the Candomblé priestesses called them? And most importantly, where was the devilish and feared Exú? How could anyone have a religion and forget to placate the god of evil? No, they reasoned, Kardek had many things in his favor but so did their ancestors. If both were right, then the most logical step would be to combine the two, taking the best and discarding the rest. Thus Umbanda was born.

The man usually given the credit for organizing Umbanda is Zélio de Moraes. He was tall and blond and white-skinned. He was raised a Catholic but was constantly bothered with visions of dead Indians. Like Arigó, he fought these visitations, then finally gave in to them. He gave advice while possessed by the spirit of a Brazilian Indian half-breed named Caboclo of the Seven Crossroads. Caboclo was part Negro and part Indian. He was in direct communication with the African spirits of the Candomblé group and also on excellent terms with the spirits of the local Indians. The people who came to Zélio for consultation believed everything Caboclo said, for after all, he was one of them. He was not the ghost of just any dead half-breed but was a half-breed spirit in the tradition of the African jungle spirits. He was a mixture of bloods. The Brazilians who talked to him were also a mixture of bloods. He knew their nation and had witnessed their history. He spoke their language, not some African tribal dialect. In short, he was theirs. He was one of them. That was terribly important.

Zélio had heard about Kardek and had been to some of the macumba meetings that were held in Rio à la Candomblé style, but Caboclo told him that neither creed was right and proceeded to dictate a brand-new set of rules, regulations, rituals, chants, drumbeats, herbal cures, curses, dance steps, etc. Before Zélio could set up his "tent," or church, Rio police broke up the group. So he moved across the bay into the

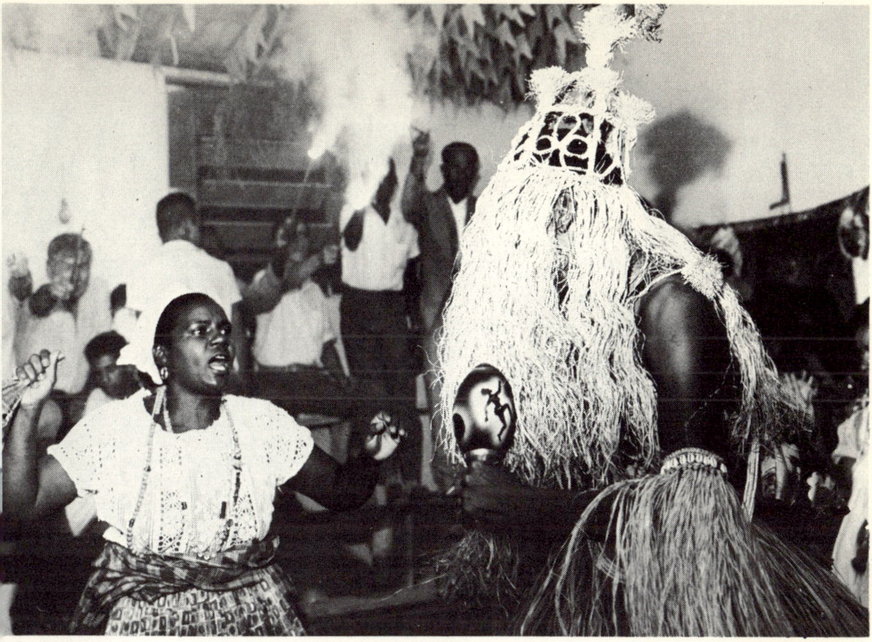

MANCHETE PRESS AGENCY

1. Omulu wears a long straw veil to hide his face, for he is the spirit of lepers and the diseased and his features are hideously scarred. He is also either St. Lazarus or St. Benedict.

2. At an outdoor ceremony inaugurating a temple in the state of Minas Gerais, an Umbanda high priestess is seized by one of the spirits.

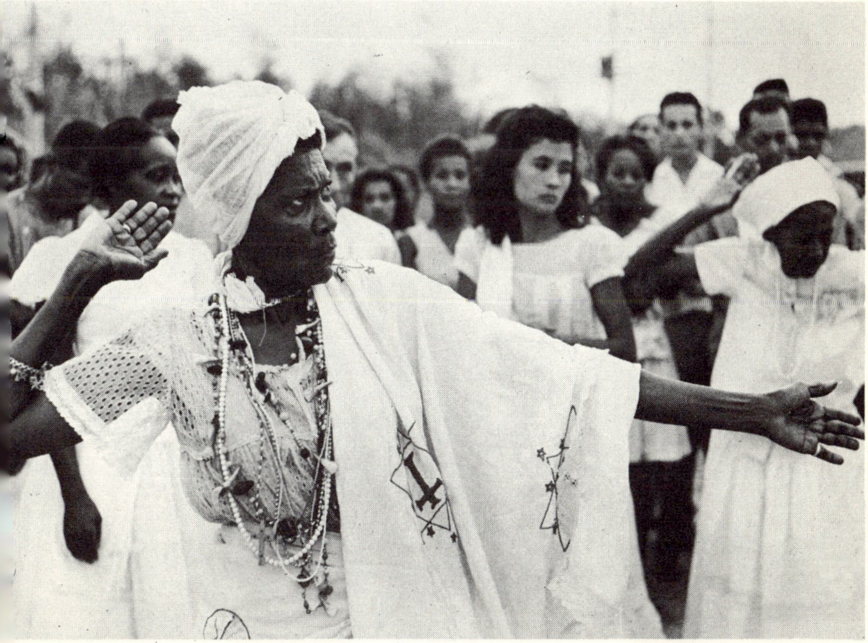

MANCHETE PRESS AGENCY

3. In Rio an Umbanda priest is seized by the spirit of the Old Black Slave. He puffs on a cheap cigar and rolls his eyes back into his forehead.

4. Color and social position are forgotten at an Umbanda session as this elegant Rio woman is "cleansed" by the spirit of the Indian Jurema.

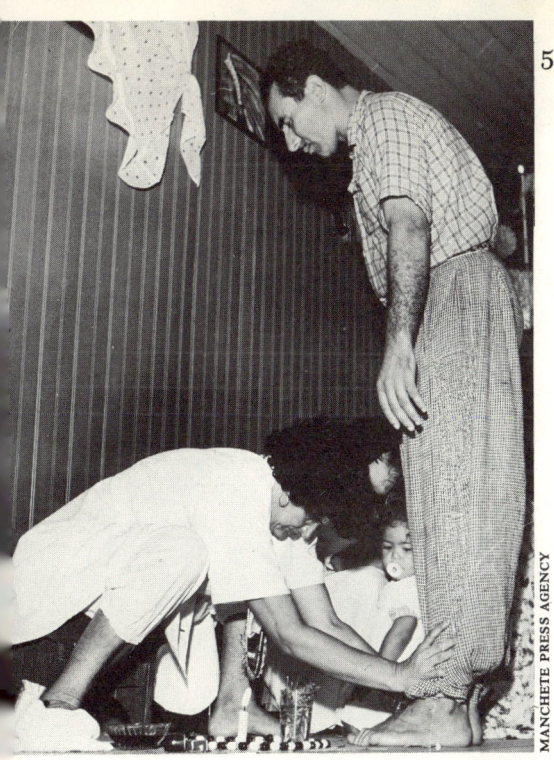

5. In Rio Grande do Sul, where Negro blood is rare, the Umbanda temples are staffed by whites. Here a gaucho, right off the pampas, gets "cleansed" by a possessed medium.

6. In Rio Grande do Sul this big blond priestess blesses a little boy exactly in the same way that her black counterparts would do in Rio or Bahia.

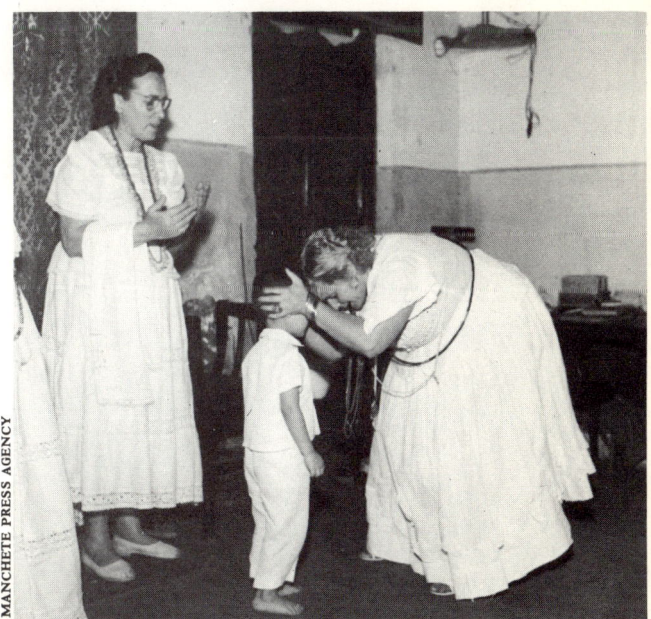

7. A Saturday night meeting at one of the larger Umbanda centers in modern industrial São Paulo.

8. At a hidden Quimbanda (black magic) session, a man kneels in a circle drawn for the devil, Exú, and tears the entrails out of a live black chicken with his teeth.

neighboring town of Nieroi. The police were easier on him there, and his congregation grew with each session. People came to him for advice, for cures and to be comforted. His assistants began to be possessed by other native Brazilian spirits, spirits who represented Negro slaves and other Indians. The Yoruba deities also came down and possessed his helpers, and so did the spirits of the Roman Catholic Church. In one session there would be whites, blacks and Indians rolling and chanting, dancing and shouting and all ready to be consulted and to help the poor and uneducated.

Where the word "umbanda" originates is also in doubt, but it could have come from the Sanskrit (!!) *Aum-bandha,* which means "the limit of the unlimited" or "the divine principle." When Zélio inaugurated his church he did not name it after either African or Indian spirits, but chose to call it "The Tent of Our Lady of Piety."

Here indeed was Brazilian miscegenation brought to the highest form. The early Portuguese with their Moorish heritage who mated with both the local Indians and the imported Africans would have understood completely.

But the police did not understand and they kept harassing Zélio's followers and anyone else who tried to set up a tent of his own. The movement was forced underground, although everyone knew where a session could be found. It thrived because it appealed to all classes, and barefoot Negroes more than once had to walk around the fancy automobiles of white believers in order to get into the tents. Skin color was not important to the spirits who gave advice, nor was money or social position. Of course, each tent bragged about the visits of the wealthy lady or the politician who frequented their sessions, but the blacks and mulattoes noted that when it came time to talk to the spirits the rich stayed right in line with the poor.

An Umbanda tent is not unlike a Candomblé hut, except that it may be in an apartment building, a house or a converted store. It does not have to have ground around it to appease Exú and the spirits of the dead. When Exú shows up they know how to get rid of him by singing and flattery. Thus any ample area can become a tent, and it has been estimated that there are some thirty-two thousand of these tents in the city of Rio de Janeiro alone!

The room is divided for the men to sit on one side and the women on the other. The benches are not unlike church pews. The congregation sits facing an empty floor space where the "Father of the Saint" and his assistants will dance. Against the wall there will be an altar with the usual collection of plaster Catholic images and another dozen or so Indian and African spirit images. The largest image is always in the center and always of the tent's patron saint. Sometimes it will be Ogun/St. George astride a handsome horse and sticking a spear into the neck of a terrible dragon. If it is Oxóssi/St. Sebastian it will show the young man bound to a tree trunk, his arms tied over his head and his nearly naked body pierced with arrows. Yemanjá will be either rising up out of the sea in a magnificent blue gown and a crown on her head or else lying on a huge sea shell in the form of a mermaid, her long black hair making no attempt to conceal her naked breasts. Around these statues and images will be framed pictures of saints, strings of beads, paper or plastic flowers, lighted candles, glasses of magnetized water, good luck symbols, paper stars and crescent moons and a large crucifix.

The sessions are open to the public (police action today is restricted to Quimbanda black magic and denounced charlatans) and are usually held three times a week. Often other sessions are held to honor a certain spirit or saint on his or her particular day. The sessions are almost always at night, around 9:30 P.M.

The session usually begins with the Father of the Saint (who is supreme boss of the tent) praying to God for guidance while an assistant walks to the four corners of the room waving a smoking incense burner much the way a Catholic

Drum and Candle

priest would do. Then the assistant walks through the congregation, purifying the air there as well.

There is one drummer instead of the Candomblé three, and he begins when the Father gives the signal. Then the assistants, both men and women, chant the first hymn to the patron saint of the tent. They sway with the drumbeats but don't try any of the fancy dancing that Candomblé Daughters do. These assistants are dressed in white. The men wear hospital-type jackets and trousers and the women have white blouses but larger, full skirts.

(Before tourists and resident Brazilian experts jump on me, let me quickly say that there is probably no religion with as many exceptions to the rules as Umbanda. Several sets of codes have been drawn up and there have even been national congresses to discuss the standardization of the rituals, but Brazilians being Brazilians—i.e. highly individualistic—they go ahead and do things their own way. There is a "high" and "low" Umbanda as well as an unnamed "middle" Umbanda. In the low they bring out snakes, drink rum, walk barefoot on broken glass and scribble cabalistic chalk marks on the floor. In the slightly higher they do away with the animals and reptiles, but keep the alcohol and walk through fire. They may also wear any color they choose. In the high sessions they try to be as much like the Kardek believers as possible in dress and comportment while at the same time paying homage to the primitive spirits who smoke cigars, roll their eyes and crawl on the floor.

It should also be pointed out that both men and women participate in the dancing and receive the spirits into their bodies, unlike the Bahian Candomblé, where women rule completely. In Rio de Janeiro, São Paulo and interior cities the Umbanda sessions are almost always organized and run by men. But, of course, there are exceptions.

These exceptions and confusions have created rifts among the Umbandistas themselves, and it is possible that within a few generations there will be *one more* new sect formed by the far extremists. This can all be excused by the fact that Umbanda is not more than fifty years old and that a much longer period of time is needed before it clearly defines itself. Christianity took centuries to get organized and then proceeded to splinter off into a dozen different groups. Having this in mind, we have no right to accuse the Umbandistas of mismanagement.)

Then begin the songs. The first one is to St. Michael to stand guard and close off the evil that may want to come into the tent. Depending on the various assistants and the spirits that normally possess their bodies, certain songs are sung to bring the gods down to the floor of the temple. Each spirit has his own song and must be invoked by this song before he will appear. Each spirit has his own drumbeat as well, and only those who are really initiated into the service can note the subtle differences. These songs are called, of all things, *sambas,* and their rhythm and liveliness have profoundly affected the music of Brazil and, for that matter, of all South America.

Having been called, having heard their songs and having danced to their drumbeats, the spirits come down. As in the Bahian Candomblé, they come one at a time, grabbing the unwary dancer, throwing her into a trance, making her tremble, shuffle, gasp, moan, cry out, weave, totter, extend her arms, clench her fists, roll her eyes, pull her hair, fall on the ground, shout, scowl, whisper or laugh. The confusion, at times, is great as ten or twelve overcrowded spirits plunge and dance in the small area in front of the altar. When the Father of the Saints (who may or may not be possessed himself) feels that all the saints who are going to show up have arrived, he makes a motion to sing another song:

> *Who comes, who comes from so far away?*
> *They are our guides who are here to work.*
> *Oh give me strength, for the love of God, my father,*
> *Oh give me strength for the work that I must do.*

Drum and Candle

The music stops and the Father of the Saints makes each possessed medium sit or stand in a certain place. Then an assistant who has not been possessed lets the public onto the dance floor one by one. Adepts of Umbanda know which spirit is good for what problem.

I have seen Brazilians (and not a few foreigners) of all social classes consult the Umbanda spirits. I remember a woman in a tattered sweater and a faded skirt who, after listening carefully to what the Old Black Slave whispered to her, broke down and sobbed like a baby. They had to carry her out of the tent. I recall an Englishman who went to a session just for a joke and came out amazed at what he had been told by the Indian woman Jurema. She gave him an accurate picture of his marital life, which was none too good. She told him that while he had come to Brazil with the British Foreign Service, his wife had stayed on in London to arrange the packing of the apartment furniture and to make sure the children were enrolled in the right schools. She also told him that his wife was being unfaithful to him, and that he suspected it and this worry was giving him headaches and causing him to drink while on the job. She asked him if he were not adult enough to throw away the bottle of scotch that he had locked in his desk drawer and to stop having three martinis every night when he came home. He told me all this while trying to keep his British aplomb, but at the same time he admitted that he was afraid his wife had a lover in London and that he *was* harming his work and his health by his constant drinking. As for the martinis, he had promised himself never to drink more than three each evening!

Sometimes the advice the spirits hand down can be deadly. Newspapers often run stories about murders and suicides that have happened because of a visit to an Umbanda session. A woman suspected her lover of being unfaithful and a spirit told her that her rival was her next-door neighbor. She shot the innocent neighbor. A man was worried that he was going to lose his job. The spirits said that one of his office companions was carrying tales about him to the boss. The man confronted his colleague with the story and was greeted with laughter. He stabbed the man with a pair of scissors. A teen-ager was constantly getting failing grades in school, in spite of the fact that she studied night after night. A spirit at an Umbanda session said that the girl who sat behind her in history class was putting the evil eye on her. After carrying out several *despachos* her marks failed to improve, so she threw acid in her classmate's face.

A *despacho* is the special Umbanda way to get through to the gods. It is a prayer, an offering and a cure. It is always accompanied by candles. It was a *despacho* that I saw burning on the Copacabana street corner shortly after I arrived in Rio. Tourists find the flickering candles on Copacabana beach "picturesque," but they are *despachos* to a certain god, in this case usually Yemanjá.

Despachos are as varied as the many requests and the many spirits can make them. You never know what the god wants for helping you with your problem, so you must consult with him at an Umbanda session. Maybe he will tell you to buy a black chicken, slit its throat with a razor blade and tie a blue ribbon around its left leg, then take the chicken to the front door of the one who has done you wrong. Leave it there with three burning candles. Your enemy will repent and your bad luck will change.

Does the one you love not love you? Find a huge shady tree and pour *cachaça* cane alcohol around its base. Then place three candles in a row. Take a small photograph of yourself and write his name on the back of it. Now burn this photo from the flame of the center candle. The smoke will unite your face and his name. You will be married soon after.

Your child is not eating? Place such-and-such herbs in a leather pouch and tie it around his neck. Your debts piling up? Light a candle at your front and back door and bathe daily with the "soap that calls money." Need a job? Light a candle to your guardian angel, take a bath with white rose petals and whole cloves, drink a tea called "open the path" and go to three Masses in one day only to assist the raising of the Host.

Umbanda has worked out most of the rituals that are found in other organized religions. When a child is born its parents tell the local Umbanda Father of the Saints and he puts a protective smoke screen of lavender, myrrh and benjamin incense around the child. When it is one month old it is taken outdoors and presented to the full moon. At the third month the child is taken to the Umbanda tent and there the priest consults the stones to see who is the infant's guardian angel. The parents name a godmother and godfather. Then the priest writes out a baptismal certificate, which is duly registered with the federal authorities.

When a couple wish to be married they go together to consult the Umbanda priest. He throws the stones to see if their guardian angels are compatible and will not object to the union. Then he marks a date for the ceremony by consulting a lunar calendar, for the phase of the moon must be right for both of them, not just for one. Then the couple choose a bridesmaid and a best man from among the tent's congregation and start planning for the wedding. On the day of the ceremony, the pair shows up at the tent dressed as if they were going to be married in a Catholic church—long white gown, striped trousers, veils and a top hat. They enter the front door and walk slowly around the room together, passing over the symbolic signs of their respective guardian angels, which have been chalked onto the floor. Beside them walk the bridesmaid and the best man. The best man carries a square ceremonial cake, the bridesmaid carries a triangular cake. They approach the altar, which is ablaze with candles reflecting the features of the myriad saints and spirits, and the cakes are given to two assistants of the priest. There is also a white cloth, almost like a sheet, extended on the ground in front of the couple. The priest prays to their guardian angels as he spills a blessed liquid over their united hands. Then the cakes are broken into seven pieces and placed on the sheet. The groom eats a piece of the bride's cake and she eats a piece of the groom's cake. Then the guests of honor are served the remaining portions. The priest declares them man and wife and the drums break into a joyous beat. The happy couple walk slowly from the tent under a hail of mango leaves. Then everyone congratulates the newlyweds and eats and drinks far into the night. (This ceremony, however, is not sufficient under Brazilian law to make the couple legal man and wife. They must still be married by a court justice. But then, Brazilians don't consider a Catholic marriage legal either. The only legal ceremony is the one performed by a civil justice. It is not unusual to hear a Brazilian woman proudly claim that she was married "two times," once by the court and once by the padre. It is also not unusual for a woman to brag that she was married "three times": once by the court, once by the padre and once by the Father of the Saints.)

When a Father dies his body is placed in a coffin in the center of the tent and the congregation meets to pay its last respects. Each spirit is invoked and the drums beat in a muffled voice. Then the casket is carried to the cemetery— the Catholic cemetery! The casket is carried seven times around the grave and then raised and lowered three times before it is finally placed at the bottom of the grave. Back at the tent all the worldly goods used in the various rituals are cleansed by incense and repeated chantings for seven days. From six in the evening until midnight no electric lights are turned on, only candles are permitted. The spirits are sung to and asked to take the dead man's soul to its final rest. After seven days have passed, the second-in-command throws the stones to see if the possessions of the dead man are to remain in that particular tent or are to be sent away. Then the stones are thrown to indicate who has been chosen to take his place. Once the new Father has been named, the Sons and Daughters of the temple go through a special ritual in which the guiding "hand" of the dead priest is removed from their head and the "hand" of the new priest is placed on it.

It is not easy to become one of these Sons or Daughters, and while the process is not as bloody as it is for the Candomblé Daughters, it is complicated and costly.

Senhora Doraci Almeida is a hard-working Negro woman who was widowed years ago. She managed to bring up her three children by washing and ironing clothes. She came to my Rio apartment once a week and I got to know her quite well. One day I asked her about Lucia Maria, the oldest and most attractive of the children. "Oh, Senhor David, I'm so proud of her! She's going to become a Daughter of the Saint." Her eyes filled with tears just as if she had announced that her eldest child was to enter the Convent of St. Mary. Poor Dona Doraci had no idea what being a consecrated medium of Umbanda meant.

First of all the girl entered a sort of voodoo convent, and her mother had to prepare and send all her food daily. Often, depending on the demands of the "Father," they were the costliest imported items from the most expensive delicatessens. Dona Doraci had to buy three floor-length satin skirts, six multicolored silk slips, six lace blouses, two fringed shawls, plus a quantity of beads for necklaces and arm bands.

She also had to send, live, to the temple farmyard two white hens, four red hens and one black hen. I helped her go to a nearby small town and bring back a pair (male and female) of goats, a pair of ducks and a Bantam hen and rooster. An uncle who owned a farm near Brazília shipped in one live cow! As if that wasn't enough, once the animals were all delivered, poor Dona Doraci had to keep sending money to feed the menagerie until the day of the sacrifice.

On the day of ordination Dona Doraci had to cook twelve pounds of beans and boil ten gallons of palm oil, plus supply eight pounds of fresh shrimp and six pounds of dried shrimp. This spirit "food" was served to the hierarchy, while the animals that the poor woman had worked so hard to buy were blessed, slaughtered, cooked and dished out to the throng of guests who had come for the ceremony. The feast was lit by 290 special white candles and the guests were lit by 25 gallons of fiery cane alcohol. Dona Doraci also had to pay the woman who took care of Lucia Maria in the convent and the three men who beat the ceremonial drums.

All in all, this mother, who charges a mere $2 to do a family wash, spent $610 on her daughter's "education." She declares until today, while she's still paying off her debt, that it was all worth it.

Brazilians have taken to Umbanda by the thousands in the past few years, and everybody has either a friend or relative who is a member of the religion. Everybody knows where an Umbanda tent can be found and everybody knows of people who have been "cured," "saved" and "redirected" by the Umbanda spirits.

The Brazilian government, on all levels from municipal to federal, leaves Umbanda strictly alone. Gone are the days when Fathers and Daughters were arrested, beaten and heavily fined for calling on the spirits. Gone are the police payoffs and the underground sessions. Politicians openly solicit the Umbanda believers, asking for their votes and promising to pass laws that will make Umbanda even stronger. The police even resort to asking Umbanda spirits to help them solve crimes. The biggest jail in Rio has a room that is decorated with a huge grinning statue of Exú, the Umbanda devil. Prisoners who won't talk are often placed in there under the constant eye of this demon saint. Few are the convicts who don't confess and ask to be transferred to another cell.

(Quimbanda is the left hand of Umbanda and devoted only to the evil spirits and the bringing down of curses and hexes. The cult is frowned upon by serious Umbandistas but recognized as a necessary part of their beliefs like day and night, fire and water, yin and yang. Quimbanda tents are almost always far out in the countryside, where the patron saint, Exú, can have his outside dwelling and be appeased when he gets out of control. The people who frequent Quimbanda are mostly illiterate Negroes and whites who have not found solace in Umbanda spirit messages and who are desperate for a solution to their problems. Ignorance causes hatred and revenge, and only in Quimbanda sessions can revenge be carried out. All of the outward appearances of Umbanda are present: the drums, the altar, the long outfits of the male and female dancers, etc. But there are no places for the spectators to sit—and they are not a congregation but rather just individuals who have shown up at that particular session to ask for a favor. Quimbanda practices no charity or social work, as does Umbanda. Quimbanda is not free, as is Umbanda, and the Mothers and Fathers who run the temples try to gouge as much money as they can from the frightened believers. Those who do not comply with the demands of the priest know that all the evil they have wished on their enemy will boomerang back onto them. Frightened from the beginning, they become even more terrified when confronted by the devil Exú and hear what evil they must do to win over their enemies. The disgusting murders and horrible misunderstandings that have arisen because of these Quimbanda practices have kept the cult under constant police observation. But since policemen, almost to a man, are also terrified of this black magic, very little is ever done to arrest a priestess or destroy a temple. The Umbandistas themselves hope to convert the cult by love. As long as there is malice and jealousy in the world, it won't be easy.)

Umbandistas, like the Kardekian Spiritists, concentrate on charity and on bettering the lives of those who believe. The clinics, orphanages, drugstores, and rest homes for Umbandistas are more numerous than the Catholic and government-grant charities. The Umbanda doctors perform a great service in a nation where the ratio is something like one doctor for every five thousand Brazilians. Without these spiritual healers, millions of the sick and infirm would get no medical attention whatsoever. In the vast interior a doctor may be hundreds of miles away. The Amazon municipality of Codajás (just to cite one firsthand example) stretches over 14,312 square miles. The town of Codajás has about 1500 people. The entire municipality has about 11,000. Yet there is not *one* doctor in the entire area. The government health clinic is being used as a goat shed. The town male "nurse" often doesn't even have a bandage or a bottle of mercurochrome. The one or two Catholic priests cannot spend all their time curing bodies when their mission is to cure souls. So the people call upon their spirit doctors and priests. Whether the treatment is 100 per cent effective or not is not the question. What is important is that they do not think of themselves as being abandoned. That fact alone keeps them going.

Umbanda has many faith healers, and they work on a lower level (i.e. with the masses and often under terrible conditions) than do the high Spiritist healers. One such man is known only as Palmério and he works his "miracles" in the far north and at the mouth of the Amazon. A tall, thin man with deep lines on his face, he gets about three hours of sleep each night and spends the rest of the time curing anyone who comes to him. He does not use a knife like Arigó, but cures by prayer and the laying on of hands. I once had a chance to see him in action in Belém, Pará, the hot, tropical Amazon city at the very top of Brazil.

He had come to Belém from São Luís, where his fame had grown so that he had to flee from pursuing mobs of the sick and ailing. Given refuge in an Umbanda tent in Belém, he remained inside while the Father of the temple controlled the crowds outside. Palmério's medicine was nothing but a glass of magnetized water. He didn't believe in drugstores and all their pills.

He was against having me in the same room with him. He was leery of strangers and especially leery of the press. Belém newspapers had misquoted him as condemning licensed doctors and medicine and the article had caused an uproar in the local Regional Council of Medicine. He refused to let me take notes and refused to let me into his operating room with a camera. I was told to stay in a far corner and not to make the slightest noise. Above all, I was not to get in his way or destroy the electric impulses that his guide, Caboclo of the Seven Arrows, used in the cures.

I was interested in watching him because I had heard of an operation he had performed on a white high-society woman in Belém the day before. The newspapers said that the woman was suffering terrible pains in her appendix and was terrified of surgery. Her husband had come for Palmério in a Cadillac and taken him straight to their sumptuous home. The woman was stretched out naked on a bed, with only Palmério and the husband as witnesses. The spirit healer examined her, then asked for a raw egg and three candles. Then while the husband pressed the egg to his wife's abdomen, Palmério lit the candles and went into a trance. He passed the three candles over the woman five times. She cried out in pain and the husband kept up the pressure with the egg. When Palmério came out of the trance he told the woman she was cured. She admitted the pains had gone and that she felt much better. Then he gave orders for the egg to be broken. When it was poured into a saucer the egg was filled (claim the newspapers) with balls of matted hair and thistles. "That is what was causing the pain," the healer supposedly said, and he went back to his Umbanda headquarters.

I waited in the semidarkness of the room, smelling the strong incense and hoping that another egg operation would take place. A boy came in, aided by an older man. The boy could hardly stand. His feet turned in at such an angle that he was almost walking on his ankles. He was dark-skinned and poorly dressed. He must have been about eight years old. Palmério lifted him up onto an ordinary kitchen table and examined the tortured feet. Then he closed his eyes and swayed slightly, his voice becoming deeper and deeper as he mumbled a prayer to one of the Umbanda spirits. The boy's eyes, which had been filled with terror at first, closed and his head slumped forward. Palmério pressed the deformed feet together and shook them, violently. Then he shouted something and glared at the twisted ankles for a full minute. Brusquely he raised the feet toward his face. Softly he kissed each foot with his lips. Then he shook the feet again and allowed them to swing back down by themselves. He spoke to the boy, who came out of his doze and smiled. The doctor patted him on the shoulder. "You can go now," he said gruffly. "Others are waiting their turn too, you know." The boy slid from the table and landed with both feet firmly on the floor. His knees shook for just a second, but Palmério was behind him, almost pushing him across the floor. The boy took tentative steps, then bolder steps and finally crossed over to the door unaided and walked away with complete confidence.

There were dozens of questions I wanted to ask, but he glared at me and I slunk back into my darkened corner. A woman came in and when she started to tell him of her troubles, he told her roughly to shut up and get on the table. He unbuttoned her blouse and brassière and her two big breasts flopped into view. One of the breasts had a sickening greenish-brown bruise. Whether it was cancer, an accident or a birthmark I never did know. But Palmério knew and after passing his hands over her breast and flinging some invisible filth from the disease onto the floor, he told her to get up. The room was not well lit but as she dressed I could see that the stain had disappeared. When she left the room Palmério told me I could go. I thought of protesting, but changed my mind. I thanked him for letting me assist him but he didn't seem to hear. It was way past midnight and yet I had to push my way through the crowds that blocked the front of the house.

Isaltina is one of the more famous Umbanda healers. Thirty-four years old now, she was a devout Catholic until she was thirty. Her parents were middle-class and respectable, from the city of Natal, in far north Rio Grande do Norte. Her childhood was just like that of all the other girls in the area, and she managed to get an elementary education, a job in the post office and a nice, average guy for a husband. Shortly after her baby was born Isaltina awoke one night with terrible body pains. Every joint and muscle ached and because she didn't want to alarm her young husband she said nothing and tried to sleep. The attempt produced a nightmare. In the dream Isaltina was running across an open field. Her legs ached and her lungs were bursting. She saw the edge of a cliff. She tried to stop but her legs refused to obey. She screamed as she fell into the abyss and this scream awoke her husband. All the next day the pains stayed and that night the same dream, over and over again. On the third day her husband took her to a doctor, who examined her, found nothing wrong and prescribed painkillers for her aches and sleeping pills for her dreams. Her mother, worried because Isaltina had never had any ailments whatever when she was growing up, remarked about the problems to a neighbor. "Ah," said the woman, "this is the sign of a medium. Your daughter is being possessed by a spirit. A friend of mine in the interior had a sister who went through the same thing. She had to join an Umbanda group to get rid of the pains." The mother, furious at such a pagan idea, broke relations immediately with the neighbor.

The pains did not stop and Isaltina grew weaker each day. She lost weight and had circles under her eyes, and her mother had to come and help her take care of the baby. She went to other doctors, and she was X-rayed and examined. None of them could find anything. Then one day her husband went to get the report from one of the few remaining doctors in the city who had not given his opinion as yet. The doctor told him plainly: "Your wife is going to die. I don't know what her ailment is, but she is doomed." The husband broke down and sobbed. "Crying is no good," the doctor said. "May I give you some advice? Try other ways. Your wife is not a case for a medical doctor."

The only "other way" that the distraught husband knew was to go to the Umbanda center. It was the first time in his life that he had ever entered one of these places. It was against all his upbringing as a Catholic and against everything that Isaltina believed in as well. But it was the one and only last chance. The nurse in attendance said that there would be consulting sessions the following day and she wrote the name of the head doctor, a man who had just come from an Umbanda center in Rio, one Sebastião Pedra d'Agua.

When he returned home he became ashamed of what he had done and said nothing to Isaltina about the spirit center. That night as they were getting ready for bed she noticed the slip of paper in his shirt pocket. "Who is this man?" she asked. Her husband said it was a business contact and that it wasn't important. For some reason Isaltina put the slip of paper under her pillow. That night she slept without awaking once with pain.

The next day her husband told her the truth. Pedra d'Agua

was an Umbanda medium and he thought Isaltina should see him. She cried and said she didn't believe in any of that nonsense and was so shaken by what he had done that she had a relapse and had to be put back in bed. That afternoon her father-in-law arrived with a brand-new doctor. After examining her the doctor called the old man aside and told him that Isaltina was dying. He gave her a few days at the very most. Isaltina overheard the conversation. When they returned to her room she pretended to be asleep and they went into the living room. She rose quickly, dressed and left by the rear door to seek Sebastião Pedra d'Agua.

She had to wait her turn in line but when it came the stern little faith healer stopped short and stared at her. She told him what her problems were and after an assistant took down her name and address he made her stand in front of him. He passed his hands in the air around her body, then told her to close her eyes. He put her hands on her forehead and she shook, violently. Then he dismissed her. "You are cured," he said. As she left he turned to the assistant. "Be careful you don't lose her address. She interests me."

If this were a fairy tale and not a true story, the next step would be to relate that Isaltina got better and never had any more aches and pains. That her weight returned to normal, her eyes lost their dullness and her old personality returned. Well, it's a true story and that's exactly what happened. From the moment she walked out of the Umbanda tent she was cured.

Less than two weeks later Isaltina was surprised by a visitor. It was Sebastião. He had come to tell her that she was an exceptional case. "You are the possessor of a mediumship that is extra-special. You could be of great service to the people if you wish. But it means you must learn many things and give up much of your private life for the good of others. Are you willing?"

Drum and Candle

Isaltina thought it over and discussed it with her husband and her parents. Her mother was against it but her husband said he would abide by whatever decision she made (rare for a Brazilian husband!). A week later she showed up at the spirit center, ready to develop her powers.

The young housewife learned quickly and soon she was performing operations on the "fluid" of the patients. Again, unlike Arigó, she didn't use a knife, only the laying on of hands.

It was revealed to her and Sebastião when she was in a trance that she was being used by the spirit of a German doctor named Artz Scovsck. He had been a surgeon and died before "his work could be completed." He used the physical body of Isaltina, he told her, because "he had unfinished business to transact."

Isaltina would go into a trance when she operated. She would mumble in German and scowl as she brought her hands over the patient, again and again. When the operation was over she would come out of her trance and look around in a daze. Often she burst into tears. Her first patient was a woman who, each time she became pregnant, would lose the fetus at the fourth month. Dr. Scovsck, through Isaltina, diagnosed her problem as a sharp growth in her uterus that pressed against and destroyed each fetus when it enlarged to the fourth month. Isaltina went into a trance and operated on the fluid body of the woman; weeks later the woman entered a new pregnancy and eventually had a child.

Isaltina's fame grew in Natal, but Dr. Scovsck wanted to move to Rio de Janeiro. The young woman had no choice but to obey. She left her husband and baby and went with Sebastião. They installed themselves in an Umbanda temple on an overcrowded slum *favela* hillside and began to practice.

Literally thousands of people came to Isaltina. Stomach cancers disappeared, cripples walked, blind men saw, cleft palates vanished, painful varicose veins diminished, growths in throats were eliminated, tumors evaporated. The crush of the crowds forced Isaltina and Sebastião to call the police to keep order. Rich and poor, black and white, famous and humble lined up day after day to go under the hands of the almost girlishly young medium.

It was then that a Rio TV station tried for a sensational scoop, a journalistic first. Newsmen are notorious scoffers, and these Brazilians with all their newly purchased electronics were bigger disbelievers than all the rest. They wanted to put Isaltina on live TV. They wanted to prove that she was nothing more than just the stuff legends are made of. To their delight, Isaltina accepted the challenge.

The big night came. Cariocas had their TV sets turned on all over town. Families grouped together to see the show, bars turned on their sets to capacity houses. Isaltina was presented to the public and she, shyly, thanked them for their faith in her. Then the doors were opened to an adjoining studio. On a table under the bright lights and unfeeling cameras lay the patient: a doctor himself and ex-secretary to the governor of Isaltina's own state of Rio Grande do Norte. He was a well-known figure in the north of Brazil. It was also well-known that he had been a cripple for years. As if this test wasn't enough, around the table stood seven medical doctors, chosen by the TV station from the top hospitals in Rio.

Isaltina and Sebastião approached the patient. It was obvious that this humble housewife had a great deal of respect for such an esteemed local politician. She chatted with him for a few seconds and told him not to worry. Then she went into a trance. The lights glared, the cameras swooped in and recorded from every possible angle. Isaltina passed her hands time after time over the strangely semiconscious form of the man on the table. The doctors watched her every move. There was no possible chance of fraud. Isaltina

Drum and Candle

grumbled in German (a language she had never studied or had a chance to hear spoken), and after perspiring profusely, she went limp and almost fell against Sebastião. "It's over," she sighed softly.

The lights remained lit and the cameras went in for a close-up of the middle-aged politician. Slowly he sat up and shook his head, as if he had been drugged. Then he swung his legs over the side of the table. With deliberate care he put one foot on the floor and then the other. The cameras recorded. The silence of the studio hung heavy. Then he shuffled one foot, putting his body weight on it. There was no pain. Then he shuffled the other foot. He stood up. Not knowing whether to laugh or to cry, he placed one foot in front of the other, and while the entire city of Rio de Janeiro watched in breathless fascination, he *walked* across the room and embraced Isaltina.

The most important aspect of any of these religions or cults, be it Candomblé, Spiritism or Umbanda, is that the *people* are reached. The common, ordinary man in the street is able to get closer to the world of spirits, is able to communicate with the dead, to ask favors of the African and Indian entities and actually to *see* the spirits descend and take over the body of a Son or Daughter of the saints.

The Catholic Church, although steeped in its own brand of mysticism and with its own martyrs, heroines and ritual, is still very far away from the uneducated or spirit-minded Brazilian. The priest wears a long robe, lives by himself and until recently chanted in Latin. The Brazilian Fathers and priests wear ordinary white cotton shirts and trousers, are married and speak to the congregation in their own language. There is no gold in a spirit or Candomblé temple to remind the adept how poor he is. There are no massive cathedrals in spirit worship to remind the adept how insignificant he is. There are very few sins that will throw the spirit believer into hell. There is no need for confession, no need to memorize a catechism or to finger a rosary. And there is no one leader of them all who resides far across the ocean amid splendid palaces and lavish jewels and who is white and speaks Italian. Brazilian spirit belief is the belief of the Brazilians. It is theirs without any outside interference. It is as much a part of their lives as their own families, their friends and their country. They accept it and take it seriously. Foreigners may laugh and criticize but they don't understand. The Brazilians understand. The spirits understand the Brazilians. The two planes—worldly and unworldly—work together and help each other. It's that complex, and yet it's that simple.

8

I saw the important-acting little man drive up in his battered Volkswagen, knock at the neighbor's door, then hand her a piece of paper. There were the motions of a discussion, she signed another paper and he drove hurriedly away. That evening she stopped by my house.

"I want you to loan me a box of matches," she said, then added, "If you wish, you can come with me."

"Where?"

"To a crossroads where there is a tree. That old bitch who owns my house has given me an eviction notice. And I don't intend to leave!"

This woman, whom I'll simply call Helena, was furious and rightly so. Six years previously she had rented a small house in the mountaintop town of Teresópolis and had brought her three children up from a Rio slum section to a life of better schools, fresh air and better food. Her husband had abandoned her for another woman. She didn't care about that. What she did care about was her children, and once she had arranged a daytime job in a chemical factory and a nighttime job as ticket seller in a local movie theater she rented the small house and started a new life. Now the owner of the house wanted her out, contending that her married son needed to live there. The son had his own apartment in Rio and the legal paper was just a ruse to get my friend and her children out so that the house could be rerented with a new contract for a higher price.

"If that old bitch thinks that I'm going to fall for this, she's crazy! I've painted that house and put in new wiring and planted a garden. She gets her rent on time! What more does she want?" We were walking quickly away from the center of town toward a wooded section. It was warm and muggy in spite of the altitude and the huge full moon. "She thinks just because I don't have a man taking care of me that I'm helpless. Well, she's got another think coming! I have someone more important than a man on my side! I have Exú!"

I stopped short on the dark dirt road. "Exú? You mean the devil?"

She gave a short laugh and nodded. "Exactly. I don't call on him often, but when I do he knows it's important and he listens to me." She glanced at me. "You don't believe in the devil?"

"I don't know," I answered. "I'm not sure."

"Not being sure is better than denying him altogether. I couldn't do this offering with you if you were a complete disbeliever." We walked past the last house on the road. Pitch-blackness lay all around us. "I think you are a spiritist," she said. "You have all the signs."

"What do you mean, 'the signs'?"

"Your respect for things religious. The peace that is in your house. The way sometimes your body is bathed in a white aura."

"Me? You've seen a white aura around *my* body?"

"Many times. When I was living in Rio I used to work in a spirit center. Up here I don't have the time. But I know a spiritist when I see one." She started to say something more, then stopped. "Over there," she pointed. "That tree on the crossroads. It's perfect."

The tree stood on one of four corners that had been cut through virgin woodland by a real estate company a few years ago. They bought the land and parceled it out into

With modern Copacabana celebrating New Year's Eve in tall apartment houses in the background, members of an Umbanda temple celebrate the night of Yemanjá on the beach.

Copacabana beach and the thirty-first of December. The spirits have seized these Umbanda worshipers as a crowd looks on.

MANCHETE PRESS AGENCY

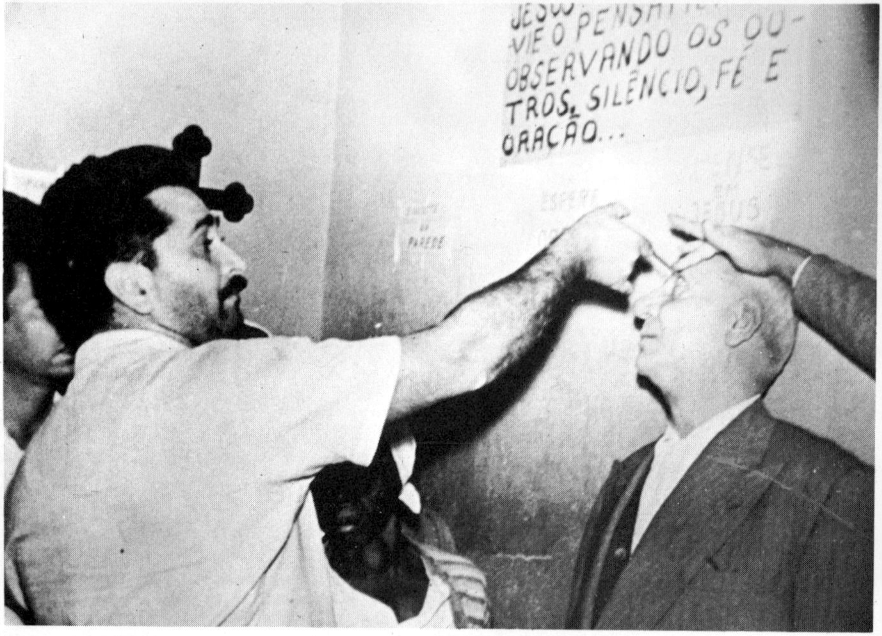

11. An actual picture of the famous spirit healer José Arigó shoving a kitchen knife in the eye of a patient.

MANCHETE PRESS AGENCY

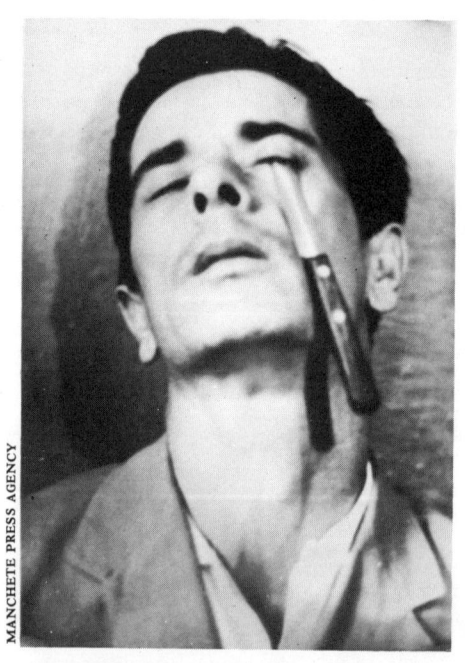

12. Arigó stuck this knife into a patient's eye, then stepped back and let photographers take a rare picture.

13. The author with two Umbanda statue friends in Rio de Janeiro.

14. The Black Pope of Brazil, Tancredo da Silva Pinto.

15. The lone crusader, Father Boaventura Kloppenburg, minus his Franciscan habit and surrounded by Umbanda images of the devil, Exú.

16. Edu, the Umbanda high priest of Olinda and Recife.

17. Dona Leda, the medium who reads cards and talks with the dead in Pôrto Alegre.

18. The postage stamp issued by the Brazilian government in 1957 to honor the hundredth anniversary of Allan Kardek's work *The Book of Spirits*.

19. Some items used in spirit rituals. The figure of Yemanjá is carved from the bone of an Amazon River sea cow. The bead necklace around her is from Rio for the god Oxóssi and it holds various good luck symbols. The three antique *figas* are of ivory, onyx and coral and ornamente in gold. The necklace is antique and go coral and belonged to a Candomblé priestess of the colonial era.
The long necklace enclosing all the oth items is of African cowrie shells and gla beads. It was used in Umbanda rituals in Rio.

COLLECTION OF THE AUTHOR

individual lots. Then the company went broke and the whole project fell through. The tree, a magnificent full-leafed thing, had been spared. The other three corners were bare.

Helena crossed over to it and gazed at it for quite a while. I stayed at a distance, leaving her alone with her prayer. "O Exú," she said aloud. "Exú of the crossroads! Exú of the trees! I need your help. I need your intervention. I have been given a legal paper. This paper says that I and my children must leave the house we are in. We have no other place to go and no money to move. Our lives will be disrupted. O Exú! The woman who sent this paper against me is wrong. She is a liar. She is not a good woman. I wish her no harm, even though she wishes me and my children harm. The only thing I wish, O Exú, is that you make her take back this paper. That she sees that she is wrong and sees what damage she is doing. I ask for your help. I believe in you. I need you. Look," and she rummaged in the bottom of a shopping bag she had been carrying, "I have a present for you. A bottle of *cachaça*. You like *cachaça*, don't you? It's the best sugar-cane alcohol on the market. I bought it just for you. Here! Have a drink."

She uncapped the bottle and started pouring it into the ground around the base of the tree. It glistened in the moonlight as it soaked into the wood and the stench of the raw alcohol overpowered every other perfume in the night air. "Wasn't that good?" she asked. "The best on the market. I bought it just for you. Now listen, Exú. I made a Xerox copy of the legal papers. I'm going to leave them with you. I want you to read them and then to work on them for me. Okay?" Her tone was conversational, as if she were talking to a friendly human being instead of the Brazilian spirit of evil.

Into her shopping bag once more, and out came a package of white wax candles. She placed six of them upright in a circle about a foot around. Then she lit them, one by one, and each one with a fresh match, until they were all ablaze and making strange shadows on the still wet tree trunk.

"This," she said, holding up a white folded paper, "this is a copy of the process. Read it and tell me what can be done." She took the paper and placed it carefully in the center of the burning circle. Then once more into the bag. "I brought you a cigar too. The man said it's the best one available here in Teresópolis. I hope you enjoy it." She took the cellophane from the cigar and laid it on the legal process. Then she took a fresh box of matches (the one I had given her) and opening the box to expose the match heads, she placed it alongside the cigar. "The matches are from my friend over there." She motioned toward me. "He's a good person and someday if you need anything you can count on him for help." I took a few steps backward into the shadows, hoping that the devil hadn't seen my face and wouldn't be coming around asking for any favors.

Helena turned away from the tree and the burning candles and came over to me. "Let's go," she said. "No, don't look back! Now we just walk home the way we came."

Three days later Helena was in her front yard planting a rosebush. "Hey," I called to her, "you can't take that thing with you when you move, you know!"

"I'm not moving," she called back. "Last night he called me."

"Who called you?"

"The son of the old bitch. He said his wife didn't want to move out of Rio and that I could stay in the house as long as I liked. He made his mother withdraw the process."

"Thank God!" I shouted.

"Thank God nothing!" she shouted back. "Thank Exú!"

Brazilians have a way of getting what they want from the devil . . . or any of the hundreds of other spirits that roam the astral planes. They do not hesitate to call on them and are not ashamed to tell about it. They will usually try to solve their problems without spirit intervention, but if it is a case beyond human effort, then the spirits are sought.

There are good spirits and bad spirits the way there are good people and bad people. Many spirit leaders and writers contend that since spirits are in reality nothing more than souls of the departed, they have all the frailties of the mind without the frailties of the flesh. If a man was worthless, a murderer, a liar, an ignoramus while on the earth, he will be the same in the spirit stage. Of course, when his spirit leaves the worldly plane and enters the stage where he rejoins the other spirits and awaits a new incarnation, then he becomes the sum total of all his other incarnations, and bad done in the last life is balanced out against the good done in former lives.

There is one very popular theory that *all* of us are fallen angels. When the two right-hand archangels of God had a clash, one of them was thrown from heaven down into hell. He became the devil, Satan, Exú. The other one, the one who remained beside God, became the Holy Spirit, Jesus, Oxalá.

Now Exú, when he fell, took along a large number of other angels. Whole armies of them, as a matter of fact. These angels were not as bad as he was, but were tainted because of their allegiance to him. The nether regions of hell were crowded with them. Few of them liked it there; many wanted to be returned to heaven.

God was unhappy that so many fine angels had chosen sides against Jesus/Oxalá but knew that they could not be trusted to be merely brought back into heaven. They had to know and appreciate the value of heaven. In order to return to a place that was purely goodness and light they had to spend time in a place that was darkness and trouble, but a place where doing good would be carefully noted and added up in a giant ledger. When enough points had been tallied on the "good" side, vastly outweighing those on the "bad" side, then the fallen angel would be allowed back into the kingdom of heaven.

So God created the earth. He made it exclusively as a testing ground for the fallen angels.

He put everything on the earth that the angels would need, but in such a way that they would have to work for it and co-operate with each other in order to survive. If they could not live with one another on a planet of plenty, he reasoned, then how could they live with the angels of heaven, where plenty was taken for granted? Nobody ever heard of an angel in heaven having to plant rice, keep milch cows or build a house to keep out the rain. Heaven was . . . well, heaven. And well worthy of a struggle to gain readmittance.

So what happened? He put two clay figures on the earth (the place was Africa and they were *not* figures in His image, in spite of what the Jewish-Christian Bible says) and let two of the fallen angels come in and incorporate with the figures. They started almost immediately to disobey Him. They argued with Him and their children lied to Him. He put other bodies on the earth and let in other spirits, and soon they were cheating, stealing and even killing each other for the plentiful things He had placed for them.

God was smart. He didn't tell the spirits, when they were in human form, how He was testing them. They didn't know the value of a good deed to a fellow human. It was only after they had finished their allotted time on the earthly plane that they were shown their ledger pages. They were told then how important doing good really was and told that they would be given another chance, in another lifetime, to make up for their evil and to improve their scores. They were allowed to mingle with humans and to use their knowledge to make their embodied spirit friends sense the right way of doing things. If an embodied spirit called upon one of them, they were to answer. If the embodied spirit wanted to do good then they were to help him. It would be a mark in their favor as well.

But if the embodied spirit asked for evil to be done, and they helped, then both embodied and disembodied spirits would earn a black mark in the ledger.

When they returned to earth and to another body (i.e. reincarnated) they were on the human-spiritual level that was the sum total of their former lives' deeds. They were to remember the value of doing good and were to remember how evil could put them back into hell again. Those who learned their lessons advanced, did good to one another and eventually got back into heaven. Those who forgot their lessons or deliberately chose material advances over spiritual advances had to return to earthly lifetime after lifetime. If it seems to be a long process: too bad. God has been around for an even longer time. He is in no hurry. He can wait dozens of lifetimes to test a spirit. He has nothing to gain by it. The spirit gains—or loses—everything.

Now one would suppose that every one of the fallen angels would want to get back into heaven. But that's not the case. There are many of them who are quite happy with Satan/Exú. They like that existence. He treats them well. Those who have his confidence exert enormous power over the others and are sent to earth to keep vast throngs from deserting the devil and his band. For after all, if the devil is to remain strong he must have supporters behind him. He cannot hope to hold out in his battle against Jesus/Oxalá and God if he is all alone. He treats those who remain with him very well indeed.

That's why there are both good and evil on earth. That's why when wars start, or murders are committed or evil plagues the land God does nothing to stop it. He is testing the incarnate spirits. If they want to wage war against each other, let them go right ahead. He writes it all down on the debit side of the ledger. Wars don't bother Him. When the innocent suffer they are compensated in the next life. When an evil man seems to be gaining you can rest assured that he will suffer the next time around. A man is born a cripple? He must have earned the punishment. A woman is beautiful? She earned this beauty in other lives, but let's see what she does with that beauty this time around. If she uses it wrongly, she may be ugly the next time she is born. Are you poor? You are being tested. Are you rich? You are being tested. Are you white? Are you black? Are you a member of a progressive nation? The citizen of a backward nation? Are you smart? Are you dumb? Are you happily married? Are you proud of your children? Are you ambitious? Are you satisfied? No matter what you are, you are being tested. No matter what you are in this life, one thing is certain: You are different from what you were in your last life and what you will be in your next.

God knows that being "only human" is to be weak, to be filled with doubt and all sorts of frailties. That's why He has allowed the spirits who have been on earth before to help you in this life. They are all around us and are waiting to be called upon. After all, it's to their advantage to listen to us, be they working for God or the devil. We must get rid of the materialistic notion that "what we cannot see does not exist" and call upon them for help. In the past few generations we have accumulated "things" to the point where we have completely forgotten the reason for being alive and on earth. Material objects and scientific things have obscured (in just a few short years) all spiritual teachings. We are being drowned in worldly matters. It's time to look inwardly once more. It's easy. The Brazilians do it all the time.

Umbanda believers leave no religious stone unturned. They have freely borrowed the Catholic saints and prayers, have taken up with Candomblé African spirits, have gleaned what they wished from Kardek's investigations and have gone back into medieval lore for cabalistic signs and astronomical charts. They offer a little bit of everything and have a giant following because of it.

They place great store in triangles, circles and symbols.

Each of their saints/spirits has his own symbol. Each of their many Exús does also. And each of us here on earth has a triangle that he can use when he wishes to get closer to the "spirits of nature" (which are not to be confused with the spirits of the dead). These triangles are used only for good, never for evil, and they must be used by the right person and in the right position.

If you were born under the astrological sign of Leo (July 23–August 22), Sagittarius (November 22–December 21) or Aries (March 21–April 19), then your nature element is *fire* and your protective spirits are Oxalá/Jesus for Leo, Xangó/John the Baptist for Sagittarius and Ogun/St. George for Aries. Your life force or cosmic current comes from the *south*. Take a large new white cloth and cut it into a triangular shape. Now with yellow paint draw this triangle in the center of the cloth, making sure that the top point is in line with the top point of your scissored cloth and that the design is large enough for a human being to kneel inside it without his feet touching the edge of the design:

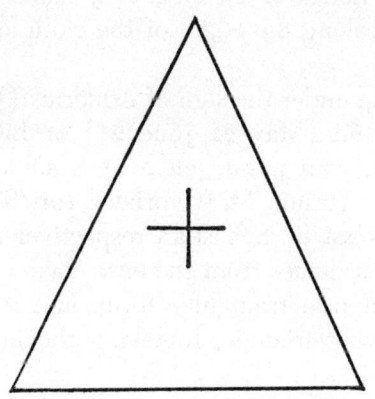

Drum and Candle

When you wish something, take this cloth and place it on the ground (bare earth is more powerful than a man-made floor) with the apex of the triangle pointing *exactly* south. Take off your shoes and stand behind the base of the painted triangle without touching the design. Ask protection and guidance of your particular spirit/saint, telling him how much you believe in him and how much you need him. Then ask your favor. If you wish a material favor (a new house, a car, more money, etc.), place an even number of candles at each point of the triangle. If your request is non-material (health, love, friendship, etc.), place an odd number of candles at each point. Strike a fresh match for each candle and repeat your request each time a candle begins to burn.

If you are trying to get rid of the evil eye, bad luck or bad health, then stand with your feet touching the apex and your back to the south. Bend down and touch the apex with your hands and light an odd number of candles.

Now should you be working with a medium, she (or he) kneels in the center of the triangle, always facing south, and if she says the spirit demands a special offering like a chicken, some beads, a bottle of alcohol, etc., make sure that these gifts are placed along the edges of the cloth and never on the cloth itself.

For those born under the sign of Aquarius (January 20–February 18), Gemini (May 21–June 21) or Libra (September 23–October 23), your nature element is *air* and your protective spirits are Yorimá/St. Cyprian, Yori/SS. Cosmos and Damian and Oxóssi/St. Sebastian respectively. Your life force of cosmic current comes from the *east*. Take a large new blue cloth and cut it into triangular form, and with green paint draw the following triangle, following the instructions given for the preceding one:

Drum and Candle

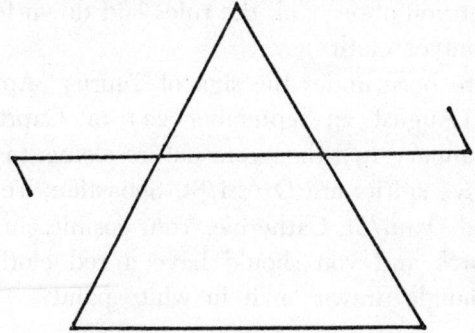

When ready to make a request, make sure the apex is toward the *east* and obey the rules of odd and even candles and the position of the medium inside the drawing, as well as of the placings of the offerings.

If you were born under the sign of Scorpio (October 24–November 21), Cancer (June 22–July 22) or Pisces (February 19–March 20), then your nature element is *water* and your protective spirits are Ogun/St. George, Yemanjá/Virgin Mary and Xangó/John the Baptist. Your cosmic current comes from the *west*. In this sign a yellow cloth must be used and the following triangle drawn upon it in white paint:

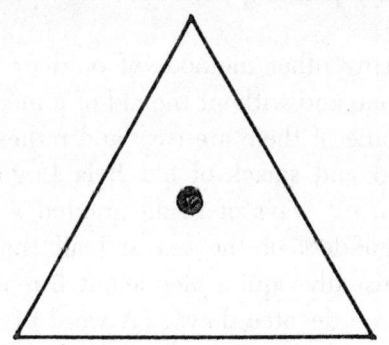

Drum and Candle

Make sure that the apex of the triangle is always pointing *west* and that you observe all the rules laid down for the first-mentioned prayer cloth.

If you were born under the sign of Taurus (April 20–May 20), Virgo (August 23–September 22) or Capricorn (December 22–January 19), then your nature element is earth and your protective spirits are Oxóssi/St. Sebastian, Yemanjá/Virgin Mary and Oxun/St. Catherine. Your cosmic current comes from the *north* and you should have a red cloth with the following triangle drawn on it in white paint:

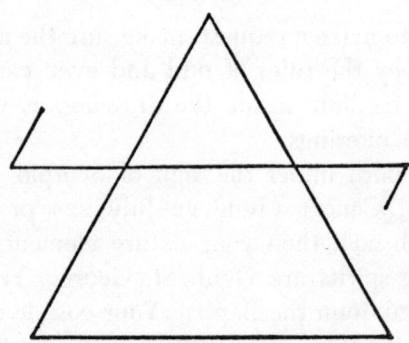

When you make a request, be sure that the apex of the triangle is always pointing north and that you follow all the rules.

There are many other methods of outdoor praying, which can be done alone and without the aid of a medium or Mother of the Saint. Some of them are easy and rather poetic. Others are complicated and smack of old Bela Lugosi movies.

One of the nicest ways of being granted a favor is to ask Yemanjá, the goddess of the sea and all the waters of the earth. She is (usually) quite nice about listening to you and seldom lets a true devotee down. (A word of warning: Don't try to hoodwink her or any other of the spirit gods. They know whether you are being sincere or not. A facetious prayer will almost always blow up in your face.) Yemanjá likes presents and since she is most decidedly feminine she likes to be given things like mirrors, combs, perfumes (imported French ones are best), hair ribbons, necklaces, bracelets and small white birds or animals. Since she is also a woman of the world she likes an occasional glass of scotch, champagne or cognac. A package of filtered cigarettes may also be accepted.

You take these offerings to a beach, a riverbank or a waterfall. There you spead out a white cloth—a new tablecloth or bed sheet is perfect—and place your offerings on it. If you give her food (filet mignon, white rice, a baked chicken), make sure the plates are white and brand-new. Then call upon her. Tell her what you want and why you need it. Then light candles in accordance with your wishes: even number for a material request, odd number for an non-material one. The candles should be between the offering and the water and *never* directly on the cloth itself. It wouldn't do to make the request and then burn the gifts before Yemanjá has a chance to claim them!

In this offering, as in all others, once you have lit the candles and have finished asking for what you want, walk away from the scene and *never* look back.

Xangó is another spirit that intercedes directly when you ask him for a favor. He is a specialist in "opening" your path when someone has "tied" you with a curse. If you feel that your life is getting nowhere, find a rocky cliff (or a large boulder), then open a bottle of black beer and spill a little on the ground in the form of a cross. Put the bottle down (it should still be half full) and light a single candle beside it. Then say aloud, "My father Xangó! I beg you to accept this humble present in your honor. Accept it and help me. Please open my paths."

The spirit of the Old Black Slave (Preto Velho) is most

powerful in Umbanda rituals. He is a wise old man who incorporates the souls of many dead slaves. He knows all the answers, but is able to explain them only in broken Portuguese mixed with a few African words. He is good and kind, for he has suffered and knows how difficult life on this planet can be. He should be treated with the greatest respect, for he is able to accomplish many things.

To reach him, go into a forest or wooded area and find a tree stump. Spread out a brand-new Scotch plaid towel (or any design with square blocks) on the ground and place an open bottle of wine (he prefers muscatel) on it in an upright position. Make sure you have poured some of this wine onto the tree stump beforehand. Now on the towel place a new pipe and an open package of pipe tobacco. Light a single candle and place it on the ground between the towel and the stump and ask him for whatever you wish. Then apologize that you have given him such an insignificant gift but add that if he grants your wish you will return with a bigger and better present. (When you get your request you must keep your part of the bargain. Go to the same stump with a new towel, a bottle of fine cognac, a bottle of good wine, a fancy pipe and some imported tobacco. Light a single candle and thank him, but don't use this as an excuse to ask for another wish. Don't be greedy!)

Exú has many workers on his evil astral plane, as we now know. The chief Exú is, of course, Lucifer, who is known in Umbanda and Quimbanda black magic circles as Exú Rei or King Exú. He has two private secretaries who were known in medieval times as Put Satanakia and Agalieraps. In Brazilian magic they are called Exú Marabo and Exú Mangueira.

Directly under King Exú comes Beelzebub/Exú Mor and Ashteroth/Exú of the Crossroads. They in turn command Tarchimache/Exú of the Closed Paths, Fleruty/Exú Tiriri, Sagathana/Exú Velvet Night and Nesbiros/Exú of the Rivers.

Under their command come twenty other devils, each with his own cabalistic and Brazilian name. For instance, Merifild is the Exú of the Seven Crosses, Hicpacth is the Exú of the Forests and Morail is the Exú of the Shadows. They all have definite jobs and spiritual obligations, and those wishing to practice pure black magic must learn who is who on this evil list.

King Exú is almost never called down (or up!) to grant a request. He is just too powerful and too busy trying to outsmart Jesus/Oxalá. Those mortals who have dared to disturb him have all suffered terribly. His sign (and don't ever draw it and invoke it unless you really know what you're doing) is:

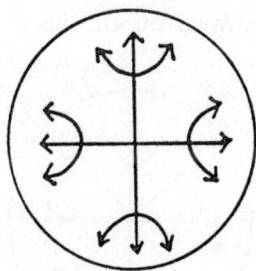

Exú Marabo, the immediate assistant of the King, often shows up at black magic sessions without being called. You can tell him by the smell of sulphur and the way he seizes a medium with great force. Yet once inside the medium he carries himself erect, uses the very best manners and speaks delicately and with long pauses between his words. Sometimes he speaks only in French. He likes the best cigars and uses absinthe as his curing fluid. There is no disease he cannot cure if he wishes. But he can kill just as easily. There is also no way you can get him to go away once he has arrived. Gifts

Drum and Candle

and prayers will placate him. His sign, drawn on the ground or painted in white on a red cloth, is:

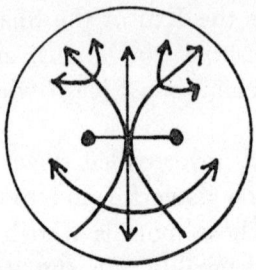

The other devil who forms the "unholy trinity" with Lucifer and Exú Marabo is Exú Mangueira. He usually comes to a black magic (Quimbanda) session when his name is called out and this sign is drawn on the floor:

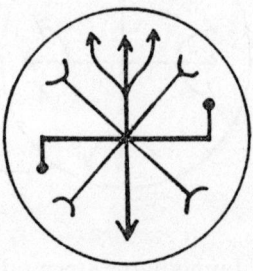

He also kills or cures, speaks French and likes fine wines or pale beer to use as his curing liquid.

Exú of the Closed Paths is a constant visitor to Brazil. To "close the paths" of someone means to make everything go wrong. If you do this to your enemy his business will fail, his girl friend will leave him, his wife will become ill, his health with get bad and nothing will go forward. He will not die, but he will be most unhappy.

To make this devil work for you buy a piece of red satin

Drum and Candle

and cut it into an exact three-foot square. Then hang a three-inch fringe of black satin thread all around the borders. In the exact center of this towel you must embroider in white satin a circle of 17 inches in diameter and then embroider this design in the center of the circle:

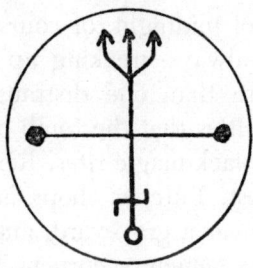

This done, take the towel to a crossroads and place it in the center where the two roads meet. Take two new candles, cross them, and tie them together with a ribbon of red satin and another of black satin. Place them on one corner of the towel. Now do the same for the other three corners. In the center of the design, place a brand-new ceramic serving bowl (a crude fired clay bowl is best) and in this bowl place a black rooster (uncooked please, the devil has his own cooking fires!) that you have cleaned of its intestines and filled with yellow corn meal and ground black pepper. On one side of the bowl place an open bottle of cane alcohol (whisky or bourbon will also serve) and on the other side seven cigars tied with black and red satin ribbons. These cigars should be out of their wrappers and placed in X's, one across the other. Then in front of the cigars place seven boxes of matches, each half open and with seven match heads pulled slightly forward.

With this done, take fourteen new white candles and light them one by one, placing them on the ground around the edges (but never on top of) the red towel. Each time you

Drum and Candle

light a candle say the name of the person whose "paths" you wish to have "closed." Now walk away and don't look back.

There are still more devils in the Brazilian hierarchy (as if the original gang wasn't enough!), and they work exclusively in cemeteries. Don't go calling on them at crossroads or tree stumps, because they have no power there, but seek them out (right at the stroke of midnight, of course) in any graveyard. Brazilian police are always breaking up midnight sessions in cemeteries, and more than one distraught family has complained to the authorities that the tomb of their loved one has been desecrated by black magic rites. Rentals near a cemetery are always the lowest. Butcher shops and fruit markets are almost never found near a graveyard, and don't wait at a bus stop at midnight on a cemetery corner: The driver will never pick you up!

Chief of the graveyard spirits is Omulu, who is known in Rome as St. Lazarus. It figures. Many spiritists and black magic practitioners claim that Omulu/Lazarus is not evil but merely oversees the rituals and gives his permission to grant a request. Don't call on him, he has lots of assistants.

Assistant number one is Exú Skull. He commands seven other Exús, each of whom in turn commands forty-nine Exús, each of whom also commands forty-nine Exús, each of whom . . . etc., etc. That's why a prayer in a cemetery is so powerful. There are more devils waiting there to serve you than you can shake a pitchfork at.

Exú Skull can give you the battle plans to win a war and can help you conquer any enemy. He lies in wait at the graveyard entrance, and therefore you must get his approval even to enter the place. To please him, place a raw beefsteak or a raw ham steak at the graveyard gate. Give him a handful of corn meal mixed with *dendê* palm oil (a good olive oil will also serve) and a glass of whisky mixed with a shot of sweet oil and a shot of bitter vinegar. Light at least seven candles around this offering. Then—and only then—should you

Drum and Candle

go into the cemetery and start your requests to the other devils.

Exú of Midnight must be invoked when the church bells strike the bewitching hour. He is so powerful that very few people ever call upon him. It was this devil, say the Quimbanda experts, who came and tortured Christ when He was on the cross, and who was the first to tell Lucifer of Christ's death.

Exú of the Skulls (different from Exú Skull) likes big black cigars and works best when putting a curse on an alcoholic or a drug addict.

Exú of Hot Ashes likes an offering of whisky mixed with black pepper, and to make him pay attention you must write your request (evil, of course) on paper and then burn it along with a piece of dry wood inside the cemetery. He lives near the incinerator of any graveyard. Mediums who have been possessed by this devil in cemeteries have been known to drink a glass of whisky mixed with gunpowder and suffer no ill effects.

Exú of the Pitchforks is a dangerous devil. He can make or break a love affair. He appears when you draw the following on the back of a tombstone and light three black candles:

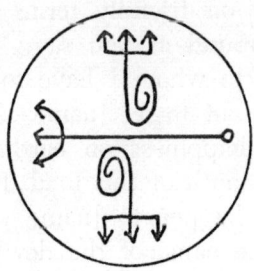

Exú Pagan is called upon all the time by couples who have become separated because of extramarital affairs or jealousy. He increases the hate and misunderstanding of a married couple and almost always succeeds in breaking them up. A husband wishing to get rid of his wife often calls on this devil. The "other woman" uses him to her advantage as well. He enjoys his work so much that you don't have to give him any gifts at all, just draw his sign on the graveyard ground:

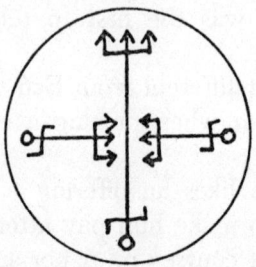

If you really have an enemy, and don't have time to go and talk to an Exú or black magic medium, there is a do-it-yourself curse that almost always works:

Grab a black toad and sew his mouth shut with black thread. Then tie a long black thread to each of his toes on all four feet and hang him upside down (as if he were an inverted parachute) over a thick-smoking fire. At the stroke of midnight call on the evil spirits (one or more, depending on how many you are on friendly terms with) and spin the toad around and around as you say: "Filthy toad, by the power of the devil, to whom I have sold my body but not my soul, I beg you not to let [name of your enemy] enjoy one more hour of happiness on earth. Let his health be trapped inside the mouth of this toad. Let him wither away and die. Make this happen to [name your enemy] as soon as I finish saying the name of the devil three times. Satan! Satan! Satan!" In the morning put the toad into an earthen jar and seal the lid with candle wax. (Should you repent of what you have done before the toad dies, then take the poor thing from the jar, remove the stitches from its mouth and give it fresh cow's milk to drink for seven days.)

Drum and Candle

Now with all these ways to louse up a person's life, there are an almost equal number of ways for him to get free again. The law of give-and-take applies in the Brazilian spirit world as well.

Suppose that you know that someone has made a "work" against you. The best way to get rid of it is to visit an Umbanda session and let the medium decide who did exactly what to you. You can describe your physical and mental condition and the reasons why you think someone is doing you wrong. She in turn will tell you what to do in order to free yourself. She may request you to light a certain number of candles at a crossroads (or a street corner if you live in a city), offer a black chicken and some corn meal to a specific spirit, buy a gift and throw it into the sea or a river, say a dozen Hail Marys while rubbing a vile green powder into your skin, wear certain herbs in a leather pouch around your neck, use a certain perfume or take a bath with a special kind of soap. Do as she says, for it's to your own good, and if she is in charge of a center/temple she has enough experience to know what she's talking about.

If you don't have time (or are far removed from a reputable spirit center) there are home cures that you can try on your own. For instance:

On Sunday pop a quart jar full of popcorn kernels. On Monday, before having anything to eat, pour the popcorn over your naked body while praying to St. Lazarus to rid you of the evil that has been worked against you. Then sweep up the popcorn and spread it around a deserted crossroads.

Or you can look for a long-bladed plant (stiff and sword-shaped) and cut a few blades off at the roots. Then soak the blades for three days in the urine of a virgin girl between the ages of eighteen and twenty (this last ingredient may be the most difficult to find!) and braid them all into a belt that you must wear under your clothes next to your skin. You will be free of any curse.

Drum and Candle

A simpler way to get rid of evil someone has put against you (providing you know the name of your enemy) is to take a new candle and pare down the bottom so that the wick is exposed. Then light this wick and let the wax drop onto the ground as you say: "Candle, let the evil that [name] has done against me reverse itself as I have reversed you. Let whatever she has wished on me return to her." There are many old-time Brazilians (and some young ones as well) who swear this really works.

Or take four new candles and find a deserted crossroads. On the road leading to you left, place three candles in an upright < formation and light them. Take the fourth candle and break it in the middle. Stand it in the center of the other three with the broken end pointing toward the right. Light this candle and say: "May the force that is being used against me be broken and vanish into the night the same way that I have broken this candle and its smoke is vanishing into the night."

Is your house or apartment under the influence of the evil eye? Then crush a clove of garlic with a tablespoon full of ground coffee and a tablespoon full of sugar. Put this mixture into an incense burner and on Monday, Wednesday and Friday light it and wander through every room of your house.

Now suppose you have a friend who has been cursed, but he refuses to do anything about it either because he is afraid or because he just refuses to believe in such things. What do you do? You find a fresh corpse and stick it with a needle twenty-one times. Let the needle dry in the shade. Get a shirt or blouse that your doubting friend wears and using this needle and some ordinary thread sew a tiny cross in one of the far edges of the garment. Don't ever tell him you did this or the curse you worked so carefully to drive away will come back.

Romance not only makes the world go round; it makes the Brazilian spirits rush around as well. One powerful spirit medium told me that over 80 per cent of the women who come to him for advice have love problems. Some of his advice:

If you are wondering which of your many suitors you will marry, take a large onion and write the name of one of your boy friends on it. Do this with each name, i.e. one name per onion. Put them together in a ceramic bowl under your bed and cover them with a damp cloth. The onion that withers first will carry the name of the man you will marry.

If you are engaged to be married but your boy friend seems to be delaying the wedding day, do the following: Find yourself a black toad and tie your boy friend's picture to its belly with a red ribbon and a black one. Put the toad into a clay jar, close the lid and with your mouth pressing on the lid whisper: "[the name of your beloved], if you love another and not me, or tell your inner secrets to another and not me, then I consign my future to the devil and beg him to close off your days on earth in the same way I have closed off this poor toad. And I beg him not to let you free until the day you marry me, for I love you with all my heart." Every day take off the lid and give the toad a drink of water. On the day you marry take the jar to a wooded area and let the toad free. Do this very carefully, because if you harm or injure the toad your married life will be harmed as well.

If you have no one in sight at all, then you must turn to St. Anthony. He has given husbands and wives to lonely people for generations. There is no reason why he won't do the same for you. The recipe for happiness is simple. Take a rosary, and at each bead where you usually say an Our Father say: "St. Anthony asked, St. Anthony prayed, St. Anthony delivered." Then at each bead where you normally say a Hail Mary say: "I must ask, I must pray, I must receive." When you have finished tell St. Anthony just what kind of a boy friend you are looking for.

Now you have the boy friend but he doesn't seem to know

Drum and Candle

it. He keeps ignoring you. St. Anthony has shown him to you but he keeps at a distance. Don't despair. Go into a shop and buy a length of white satin ribbon. Tie it around your upper leg and looking toward the heavens say: "Three stars in the sky I see and Jesus is the fourth and this ribbon is around my leg so that [boy friend's name] will not eat, nor drink, nor rest until he has married me." This should be said three times in a row.

Let's suppose this has all worked (and it's bound to!); you are married but your husband seems to have a roving eye. You are worried about the attractive widow on the next block or the secretary who seems to get more attention at the office than you do at home. The hex is complicated but worth it. Get a foot from a dead black dog and cut out the soft pad in the middle, throwing the rest away. Take a wooden knitting needle and force it through the pad, then wrap it very tightly in red satin and sew it shut. Slit your mattress in the spot that usually divides your side of the bed from your husband's and slip in the object. Be careful that it doesn't protrude, and stitch the mattress up again. Now when you and your husband are in bed together be friendly. Agree with everything he says and with everything he wants to do. Make him laugh when he is sad and listen to all his problems. Never—but never—make allusions that you know about his mistress. Sleep in the nude and keep snuggling up to him. Each time he has relations with you have a small gift nearby to hand him (a piece of candy, an apple, a flower, etc.). In the morning get his breakfast. Let him have his coffee but also try and get him to eat a bowl of oatmeal heavily seasoned with eggs, cinnamon and cloves or else a cup of hot chocolate with lots of vanilla and nutmeg.

Are you worried about your wife? Does she seem to have secrets and smile a lot when you tell her you won't be home for dinner or have to go away for a few days on company business? Does she claim all purity and innocence when you question her? Do you want to know the honest truth? Are you sure? Well then, get the heart of a pigeon and the head of a toad and put them someplace where they can dry. Crush them into a fine powder, add a few drops of rose water and put the mixture into a small velvet bag. Lie down beside your wife and pretend to go to sleep. When you see that she has fallen asleep, slip the bag under her pillow. Fifteen minutes later she will begin to talk. She will tell the truth about her love life. A word of warning: As soon as she has stopped talking remove the sack and place it in a drawer away from the bed. If left too long under her pillow it can cause brain fever or even death. (Which may be what you want after you hear her confession!)

Now suppose you are a young man with ambition and that ambition means marrying for money. There is a wealthy widow in town who never seems to pay any attention to you. You know that her financial situation will be your salvation. Here's what to do: Catch a bat and drain its blood. Add an equal amount of rose water or cologne. Dip a clean white handkerchief in this liquid and go calling on the widow. When she greets you kiss her once on the hand. Later try to get closer and kiss her for the second time on the forehead. Then await your chance and kiss her on the lips. As soon as these three kisses have been placed, pretend to go into a faint. Swear that excess of love for her is making you weak. Take out the perfumed handkerchief and wave it under your nose (but do not breathe in), then pass it under her nose as well. When she inhales, her love (and money) is yours.

Having the will to get a lover at times is not enough. You have to keep your looks and remain attractive as well. The people who hand out advice in Brazil's spirit centers know the value of a clear skin and a full head of hair. For example:

If, Madam, you have a good figure and wish to keep it *forever*, take a pound of lean calf's meat and cut it into thin steaks. Place them over every part of your body that you wish to "keep fresh and liquid." After about an hour you can remove the steaks and will feel smooth and lovely forever. Don't wash the steaks before and don't serve them later to anyone but your worst female enemy.

Is your skin blotchy or discolored? Take a glass or two of any egg liquor and put it in a wide-mouthed bowl. Expose the bowl to the rays of the moon for three nights, then to the rays of the sun for one day. Then mix in a few drops of fresh goat's milk. Wash the blotchy and darkened places on your skin with this mixture. Guaranteed.

Wrinkles? Smash into a pulp sixty grams of fresh spring onions and an equal part of clear honey. Add thirty grams of melted beeswax and make a salve. Spread this over your wrinkles before you go to sleep but *don't* wash it off the next morning.

The best thing for your skin is "pigeon water." To make it, do the following: Take three ounces each of saffron tea, string-bean tea, watermelon juice, cucumber juice and lime juice and put them all in a clean white bowl. Then take a handful of azalea petals, lilac petals, heliotrope and bean blossoms and add them to the bowl. Then take seven or eight pigeons from which you have removed the feathers, the intestines, the tips of the wings and the heads, chop them up very fine and add them to the bowl. Now put in four ounces of confectioner's sugar, two ounces of borax, one teaspoon of camphor, the insides of twelve small white flour biscuits (still warm) and a fourth of a bottle of white wine. Let this sit for seventeen days, then bring it to a boil. Strain. Throw the solid matter away and use the liquid on your face every morning when you awaken.

Perhaps the most marvelous of all the natural substances is the fat of the eel. Rubbed on your skin it takes away liver spots. Rubbed into your scalp it makes your hair grow. Melted and poured into your ear it takes away deafness. Boiled in water and applied it melts tumors. And rubbed into your —— it clears up hemorrhoids!

There are other things that can be improved as well as physical beauty:

How to cure a drunkard. Take the gizzard from a black chicken but don't remove the tough skin. Wash it, bake it and grind it up very fine. Then put a pinch of it into each of his drinks. He will stop drinking but *you* must never eat a black chicken again.

If that doesn't stop him, try this. Take three live shrimps (or three live sardines) and put them into a bottle of his favorite booze. When he asks for a drink pour him a shot from this special bottle. Don't let him see the bottle or he won't drink from it. (I'm not sure about this last line. It seems to me the best way to make him stop drinking would be to show him his favorite brand swimming with sardines or crawling with shrimp!)

How to cure wasp or bee bites. Remove some tobacco from a cigarette and moistening it in your own saliva, apply it to the infected area. Or urinate and wash the bite in your own urine.

How to cure a toothache. Take a clove of garlic and place it on the pulse of your left wrist. Tie it tightly to your wrist with a white cloth. In a little while the toothache will be gone but the skin on your left wrist will be burned. But then, you can't have everything.

How to get rid of intestinal gases. Go out into your back yard and looking toward heaven say: "God is the sun, God is the moon, God is light, God is the total of truth. With these words which are certain and true, leave, in the name of God, these infernal gases!"

How to cure an epileptic attack. Take a live pigeon, chop off its head and make the ill person drink all the blood immediately from the severed neck.

How to bring about a delayed menstruation. Go into a

clearing, light a candle and while looking at the red flame say: "St. Mark and Matthew cutting grass in a dry field, you have blood in you like Jesus had blood in Him. Hot blood in the veins like Our Lord Jesus Christ had at the Last Supper, blood that is eternal as Jesus Christ is eternal. Blood that spurted when Our Lord Jesus Christ had His hour of death, spurt from me instead."

Sometimes you must pray and work to save yourself from acts of nature.

How to preserve yourself from being struck by lightning. When you see storm clouds gathering tie a white ribbon around your arm, your neck and your waist. Go into your bedroom and light a single candle to St. Barbara. Then wash out your mouth three times with fresh water and say: "I beg you, kind lady, to intercede for me with Him who wishes me to die. As this ribbon around my neck is pure, so is my soul and so are my intentions. Because I am worthy of your protection, dear lady, keep me free from the horrors of lightning bolts. Amen."

How to keep snakes out of your house. Mash up cloves of garlic and place them on each doorstep. Snakes will never come near (nor maybe anyone else!).

Spirits and Spiritist advice can come in handy in your everyday life as well.

How to be happy in everything you do. Get a green frog and on a full-moon Friday night in the month of September chop off its head and feet and put them into a jar containing elder oil. Leave them there for twenty-one days taking them out exactly at the stroke of midnight. Now for three nights expose them to the rays of the moon. Go to the cemetery and take a handful of dirt from the grave of a parent or loved one and on the fourth night mix this earth with the pieces of the frog. Put this into a never-used ceramic pot and place it in a quiet spot inside your home. This works because the spirit of the dead person will watch over everything you do and the eyes of the frog will remain open to give you better insight and judgment.

How to get a spirit to help you with your housework. Cut the heart out of a pure white pigeon and slitting it open, put in a live housefly and sew the incision up quickly with white thread. Bury this in your back yard on the left edge of your property. Plant a rue bush directly over it. When the bush begins to flourish a strange person will show up every day to wash your dishes, make your beds, clean your clothes and sweep your house. Do not talk to this stranger or allow your neighbors to see him, or else the hex will be broken and your servant will never return.

How to improve your business. Find a tree branch that has been formed into a perfect cross. Cut the cross from the tree and tie a white ribbon around the top. Every morning when you open your store hang the cross by the ribbon on a nail near the front door. Say (very softly, so that no one hears you): "True cross formed by God for the happiness of commerce, don't abandon me, don't abandon me, don't abandon me."

Now should this not work it may be because you are applying too much energy to your sexual relations. To improve your business you must keep the cross near the door but have sex with your wife only once every three months or (better yet) once every six months "if your health permits it." And once every third night get down on your knees beside the bed and say three Our Fathers and two Hail Marys. (What your wife will say is probably something else again.)

How to win at cards. Go visit the body of a dead friend and when no one is looking remove three nails from his coffin. Then find a frog and make him swallow the nails, sewing his mouth up immediately afterward with black thread. Put the frog into an earthen jar and keep it alive with fresh water. On the night of the big game kill the frog and remove the three nails, putting them in a black satin bag around your neck. When you start to play always bet double but *only* on the first three cards given you. As you bet, touch the bag under your shirt and silently say: "Oh [name of your dead friend], give me your calmness! Give me your calmness! Give me your calmness so that ambition won't make me hasty and lose everything." You must find a new frog in order to renew the charm every three days, but you can use the same nails over again (if that's any consolation).

To make an unwanted guest go home. When you see that a visitor is staying longer than he should and you want him to leave, take your ordinary straw broom, turn it upside down (i.e. with the handle touching the floor) and place it behind the kitchen door with the straws pointing toward the front door. Say: "Oh broom that has swept so many other undesirable things away, make [name of unwanted guest] leave too!" You will be surprised, but within a few minutes the guest will remember something he has to do and will rapidly leave your house.

I know an old woman in a small interior town who captured the heart of a young man. He was as good-looking as she was ugly, but they went everywhere together and he paid so much attention to her that it was obvious he was very much in love with her. Of course, gossips whispered all sorts of things about the old crone, and one night when I got her confidence she told me her secret.

"Every morning I make my lover an omelet. But I don't make it in an ordinary way. I lock the kitchen door and take off all my clothes. Then I light a special love incense and place it on the floor. I stand with my feet apart and let the fumes from the incense float up between my legs. Then I take three eggs, scramble them and pour them onto my breasts. They slip down the length of my body and I catch them in a frying pan right under my crotch. Then I cook the omelet and serve it to my lover. He will never leave me!"

9

"Everything is magnetism in Universal Life.
"Between the worlds is gravitation.
"Between the souls is understanding.

"Jesus placed His hands to cure. We deliver our hearts to Him so that He can fill them with the divine work of human regeneration and so that this magnetic service will be within us and enable us to reach souls rich in faith and kindness. In our hearts and lives there is an unquenchable fountain of love pouring from the rulers of heaven to the perfection and the glorification of this earth that the Lord has given us to plow and plant."

Thus wrote the great spirit Emmanuel through his human Brazilian mortal medium Francisco "Chico" Xavier in 1953. Emmanuel has become the great clarifier and teacher of the present brand of high Spiritism in Brazil. He seizes the body and writing hand of primary-school-educated Chico Xavier and expounds theories and complex doctrine that have filled nineteen books that are read by Kardek Spiritists throughout the vast nation. His words are not law any more than the writings of Kardek are law. What he has done is to orient the true believer and to help him in the difficult task of "working for charity without gain."

Emmanuel claims to have been a high public official in ancient Rome and a Catholic priest in his last incarnation.

He dictated a long, turbulent and bloody historical novel titled *Two Thousand Years Ago*, which is so detailed in ancient facts and atmosphere that unlettered Chico could never have done it with his own limited education and imagination. In another book, *The Path of Light*, he confirms the primitive Umbanda idea that all of us are fallen angels but that the Egyptians were the only ones to conserve their celestial knowledge while reincarnated on this earth. It was this "otherwordly education" that enabled them to build the pyramids and write their esoteric laws. The Hindus, Indo-Aryans and Israelis came shortly afterward, but most of them have evolved through so many lifetimes that they are now "one with God." Emmanuel claims that Israel will accept Jesus Christ as its Messiah before the year 2000 in spite of being "hampered by spiritual pride and presumptuousness."

Emmanuel's books have sold over 110,000 copies in Brazil and his readers have learned that a great catastrophe will occur at the end of the year 2000. It will not be the end of the world but the "obliteration of our materialistic age." The new era will usher in love instead of hate and those inhabiting this planet will all be of high Christian feelings. That doesn't mean that the *religion* of Christianity will survive, "for it too has become infected with the false pride of man," but that the basic ideas that Jesus preached will be the laws of the land. Jesus is the true ruler of this planet. He has appeared in many guises over the centuries. It is His planet and one day (and not so far away either) He will come back, claim it and clean it up to His liking.

What can we mortals do (when destruction comes) to stay on the winning side? Practice charity *now*. Work for the other person's good *now*. Stop putting ourselves into first place *now*.

The high Spiritists in Brazil believe firmly in Emmanuel and Kardek's teachings. The golden rule is a thing to live daily, not just to be reminded of each Sunday. The way to better yourself is to better others. The way to advance in the spirit world is to help your afflicted neighbor in the earthly world. My favorite sign is posted in a Kardek high Spiritist meeting hall in São Paulo:

"Don't put off until the next reincarnation what you can do in this one."

The Kardek followers are not on very friendly terms with the Umbanda followers. They consider themselves on a higher plane and a little bit better for their ways of doing things. Many of them object to the beating drums, the devils at the graveyard and the dead black chickens at the crossroads that the Umbandistas use to make their cures. They feel that their method, the simple method of the laying on of hands, is the much truer method. Christ used it, they point out; He did not smoke a black cigar and beat on a drum.

The laying on of hands in a high spirit session can be a moving experience. It is done with such simplicity and calmness that outsiders always doubt its effectiveness . . . until they see the results before their very eyes. The cures in Umbanda are more dramatic and more theatrical, but, say the Kardecistas, they are not permanent. In Umbanda (they claim) there is nothing to believe, nothing to keep the newly healed as a firm member of the group. The man appears at a session, is cured and goes away. His allegiance is not to any particular temple but to one particular spirit, be it St. Sebastian or the Old Black Slave. In the high Kardek sessions, the treated person must truly believe and because of this should become a member of the group. "Faith is a lifetime thing," said one high spirit leader, "not just a spur-of-the-moment medicinal pill."

Emmanuel has shown the high spirit believers exactly how Christ cured by the laying on of His hands. He gave them the outlines of good conduct, health tips so that they themselves don't contact the various ailments and step-by-step instructions on curing the malfunctioning perispirit. For unlike Arigó, who actually cuts into the flesh, the Kardek doctors cure only the invisible human aura, and this, once back into normal function, acts in turn on the flesh of the body.

A medium with powers to cure is merely the "horse," the "receptacle" of an advanced spirit. Humans are merely human. Their powers are nil. Only when they are capable of receiving a curing spirit from the astral plane are they able to cure another human. This ability to receive is not a special gift of God but comes from being advanced on the long highway of incarnations, from selflessness toward others who are *not* as far along and from having great faith in the Lord and all His powers. Wanting to cure is the first step toward actual curing, but a pure heart and an undefiled body are the next steps. Kardek mediums do no smoke, do not drink alcohol, abstain from eating meat (fish is allowed) and on days when they are to work in the centers refrain from sex. Once they have been "cleansed" by the center leader they even avoid shaking hands with other mortals.

The idea behind it all is quite simple, and the drawing on the following page should make it even simpler.

We are, all of us, constantly bombarded by cosmic forces that come from above, beside, behind and even below us. These forces give us life or upset it, keep us healthy or make us ill. Our own thoughts can also keep us healthy, but an evil thought or constant nervous tension can bring on all sorts of ailments. Everything is mental or cosmic. And it is registered in the auras that surround our physical bodies.

The figure below is in complete balance with the elements. He is right in the middle of his vertical line (A-B) and right in the middle of his horizontal line (C-D). The center of his body (E) is exactly in balance. He is bombarded by cosmic forces up and down (F-G) as well as across (H-I). Protecting him is his outside aura (K), which moves quickly in a counter-clockwise direction. It is this aura that should be bluish-white; if it is gray, this indicates illness to a medium. There is a vacuum (J), then another protecting aura that runs clock-

Drum and Candle

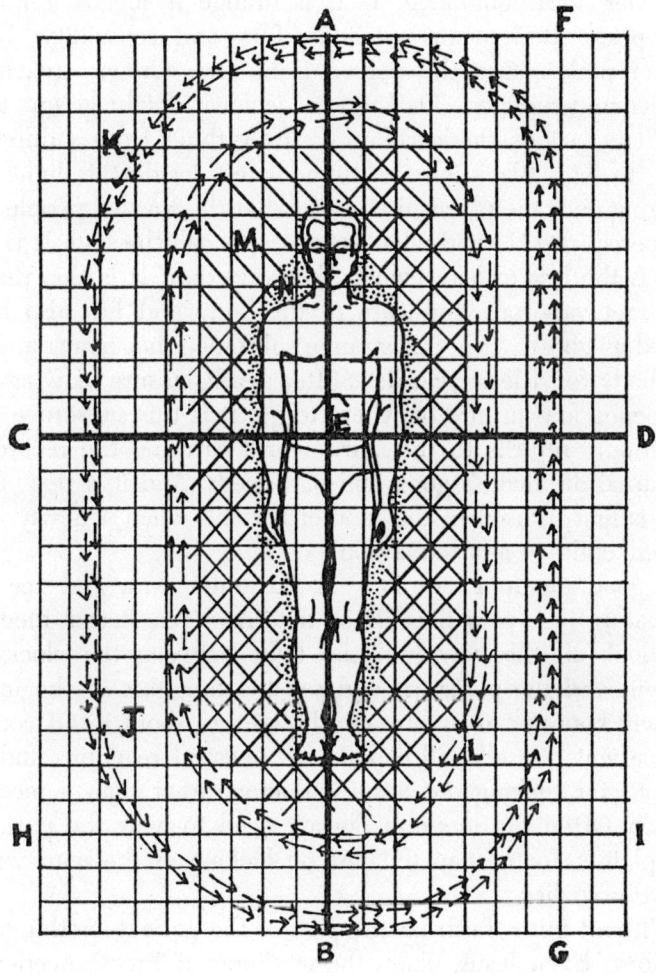

wise (L). Directly inside this current is a light (M) that by its color and force tells the medium all about the body's mental health. If this light is blue it means that the person is under spirit guidance. If it is orange it means ambition and pride. Red means passions, fury and sensuality. Deep red or pink means the person is in love. Green: treachery, artifice and rudeness. Dark green: jealousy. Light green: tranquillity. Various shades of gray: everything from sadness to lying to fear. Black is hate. Immediately inside this light and clinging onto the physical body is what the Kardek people call the perispirit (N) and what most people call the soul. It is this that is the last to leave when the body dies. It is this that is an exact vaporous duplicate of the body and has also been called a "ghost." It is this strange substance that hangs around the body for a least two days after death, unsure of what has happened and unsure of where to go. It is this substance that eventually returns to the spirit world carrying the record of its carnal duplicate's good and bad deeds. And it is this vapor that is first infused in the mother's womb when a newly conceived child is allotted a soul.

A good medium can look at the outer aura and see immediately if a person is ill or not. An even better medium can look all the way into the light between the clockwise current and the perispirit and see the thoughts of the mind. He will know what to cure and how to go about it. Of course, the patient himself will explain his physical reactions and his reasons for seeking out a spirit doctor rather than a medical doctor. Often the medium doesn't need to hear the patient's complaints, for he can tell just by looking at the man where his trouble lies.

Without faith—faith on the part of the patient—nothing can be done. Even Jesus, claim the mediums of Brazil, needed to be sure of the faith of His patients before He could cure them.

A body "out of whack" with the elements and invaded by evil thoughts or a malign cosmic vibration looks like this:

Drum and Candle

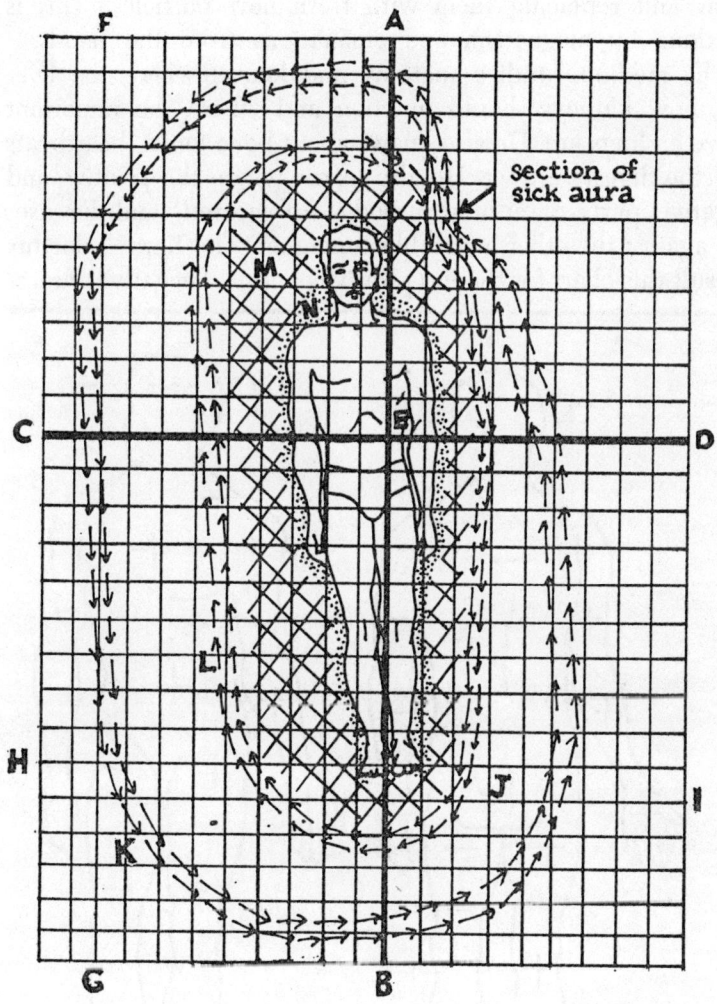

Drum and Candle

The job of the medium is to put everything back into the smoothly working order of the first illustration.

How? By pulling out the damaged cosmic particles of the auras and replacing them with fresh new particles. This is all done by magnetism and emanations from the hands.

The medium studies anatomy and knows where the liver lies, how kidneys should function and where the important nerve endings are. He also knows about bone joints, heartbeats and the digestive tract. He also learns where the positive and negative parts of a human body are located, and he uses one against the other, much like a magnet. The Kardek doctors consult this chart for the + (positive) and − (negative) areas:

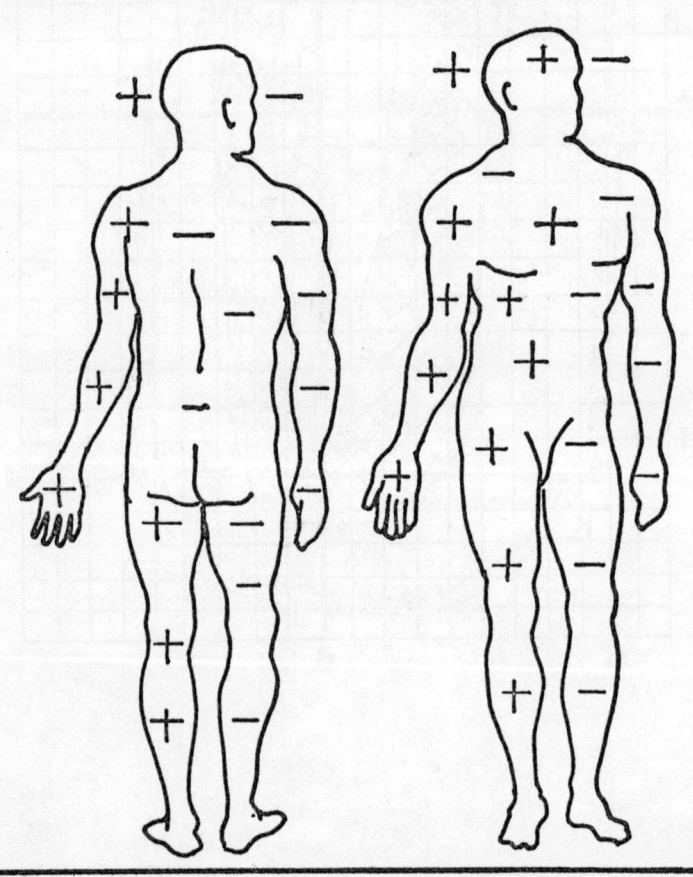

Once a session has been opened, the necessary prayers have been chanted and the necessary spirits are possessing the mediums, the doctors can get to work.

A medium's hands, when they begin to discharge magnetic fluids, turn a slight light-blue color and emit rays (which only other mediums can see) up to a distance of twelve or fifteen inches. Three separate rays shoot out from each finger and thumb and must (if we could see them) look like the triple shower head at work. When the fingers are held close together the rays combine like a laser beam and dig into an aura and into the human flesh with terrific force.

A medium knows when she has made contact and is emitting forces when she feels her limbs to be enveloped in a kind of invisible fog. Or when the skin on her arms, hands and face begins to tingle as if it was "going to sleep." (I have felt this myself various times when I have been introduced to a medium or have come into a room where a highly sensitive spiritist was. With practice I got to the point where I could pick out spiritist strangers in a crowd. Which proves that there must be something more than just "mental" about a good medium.)

The patient also feels his skin tingle. Sometimes he becomes faint and other times he will go into a deep trance/sleep. A patient can be treated in three positions. One: sitting down in a straight-back chair, his legs and feet slightly apart and his hands resting lightly on his knees. Two: lying flat on the floor, legs straight out and feet slightly apart, with the arms lying next to, but not touching, the body. Three: standing with the feet slightly apart but with the weight evenly balanced on both legs. The arms should hang loose at the sides. It is most important to be completely relaxed and to never cross your arms, hands or even your fingers. This disrupts the continuous, even flow of the magnetic fluids.

(Some mediums can cure *in absentia!* If the patient is too weak to come to the spirit center or too far away for the medium to travel, the patient and the doctor agree upon a consulting time. At this hour the patient relaxes and thinks of good things or concentrates on the parts of his body that are ill. The medium sends his curing fluids at the same moment, much like the way CBS sends Ed Sullivan into your living room every Sunday night.)

The most common posture is this one:

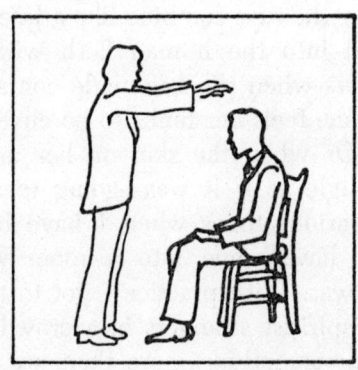

The patient sits in a chair; the medium places his hands together and, palms downward, allows the magnetic fluids from his slightly separated fingers to enter the aura over the patient's head. The medium should tense his own body and breathe deeply and regularly. No small talk or sounds of any kind should be made during these passes.

If the illness is in the upper region, and is not a serious one, the medium can use the "combined hand pass," in which the left hand remains hovering over the back of the neck $(-)$ and the right hand moves slowly from the top of the head down to the chest $(+)$ in front. For this the medium must stand to the right side of the patient.

The idea is basically simple and physical. For instance, if

the illness is in the kidneys the patient turns his back to the medium and the "doctor" passes his hands back and forth over the area. If it is a knee pain, ankle pain or foot pain the patient sits and the medium bends down and passes his hands in the air beside the affected parts. Eyes are slightly different: The medium places the palm of his hand over each eye. This is one of the rare examples where the medium actually touches the body of the patient. (Note that it is not necessary for the patient to disrobe, as the fluids easily penetrate the folds of any cloth. But when a patient is flat on his back in bed—thus hindering the easy flow of the aura—the body should be covered with just one light sheet rather than with heavy blankets.)

There are five basic movements to a complete body pass:

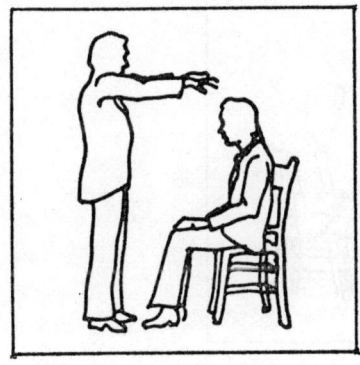 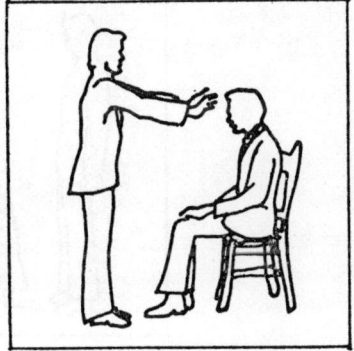

1: The concentration.

2: Letting the hands move slowly down the body of the patient to the place where the cure is to be made.

Drum and Candle

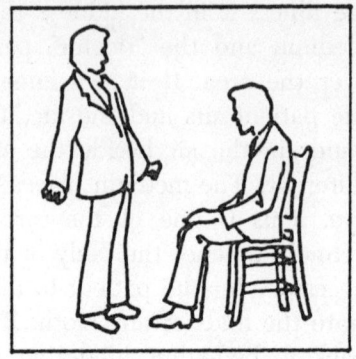

3: Ending the pass, closing the hands and stretching the arms away from the body.

4: Opening the fingers quickly, expelling the evil fluids.

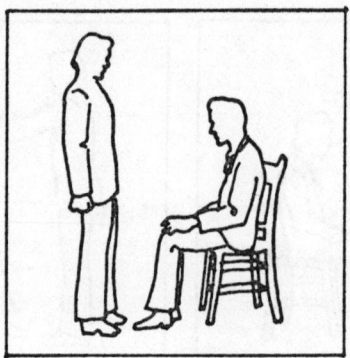

5: Rapidly returning to Position One and beginning the pass over again.

There is also something called the "hot" and "cold" breath. It supposedly goes back as far as the primitive laying on of hands. If the medium can transmit fluids from his hands, he certainly should have a large amount of beneficial fluids concentrated in his lungs. The hot breath is used against burns, local inflammations, open sores and muscular pains. The cold breath is applied to congestive areas and to people with nervous disorders; it is even used for heart attacks. The hot tends to be a cauterizer, the cold a calmative.

To blow hot, place your lips at a distance from the sore (for hygienic reasons you should cover it with a piece of gauze) and blow in short, deep spurts as if you were warming up frostbitten hands. To blow cold, take a deep breath and expel the air from your lungs as if you were trying to put out a candle from a distance.

That's all there is to it. It's that physically simple, yet there is definitely *something* there. I have seen several people recover from bad aches and miserable pains after a high spirit medium passed his hands over or blew on the sore spot. I have talked to dozens of others who have despaired of ever being cured after countless X rays, injections and high-priced medical fees and who have walked out of a Kardek spirit session completely cured. Scoffers will say these cures are all "mental" and dismiss them. Yet what today is the definition of "mental?" If "mental" means something that is only in the mind, then please explain extrasensory perception. Please explain hunches and feminine intuition. Please explain premonitions that come to pass. Please explain an artist's or a poet's inspiration. Please explain, if things "mental" are of no account, how an inventor creates a new machine, a scientist a new medicine, a philosopher a new method.

When was the last time you had an idea? It wasn't a *material* idea, was it?

10

"The Black Pope of Brazil." That's what they call Umbanda medium Tancredo da Silva Pinto. He is very black and very impressive. He has personally initiated more than fifteen hundred people as priests of this Afro-Brazilian religion. He speaks with a soft voice but with great assurance. Self-educated against impossible odds, he can discuss painting and world history right along with spirits and devil incense.

"I am not a Christian," he told me, "but I admire Christ's intelligence and His ability to preach and reach the masses. He was not the Son of God, because God is the phenomena of nature and is not flesh and blood. Christ was of flesh and blood. He was a strong spirit medium, very strong, and the world is under His influence now. It will remain so until 1999, then another great spirit leader will come. I hope that I am still on this earth to greet him. There are many things I should like to tell him."

If Tancredo is still alive when the new Christ comes he will be ninety-four years old. He just might make it, for today, in his middle sixties, he is as strong and healthy as an ox.

"I was born in 1905, in the state of Rio de Janeiro. I don't remember how many brothers and sisters I had because when I was only seven years old both my parents died. The landlord took back the house and we scattered into the wind. I lived wherever I could. Sometimes with friendly people, other times with mean ones. Many times I slept in the woods or under a bridge. I got my food as best I could. It was a difficult life, but I know now that it was preparing me for the things that were to come."

What was coming was a complete immersion into the cult of Umbanda when he was thirteen. A married couple showed him the rituals and taught him the secrets. He lived inside the spirit center doing odd jobs to earn his keep and absorbing everything he saw. Year after year he worked his way up until he was the leader of a temple of his own. Clever and a good showman, his temple expanded and with it expanded his reputation. Soon he was in charge of a huge center in the city of Rio de Janeiro and there were more white faces among his flock than black. His miracles and cures were legion. His advice was sought on everything spiritual and most things material. He read everything he could about spirits and Spiritism, studied African history and cultural movements and soon became such an expert on literally everything (and could easily write and talk his knowledge) that he became number-one man in Umbanda circles.

When the Umbandistas tried their first abortive attempt to hold a national congress and unite the various groups by writing one set of rules and regulations, Tancredo was chosen President of the Federation. Newspapers began calling him "the Black Pope." The name stuck. He doesn't deny it.

"I gave up my own temple years ago," he said. "It only produced headaches and used all my time. My mission as leader is to unite my brothers and to show them the proper way to worship in Umbanda."

To begin with, he claims that the word "umbanda" is not Sanskrit or Portuguese. It is from the Bantu word *banda,* meaning "group." Therefore *um banda* is "one group" united from the many. Tancredo gets upset when this holy name is misused: "Umbanda is not a ritual. It is not a religion and it is not a cult. What it is is a *unification* of all the rituals of the Afro-Brazilian cults, and it contains all the liturgy and the customs of the tribes from the diverse Bantu nations." (Note: Foreigners living in Brazil will often hear the word "macumba" used in place of the correct "Umbanda." Tancredo wants it clearly understood that those who use "macumba" are completely wrong. A macumba is a musical instrument that is nothing more than a plank of dried wood with a hole in it. The plank is nailed to an oblong box that stands on short legs. The musician [macumbeiro] rubs a dry stick in and out of the hole, making the wooden plank vibrate and causing a rasping and rather melodious sound. A change in pressure or speed of the stick can alter the sound.)

Tancredo is trying to get Umbanda centers to agree on a few basic principles. It has not been easy. Everything must be done according to the laws of nature and closely linked with the phases of the moon. The moon influences the earth in four separate cycles, each lasting seven days. Therefore at the end of each twenty-eight days the moon renews its powers, and Tancredo wants Umbandistas to have only twenty-eight days in each of their months (not thirty or thirty-one) because of this. He divides each year into nine months and each day into twenty-eight hours. He admits, that unfortunately, he doesn't know what the Umbanda date really is or what year of Umbanda he is currently living in. "It's all quite complicated to calculate exactly, and anyway Umbanda has been around for thousands of years. They didn't keep track of the date in the old days. That's why we can't be sure right now."

For him, everything revolves around the number seven, and a short talk with him about this will have him writing, adding, dividing and totaling an astonishing number of mathematical equations to prove his point. "It's quite simple," he says. "It's all in the cabala and in each of our lives. For instance, did you know that a child who is only eight months in his mother's womb will not live if he is born? But a child of seven or nine months *will* live. You see?"

Drum and Candle

To be ordained a priest in the Pope's seven-based Umbanda takes twenty-eight years (his nine-month years, not our twelve-month ones), and the first initiation comes when the novice has been in the group for seven years. The beginner first has his guardian angel chosen by the throwing of the stones. This guardian will be the same one who will incorporate with him when he is spiritually "open." The novice stretches out on an earthen floor for three days and is covered with special herbs and leaves. Then he stands on a pile of these leaves for an additional four days. He does not eat anything but what a priest feeds him. He is not allowed to utter or hear one word. The windows and doors of the hut are covered with dark cloths, for he is not supposed to see the sun. After these seven days have passed he dons the clothes that symbolize his particular spirit. He is then considered a "minister" of that spirit. For the next seven years he studies all branches of the Afro-Brazilian religions, and his mediumistic powers are tested time and time again. There is a second initiation at fourteen years (singing, dancing and candle burning. No more leaves in darkened huts, though!), another at twenty-one years and the last great initiation ceremony at twenty-eight years. After this one the medium is considered a high priest and should have one power more developed than all the others, be it divination by the stones, ability to initiate newcomers, healing powers, etc. Then he is free to go and open his own temple, have his own congregation and his own chorus of dancing saints. He is completely free to be his own master—except when the Black Pope shows up on a visit.

Tancredo spends most of his time traveling around Brazil inspecting Umbanda centers and "taking notes of what is wrong." He goes with a retinue of "cardinals" and "archbishops." (He doesn't call them that, the newspapers do.) His arrival is a signal for a giant celebration, and the very best wines and foods are spread for him. He gets the seat of honor and there is much bowing and attention from everyone present. He blesses little children and makes momentous pronouncements. He is referred to as Tata Ti Inkice, which translates into "the highest priest who personally knows the forces of enchantment," i.e. "the Pope."

His black holiness is quite upset over "the ignorance and the abuse" of some of the temples in Brazil. He tells of visiting one center where everything was going according to ritual when exactly at midnight the lights went out and small red candles were lit. Then (to his disgust) they started evoking the various Exús. "After several exhibitions of swallowing fire, drinking hot oil and other things, the priest in charge called upon all those who had a special favor to ask. Dozens of women came forward, each with a plaster statue of St. Anthony, the marrying saint. Then what did the incorporated spirits do but start to chew off the head of every statue! What was left of the images was thrown into a garbage can! After that they started drinking alcohol, jumping and screaming. This lasted for several hours. I had no idea what they were trying to do, but I've put them on my list. Most definitely they are on my list. You can't make a farce out of Umbanda."

Sometimes his work gives him a chuckle or two, like the time he was asked to assist at a baptism. It took place in a thick forest and the baptismal font was a concave rock formed by years of water pouring over a small falls. "Just at the moment when the priests were in the stream and in the middle of the ceremony, a huge snake washed over the rocks and landed right beside the baby. There was such screaming and general pandemonium that it was delicious." He laughs, his huge belly chuckling under a thin layer of cigar ashes. "It was just delicious!"

While Tancredo stands very high in Brazilian spiritual importance, there are and have been other great mediums and leaders. And they haven't all been Brazilians, either. In a land of strong nationalism, mediums have been able to remain international.

Pietro Ubaldi, an Italian, studied law and English because his parents wanted him to, but when he was still quite young he started hearing voices. At first he fought them, then gave in to them. When they had "convinced me of their truths" they began to dictate. Ubaldi wrote nine books with the voices whispering inside his head. They dealt with reincarnation, mental telepathy and the future destruction of the world.

He claimed that he was able to tune in on Jesus Christ because "when I delve into the innermost depths of my deepest conscience I can catch the thoughts of the superior beings who live in these elevated planes. Christ is among them and because we think in unison and think the same thoughts, I can read His mind and capture His thoughts."

"Heresy!" said the Vatican and in 1939 put two of his books, *The Great Synthesis* and *Mystic Asceticism*, on the Index of Forbidden Books.

Ubaldi contended that we all return to earth for many lifetimes until we have gained enough purity and done enough good deeds to be admitted into heaven. It is not a new idea. He also said that before the present civilization ends in the year 2000, there will be decades of wars and revolution. Also not a new idea. But *Brazil* will manage to remain at peace and will become the heart of the new world of the twenty-first century.

Brazilians, naturally, loved his doctrine and began to translate and buy his books. Spiritists of all degrees and colors considered him one of the greatest brains that ever functioned. They had been saying for years that "God is a Brazilian," and now here was a foreigner who agreed with them. In 1951 Ubaldi moved from Rome to Rio and upon arrival was feted in the São Paulo state legislature as "one of the greatest contemporary thinkers." In the records of the legislature a deputy declaimed: "This assembly is too small for the greatness of

Pietro Ubaldi. Any state legislature, be it in this country or in any other country, is too small for the greatness of this man."

Ubaldi replied that he was touched and humbled by their words and explained why he had left Italy. "My intelligence is understood in Europe, but my heart can only be understood here in Brazil. In Europe they know how to think, but they don't know how to love. To Europe, my mind. To you Brazilians, my heart."

Ubaldi chose the city of Santos as his residence and proclaimed that he was the reincarnation of St. Peter. Meanwhile an irate group of Catholics wrote to the rector of the University of Milan asking for details about this impressive mystic. Back came the reply: "Signore Pietro Ubaldi of Foligno, Italy, is a completely unknown person. Certainly he is not a scientist, neither great nor important. . . ."

Another man to capitalize upon the spirits and his ability as a medium was Alziro Zarur. In 1949 he managed to get a thirty-minute radio program and called it "The Hour of Good Will." Then eight months later, after an incredible listener response, he founded his own charitable organization, calling it "The Legion of Good Will." It was to "promote human fraternity on truly Christian bases," yet in a very un-Christianlike way he added: "No one is saved by the religion that he adopts while on earth, but only through the good works that he practices in the name of the divine spirits." He asked for donations. They came pouring in and soon Senhor Zarur not only had his own program, he bought his own radio station! Around Brazil went his voice and his brand of Spiritism. In came the donations and the requests to be a "legionnaire." By 1959 he had 300,000 contributing legionnaires and a following that was as great as any Brazilian movie star's. Soon (in order to stifle harsh Roman Catholic criticism) the federal government officially transformed the

Legion into a *religion*. Now Zarur was the high priest of "The Religion of the New Commandment," free from taxes and free from critics.

In 1960 Zarur rose to greater heights than any other spiritist leader: He actively campaigned for the office of President of the Republic. His name and the initials of his church were smeared over walls and billboards across the nation. He was acclaimed in ticker-tape processions and given testimonial dinners by some of the most influential politicians and businessmen in Brazil. Then just a few days before elections he abruptly withdrew from the race, asking his vast following to support another candidate. Rumors had it that he had been paid off by the other parties because he was so strong that his name on the ballot would have split them all. In Brazil rumors are never proved. But when the military took over in 1964 they made sure that the short, balding little medium would never try for the nation's top office again. They took away his political rights for ten years and ordered him to play down his lucrative religion.

Another who used the radio to her own spiritist ends was Rosa Micchi Aristides, but instead of ending up almost in the presidential palace she ended up in jail. Rosa lived in Rio and said she had gypsy blood. She also said she had such special powers as being able to read cards, divine the future from chicken entrails and see into the human mind. As Rio is full of people trying to make a living from the same idea, Rosa had to come up with a new gimmick for the old profession. She decided to go modern. She invested in radios, receptors and antennas. With these electronic gadgets, she advertised, she could put the hex on anyone, anywhere. No job was too distant. She set her prices at $1 for a consultation and $20 for casting a spell. Her parlor was hung with signs that promised to "resolve family problems," "tighten the bonds of friendship," "release you from bad debts and court processes," "arrange marriages" and "kill at a distance." Often clients had to make an appointment for as much as two weeks in advance, she was so popular.

The police heard about her offers (black magic is still against the law in Brazil) when a victim came and complained to them that he had paid Rosa $20 to kill his mother-in-law and all that had happened was that she had fallen and broken three ribs. The woman was not only still alive, he had to pay the hospital bill. The police visited Rosa, disguised as clients, but were unable to pin anything on her. Hers was a normal medium's parlor except for a locked back room and an overlarge radio antenna on the roof.

Then a special detective was assigned, with his own radio equipment. He tuned in on Rosa just as she was uttering some very strong incantations against a local factory owner. Her client, who had been fired from the factory, wanted the whole place to blow up and take the owner with it.

Rosa was working hard on his request when the police broke in the door and caught her at the microphone talking to the evil spirits. She tried to convince the police that they were unwise in arresting her, that she was a very powerful woman and could ruin their lives if she chose. She made a basin of powder explode into room-filling red vapors. This brought cacophonous animation from several cages filled with rats, frogs, lizards and black cats.

The police were unimpressed and took Rosa to the station house. With her went several human skulls, three crystal balls and a jug of earth from a nearby cemetery. They charged her with "a crime against the public health" and gave her a stiff fine. As she paid her debt, she cursed the detective who had caught her wave length. "I will destroy your marriage!" she vowed.

The officer, who in divorce-denying Brazil had been trying for years to get a legal separation from his wife, was delighted.

Antonio de Alva was a Brazilian Indian soldier who was killed. That was his former life. In this life he is a Brazilian spirit medium who cures by chasing away evil. His book *How to Dissolve Quimbanda Evil* has made him a household word in spirit centers. This thin, shy man who boldly faces the devil every day of his life works in Rio for whatever his clients wish to give him. He charges no fees. That, he says, would take away his powers.

Antonio has had more experience with the wicked side of Umbanda than almost any other Brazilian. Hundreds claim they have been saved by his prayers and passes. His personal tales fascinate listeners for hours. His spiritist assistants swear to his powers and stick by him through it all. Only once did a spirit go too far.

"It was in 1952, when I worked at the 'Walkers in Search of Truth' center, that a twenty-year-old mulatto boy came to see me. His name was Sebastian and he had a terrible open sore on his right leg. He said it was a recent thing and that he had been to several doctors and none of them could do anything to help him. One doctor said it was elephantiasis. Another said it was leprosy. I saw immediately that it was the work of the devil."

The session opened with the drums and the candles, and when one of his chief assistants, a man named Wilson, received a spirit it was the powerful Exú of Seven Horns. Wilson's young blond body shook with the force of the nether spirit. The veins in his face dilated and pulsed, turning his pale complexion purple. Wilson (i.e. Exú) turned on the diseased young man and said: "Do you want to know why I did this to you? Yes, me! I put that wound in your leg! Do you remember two months ago when you were walking with your girl friend and you came to a crossroads? There was a gift there for me, but you had to be brave and show your girl you didn't believe in me or in Umbanda! So what did you do? What? Answer me!"

"I kicked it," replied Sebastian in a low voice. "I kicked it off the road and crushed everything with my foot."

"With your *right* leg, yes?" demanded the devil.

"Yes. It was my right leg."

"So I did this to your leg to show you that you must never fool around with gifts that are meant for me! I am not all bad," Exú shouted to the people who were watching the scene. "I am not all bad. I did this so that he would awaken to the truth about our religion! If I hadn't proved to him that we were right and he was wrong he would have seen the truth! What I did was, in my own way, an act of charity!"

Then Wilson (Exú) crouched beside the young man and placing his lips to the wound started sucking out all the pus and decaying flesh. He spat clots of blood onto the floor and when he was satisfied with his work he washed his mouth out with *cachaça* alcohol.

Sebastian was completely cured, but someone in the group told Wilson what he had done when under the domination of the devil. It so revolted him that he stopped going to the sessions and gave up Umbanda forever.

Shortly after that Antonio de Alva was asked by the Brazilian magazine *O Cruzeiro* to write an article for them titled "Exactly at Midnight—Life and Death at a Crossroads." The following weeks brought hundreds of letters from all parts of the country asking Antonio to get rid of evil curses. He slowed his work at the spirit center and began a kind of Spiritist lonely hearts correspondence, curing by mail all those who could not come personally to see him in Rio.

"Dear Senhor Antonio" (wrote one woman in the interior):

"I saw the article in *O Cruzeiro* and I need your help. I have been suffering for six years. I had a friend whom I liked very much. One day she asked me for my photograph. Cursed day that I gave it to her! I am a poor girl who works to keep her family and a father with t.b. Each time happiness comes to me, that woman takes it away. Why she is doing this I don't know. I never fought with her. We never had any bad feelings. She asked me to loan her one of my dresses. I did. She gave me a statue of St. Anthony all tied up with string and asked me to keep it for her in my house. She begged me not to show it to anyone or tell anyone about it. She asked me to write the name of my boy friend on a piece of paper and then to write my name on the other side. In all good faith I did as she asked me. Now she has ruined my life. My boy friend left me and I can't sleep at nights. I go to work at seven in the morning and only return home seven at night. My life is pain and suffering because of this woman.

"There is another thing. I have a son. He is a monster. He is twenty-four years old, drinks and treats me miserably. He is not my real son, but a baby I took in and cared for all these years. I thought that he would help repay all my labors of the past, but he is a drunkard and vicious and mistreats me.

"At night I feel the mattress rise up under me. Then something clutches at my throat. I never get any sleep and I need to work. There is a man who is interested in me but he is frightened of this curse that that awful woman put on me. Please, tell me what I must do.

"God will repay you for everything.

"N."

Antonio replied:

"Dear Sister in Oxalá:

"That our Beloved Mother in heaven, the Divine Mother of Jesus, covers you with her Sacred Shawl is what I first wish for you. That my spirit guide Guaicuru and my other spirit friends and guides protect you and aid you is my second wish. I read, my dear sister, with feeling and great attention everything that you wrote in your letter and in reply I would like to say the following:

"1) I always work with two lights. One white (very intense) and the other red (weak). This means that, normally, I only work and use my magic knowledge for good (white), but there are certain times when I use my powers for evil (red). With this in mind, dear sister, I'm going to teach you a charm that, if done correctly, will give you great results.

Drum and Candle

"Buy a common wax candle. Scrape the opposite end of it until the wick appears. This done, light this new wick and place the candle (ordinary end down) onto a white saucer. This done, say: 'This candle, lit on the wrong end, is for the guardian angel of (your enemy's name), so that he will collapse and throw his legs into the air. I do this because she is doing me harm and hurting me without I ever having done anything against her.' She will get all the evil she has placed on you right back in her own face.

"2) Dear Sister, you must make your *own* guardian angel stronger. Beside a clear, smooth glass filled with water, place a candle (make sure you put it on something so that it doesn't cause a fire), light it and say any old prayer (it can be a simple Hail Mary), then say: 'God, I offer you this prayer and the light of this candle as spiritual force for my guardian angel. Accept, my God, this offer and show my guardian angel how he can better protect me and defend me and orient my life here on earth.'

"3) Try and find a good Umbanda center in your home town to develop and educate your mediumistic powers, which are very sharp. Also buy a copy of my book and read about others who had problems like yours and how they solved them.

"God bless and make you happy.

"Antonio de Alva."

Two weeks later came another letter:

"Dear Senhor Antonio:

"Thank you for your letter. I did exactly as you told me, but last Monday a piece of bread appeared on my doorstep and on Wednesday there was a mirror. I am very nervous and a lump has appeared on my right breast and I don't know what to do. I wish that your guide Guaicuru could examine me. I think this woman wants to kill me. Or wants to put me into a sickbed. Every day I have faith in Jesus and Oxalá. I want to know what I should do about my son, to make him stop drinking. In the name of mercy, help me remove this heavy cross I have on my shoulders.

"N."

"Dear Sister in Oxalá:

"Those things which have appeared at your door cannot harm you if you wash them away with a little water mixed with rock salt. Throw a little urine on them too, that's always good. Urine cuts the effects of almost any black magic of this type.

"To make your son stop drinking write his name on a piece of paper and stick it to the sole of your left foot with adhesive tape. Every morning when you get out of bed stamp your left foot three times and say: 'I will dominate my son and his vice! He will obey me and stop drinking!' If you do this with faith it is absolutely certain that you will obtain good results.

"Don't be shy about continuing to write to me. To pour your heart out to someone is always healthy. I hope and pray to God that the next time you have a pressing problem you will call upon me for the solution.

"Receive an embrace from a brother in Oxalá:

"Antonio de Alva."

Recife is Brazil's third largest city. It is hot, muggy and dirty. It can also be modern, air-conditioned and chic, depending on what neighborhood you are in and what economic class of people you are with. The Brazilians refer to it as "our Venice" because it is spread out between a series of rivers and canals. Just five minutes by car from the downtown section is the small town of Olinda. It was here that the Portuguese touched down on the new continent for the first time in the year 1500. They left a few soldiers and some priests and returned later with merchants and farmers to settle. Magnificent gold churches and seminaries were constructed. The first Mass was said there. If the Brazilians of today were at all religious, they might consider Olinda as "our Mecca." It is there, in Olinda, directly across the street from a beautiful colonial church, that Edu lives and evokes his spirits.

Edu has a dark skin and a soft voice. His gestures are ethereal, his hairpiece ill-fitting. He has a flair for the dramatic. He knows how to wear gaudy capes and cause attention. He knows how to solace lovelorn women. He knows how to take advantage of any situation. He knows how to keep Recife—both white and black Recife—in fear.

I first heard of him when I was invited to a Sunday luncheon at one of the oldest homes in Recife. The guests sat out on the big colonnaded porch, sipping whiskys and Coca-Colas, waiting for the several maids to finish preparing the food. One man was being toasted because the day before his horse had come in first at the Recife Jockey Club.

"Don't praise me," he said, "praise Edu. He blessed the horse just before the race."

"Who is Edu?" I asked. "The bishop?"

"Just the strongest Father of the Saints we have in Recife, that's all," bragged the horseman. "I have him bless all my horses. They never lose with his special prayers."

"Do you believe that?" I asked him.

He blushed and laughed. "Well, I don't believe in *everything* that Edu does, but I believe that his charms *work*; they *do*."

The next day, Monday, the newspapers announced as being the Day of Yemanjá and reported that great festivities would be held in the sea goddess' honor. The story added that Father Edu would be in front of the town's leading newspaper headquarters that night to guide the devout on a pilgrimage to the sea. Naturally, I was there early.

It was a good thing too, for an estimated ten thousand other people were also crowded into the street to see and follow Edu. While popcorn sellers and flavored-ice vendors pushed their way through the multitude, the people chanted and shouted Edu's name. Many carried bouquets of flowers to throw into the sea in honor of Yemanjá. While there were both black and white faces in the crowd, all were cleanly, if not richly, dressed.

A blaring of horns and a blue and white pickup truck came roaring up out of the service entrance of the newspaper. Two huge colored posters, back to back, were fixed on the roof of the cab. They were of Yemanjá emerging from the sea. In the open area (usually reserved for hauling bundles of papers) were bales of white flowers. Two young women stood near the flowers, one dressed as an Umbanda medium and the other in costume as the Queen of the Sea herself.

In the center of the flowers stood Edu. He was wearing a silver lamé suit that sparkled in the flashbulbs and street lights. A long red cape, with a huge upturned white mink collar, gave him the appearance of having just won the Miss America contest. The sparkling golden crown on his head helped the illusion still further.

The crowd screamed his name and he smiled and waved, making the sign of the cross and blessing them as if he were the Pope rather than an Umbanda high priest. He began to to sing praises to Yemanjá and the mob took up the tune. The truck began a slow process down the main avenue toward the beach, and the people walked beside, behind and in front of it singing hymns and pelting Edu with flowers.

Two days later I was ushered in to see him.

"I appreciate your coming," he said in his soft voice. "It is always good when Yemanjá and her works are reported in the international press. She is a magnificent woman! She has remade my life and the lives of thousands of those who've truly believed." He smiled and looked at a huge statue of the goddess on a side table near his desk. There were fresh flowers around her neck, Hawaiian style, and others hanging from her hands and around the base of the image. Her dress was bright blue and her skin was white. I meant to ask him about that. I had always wondered why the African spirit of the waters should have a white skin, but in the interview that followed, I forgot to mention it.

He fingered a necklace of cowrie shells that was in front of him on the desk and watched as I got my tape recorder into position. "I would prefer it if you didn't use that machine," he said. "Let's just converse."

I told him that I wanted to get his *exact* words on tape. That it was important for a foreign journalist to capture exact phrases because so many Brazilian reporters just made up their own quotes. Still he said he wished that I would put the recorder away. I argued that in such an important project as I was writing, he would want to have his exact words on paper. Finally he shut his eyes, remained silent for a few seconds and then, looking at the machine, said, "Turn it on."

Delighted, I pushed the button and the reels started to turn. But to my dismay the tape came gushing up out of the box like plastic spaghetti! I slammed at the stop button but it did no good. Soon his desk was a pile of forever-ruined tape. "This has never happened before," I sputtered.

"You see?" he said with his soft voice and an even softer smile. "Yemanjá didn't want you to use that machine either."

I got out my notebook and started writing. He started talking.

"Last month I donated ten million cruzeiros [about $3000] to the cancer hospital here in Recife. Yet the people who are against me—and I have many jealous enemies—say that I am in business to get rich. If I wanted to have money, I certainly wouldn't give it all away, would I?

"I see and give spiritual advice to a hundred and fifty people every day but Sunday. Most of these come to me with love problems. It is terrible how there is such a lack of love in this world. I throw the stones for them and read their futures. I only charge five new cruzeiros a visit." (Later I calculated that he sees 3900 people a month for a take of $4500 monthly. And this sum does not include his fees for such special services as driving away evil, bringing back a lost lover, etc. These are paid for at a much higher rate.)

Not bad for a poor boy from a slum shack, not yet out of his thirties, who has been a spirit priest for less than ten years.

Edu says that he was a devout Catholic and his one dream was to be a priest. "I would attend every Mass each Sunday and watch the padres in their robes and with their jewelry pay homage to the Christ and His mother Mary. I knew that inside the Church I would be happy. I felt that it was my only true home."

So he enrolled in the Franciscan seminary in Olinda (the lavish and oldest Franciscan building in Brazil), but after a few years and just before he was to be ordained, "I was seized at night by a spirit. I didn't know what it was. I shook and cried out and was terribly frightened. They gave me some pills, thinking I had malaria, but the illness didn't go away. Night after night the spirits came and seized my body. Finally I went and told the father superior what was happening to me."

And what did the good father do? "He threw me out of the seminary and out of the Church!" His voice wavered and his huge eyes filled with tears. "Can you imagine what this meant to me? I, a poor, humble boy whose only love was Holy Rome herself? I, who lived only for the ritual, the music, the luxury, was suddenly banished as if I was a leper, something disgusting and vile! And the novenas, ah! the novenas. How I loved them. I would creep into the church and listen to the novenas, hidden behind a pillar. But the priests would see me and throw me bodily into the street. They would curse me and chase me. They said I was the devil and filled with black magic."

He moved into a dirty straw hut and says that for over a year he fought to free himself of this devil/spirit. He couldn't sleep and couldn't eat. Finally one night, when there was a

Drum and Candle

huge full moon, he realized it was no use. "I cried out asking it if it was here to stay. I asked if it was a spirit of good or evil. A voice said to me, a beautiful woman's voice that whispered inside my head, that it was Yemanjá who had taken possession of me and that she was good and that she was here to stay."

The spirit told him that he was to found a temple in her honor and not to worry about his detractors and enemies, for he would win out over them all. The spirit said that someday the highest authorities in town would come to him for advice and that the padres who persecuted him would repent.

He began to preach and cure from his humble hut. Slowly the poor and ignorant began telling their white bosses and madames about Edu. His clientele started to grow and with it he began to build his "Temple of Yemanjá."

Then in 1964 everything changed for the better. Recife's most important soccer team, the Nautico, wanted to win the state championship. They had been losing year after year, and that year their opponents were stronger than ever. Somehow the team's managers decided that they would ask Edu to bless the players and to intercede with Yemanjá and make them champions. He promised to work the whole season for Nautico.

With Edu on their side, the team made goal after goal, and when the last game of the season came up, the game that would decide which of the two top teams would take the cup, Nautico was one of the top two. Everyone asked Edu about the outcome. He predicted that Nautico would win and that the game would be a fight right up to the last minute. But, he promised, the final goal would be made by Nautico and it would be kicked into the net from the right-hand side.

The final tie-breaking goal was made by Nautico. It came from the right-hand side of the field. Nautico became the

Drum and Candle

state champs and Edu could do no wrong. (They have paid Edu "a vast sum of money" to keep them winning. They have taken the cup every year since then.)

The believers and those wanting to believe flocked to Edu's temple. They came with problems and he gave them hope and solutions. His ministrations got him a pale-blue four-door sedan (blue is Yemanjá's color in the north), a thick gold chain with an ivory and diamond amulet at the end, a small ruby ring set in diamonds, a larger topaz set in diamonds and a still larger ring with a huge sapphire rimmed in diamonds.

"I cure ailments that regular doctors cannot reach. I cure the ailments of the spirit. I do not believe in cutting into people as Arigó does. He only serves the flesh. I serve the soul. Once a woman came to me, tied up in ropes. Her family said she had gone mad. She was screaming and cursing. She said terrible things to me and called Yemanjá foul names. I knew that she was possessed by an evil spirit. I asked them to untie her and leave her alone with me. I talked to her and worked to drive away the devils she had inside her. In a half hour she walked out of my temple, completely cured.

"My own father was suffering from a terrible disease. The doctors could do nothing. One day the state came and took him away. I was frantic because I loved him and I did not want to see him die. Then one night Yemanjá came to me and told me that she had cured him and that I was to go to the sanitarium and bring him home. The doctors refused to let him go. Finally, when their X rays showed that he was completely free of the disease, they released him. That was five years ago. He is still alive and goes to work every day."

How, I asked, can this ancient religion help the twentieth-century "civilized" man? What does it offer that other religions don't?

"The spirits are here in predominantly black Brazil to show the white man how wrong and evil he has been all these years. It was the white man who destroyed the black man's cities and cultures in Africa. They have stepped upon the black man and his religion and used the name of their own religion as their excuse for exploitation. But now his own faith is weakening. Look at the hundreds of priests and nuns that are leaving the Church. Look at the problems Rome is having between the Pope and the priests. The white man's faith is weakening exactly now when the black man's cult is reviving. Today the white man comes to me, to *me,* the black man he threw out of his Church, to beg forgiveness for what he and his ancestors did to the black man. And in doing this he acknowledges and worships at the feet of the black man's saints!

"After the procession this week, the one you saw, I was returning to my temple with the image of Yemanjá, but as I passed the seminary from which I had been expelled so many years ago I heard a voice telling me to enter. I walked into the chapel carrying Yemanjá in my arms. The Franciscan priests did nothing. It was the high point of my life."

I wandered all over Brazil looking for a "true prophet," chasing down all the leads that dozens of people gave me, trying to find a "miracle." It was then that Dona Leda found me.

I was in Pôrto Alegre spending some time with a family that had been more than kind to me. A humble family, yet one with such honor and charity that they rose above their lack of material things to near-greatness. The woman of the house told me that she was going to visit a fortuneteller. Did I want to go along? No, I was tired and had had a busy morning doing research for a magazine article. "I think you'll like Dona Leda," she said. "Everything she has ever told me has come true." So I went. I was not enthusiastic, but I agreed to accompany my friend.

We went to a far side of town and walked down a street of new, mass-produced apartment buildings. We turned into one of them and walked down to the basement level. There was only one door at the foot of the stairs. We knocked and a young girl opened the door. She greeted my friend and we were asked into the living room. We sat on a hard red sofa and chattered with three women who were there ahead of us. There was a cheap flower print on one wall and against the other wall a huge, unseeing television eye stared blankly out. One door led to a kitchen and another to a bathroom. A third door remained closed. It was through this door that the visitors entered to see the medium. We waited at least two hours, until we were the last ones in the room. Since I kept glancing at my watch, my friend let me go in first. I promised her I'd only be a minute.

I pushed open the door and found myself in a small room about eight feet square. There was a window that looked out on the gravel parking lot behind the apartment complex but its light was diffused by a white cotton curtain. A wardrobe closet sat in one corner, its mirrored door ajar and its top lined with fluffy toy animals. On one wall there was a colored print of the Virgin Mary. Exactly opposite it, on the other wall, was a cardboard cutout of Huckleberry Hound. Under this was a small plastic-topped table covered with a white cloth. Behind this table sat Dona Leda.

In all my travels I have met maybe a dozen people who put me at ease immediately. She was one of them. There was a calmness and warmness emanating from her like rays from an invisible sun. Her chubby brown face broke into a smile as she motioned me to sit at the table on a yellow kitchen chair. "Welcome. It's good to see you again," she said.

"But I've never been here before," I protested. "This is the first time I've been in your apartment."

"I know, but I have seen you before. I knew several weeks ago that you would come to me. I saw you wandering around your apartment in Rio and felt your need for a solution to your problems."

I considered it just a lucky guess that she knew I lived in Rio, but then she added, "Your apartment faces the Christ of Corcovado, doesn't it? There are many paintings on the walls and one wall is of stone. On the right side of the living room you have a gray sofa. It's ugly and uncomfortable. You want to sell it. Go ahead, you'll be happier without it."

I gasped, for that was an accurate description of my Rio apartment, and indeed, I had hated that sofa ever since I bought it. Just a week earlier I had decided to try and sell it.

She took a soiled and thumbed deck of cards and asked me to cut them into three stacks, and to make a silent wish. She turned over each pile and said, "It will come true."

"Nonsense," I said to myself. "Even *I* can do that!"

She spread the cards on the table in four neat rows. They were not ordinary playing cards, nor were they tarot cards, but a deck with ladies in evening gowns, houses with sunbursts behind them, men counting money, ships sailing across troubled seas, horses rearing up at lightning and other strange designs. She started to interpret the way the cards were positioned and made several remarks about the immediate future. "You have just had a fight with a friend." (True.) "You value this friendship but he is too proud to ask forgiveness." (True.) "When you get back to Rio there will be a letter from him asking you to excuse his bad manners." (When I returned to my apartment, there indeed was the letter!) "You are worried about money problems." (Perennially true!) "Within two weeks you will get a telegram. There is money deposited for you even now that you know nothing about." (Happily, this also came true.) She then went on to tell me about my parents and my friends in Rio, even describing one of them down to the color kerchief she wore in her hair, the kind of automobile she drove and the type of rare French poodle she owned. True, all true.

She saw a trip to the United States for me, which I had not figured on but later took on the very day she said I would, and told me of the people I would meet there and how they would be dressed. Again, it all happened just the way she saw it. Then she asked me if I had anything special I wanted to know.

At that time I had just finished work on a novel and I wanted to know if it would sell or not. My book on the Amazon River, titled *The Mighty, Mighty Amazon,* had just come out in London to very good reviews. It was a book of historical facts. I was worried about writing my first piece of fiction.

Dona Leda had never met me. She knew nothing about my professional life. There was no way she could have known. The lady who took me there knew me very well, but she was completely ignorant of what I was writing and my plans. She could never have told Leda anything about me. I decided to play it foxy, not wanting to supply her with any facts that she could use to guess correct conclusions. "I have done something," was all I said, "and I'd like to know if I have done my best."

She closed her eyes and put her right hand over them, as if deep in thought. "This thing you have done . . . you have created something."

I nodded.

"This thing . . . it's a book. You've written a book."

I was surprised, because there were many other things I could have "created." I considered her hitting upon a book as being a very lucky guess indeed.

"This book . . . it's about something here in Brazil. . . ." Again I said yes. "But why is there so much water around it? It seems to be covered in dark, muddy water! Is this book about a river? Is this book about the *Amazon* River?"

In my stunned amazement I admitted that it was indeed about the Amazon River.

"It's a history of the river," she continued. "It's not fiction. You spent a lot of time up there researching it and you wrote it with the best of your ability." She opened her eyes and smiled. "Don't worry. It is a good book. It will take you further than you have ever imagined that you would go."

(Now before anyone dismisses her statements as a reading of my mind, i.e. thought transferences, let me state clearly that at *no time* was I consciously thinking about the Amazon book. It had been written and published. My thoughts were all on the unpublished novel.)

"Yes," she said. "It is a good book. I can see it now. It has a wine-colored cover."

"I'm sorry," I replied, "but it doesn't."

"Oh yes it does! It's a soft burgundy color."

"No," I said, "the cover is black and orange. It's a picture of the cathedral in Manaus silhouetted against a sundown on the Amazon. I ought to know, for I took the picture myself."

"You are wrong," she said emphatically, "the cover is burgundy."

I talked to her a little longer, then thanked her, surprised that she had made so many correct guesses yet had gone so stubbornly far afield about the book's cover. That evening I picked up the copy of the Amazon book that I had brought as a gift to this Brazilian family and laughed about how wrong Dona Leda had been about the color of the cover.

"But David," said my host, taking the book from me. "Remove the paper dust jacket!"

For the first time since getting a copy of the book from the London publishers, I took off the paper jacket with the picture of the Manaus sunset on it. Then for the first time I saw what color the book's cover was: burgundy!

There was no way she could have known about the book and its cover. There was no way she could ever have seen the book. There were only two copies in Brazil at that time and the book was only on sale as yet in England. I felt that I had been close to a "miracle."

I began to ask questions about Dona Leda. One woman

told me that she had predicted when her daughter would be married and even described her husband, yet at that time the daughter had not even met the man. Another said that Dona Leda had told her her husband was hoarding money from her that she needed badly for an operation. She had even described the color of the bank and the corner it was on. When the wife confronted her husband with this, he confessed, went to the bank—which had been *exactly* described—and drew out the money. Still another woman told me of the time Dona Leda came to her and told her her mother was going to die. She asked her to be prepared and to make the mother's last days on earth as peaceful as possible. The daughter did not scoff at Leda's remarks, even though her aged mother was as spry and healthful as a woman of twenty. On the very day Leda predicted, the mother lay down after lunch and died quietly in her sleep.

When I got back to Rio and found everything exactly as Dona Leda said it would be, I told an actor friend, Alberto Aguas, about her. On his first free day he went immediately to Pôrto Alegre for a session with her. He returned to Rio enthused. "I asked her about my future as an actor," he related, "and she said that I would get a TV contract that I was wishing for. I asked her if it would be from a São Paulo station, because I live in São Paulo. She said no, that it would come from Rio. So I asked her when. She told me the first half of December, but you know how persistent I am, so I asked her, 'What is the *exact day* I will get this contract?' She concentrated for a few seconds and said it would be the sixth of December."

Alberto went off to São Paulo, leaving word with the Rio station where he could be reached and confident that he would be called on the sixth. When the fifth came he got anxious, and on the sixth he stayed near the phone. But there was no call. The seventh and eighth came and went and still no call. On the ninth he returned to Rio and told me how disappointed he was in Dona Leda. On the tenth he went in person to the TV station to see what had happened to his contract. As soon as he walked into the casting director's office the secretary said, "Where have you been? We've been trying to reach you to come in and sign your contract. We called São Paulo but that number you gave us doesn't answer." When she showed him the number he had written he saw that in his haste he had inverted two figures. "But *when* did you try to call me?" he asked. Back came the reply: "On the sixth of December."

The next time I entered Dona Leda's apartment it was with the express desire to interview her for this book. Before I could tell her why I was there, she told me. "You are going to write something very important about the spirits in Brazil. I'm glad you are doing this book, for you were chosen long ago for this work. The years you have spent in Brazil investigating Spiritist works have been a long apprenticeship. You have learned much and your studies will be a great enlightenment for your non-Brazilian readers. You will talk to many people and from it all the truth will be filtered through. You are going to interview a man for your book who lives in a big house. There are also many trees around his house. Oh, what beautiful trees! Pay attention to what he says, for he is a very wise man. He is also a very powerful medium, but he is afraid to admit it even to himself. What do you want from me?"

"Your life story."

She agreed.

"My full name is Leda Silva Simonele. I was born in the town of Jaguarão in the state of Rio Grande do Sul on April 8, 1928. My father was a Brazilian. My mother was a pure Paraguayan Indian. I am an only child.

"My father ran away with another woman when I was only four years old. He left my mother with absolutely nothing. She rented a small house and started to wash people's clothes. She also washed clothes in a nearby hospital. She was a beautiful woman and all the men were crazy about her, but she said that after her husband left her she didn't want anything more to do with men. She never remarried, never had any lovers.

"One day, when I was just four years old, I was playing inside the house and a man came into the front room. He was tall, bronzed from the sun and wore a dark suit. He smiled at me and put his fingers to his lips, as if I was not to say anything. Then he walked through the house and out into the back yard. When he passed me it was like paper rustling. He leaned against a tree and kept smiling at me.

"I went running for my mother, who was washing clothes at a nearby house. I told her a strange man was in our back yard. Quickly she accompanied me back to our house. 'There,' I pointed. 'There he is.' But Mother couldn't see a thing. I went right up to the man and almost touched him, but still Mother couldn't see him. She was furious that I had taken her away from her work and locked me in my bedroom as punishment. A little while later she asked me if I would not tell any more lies if she unlocked the door. I promised. But when I looked into the back yard the man was still standing by the tree and smiling at me. I again asked my mother if she didn't see him. She called a neighbor woman and the woman couldn't see him either. I led both of them right to the spot where he was standing, and as my mother reached out her arm, he vanished.

"A few weeks later Mother and I were walking home along the railroad tracks. It had been raining and we balanced carefully on the ties so as not to get our feet dirty. Suddenly in front of us I saw a white girl wearing a white lace dress. She was walking toward us, her nice white shoes covered in mud and the hem of her dress soiled and frayed. I asked my mother why that girl was allowed to get so dirty, and mother said she didn't see any girl. I pointed to her and got more and more excited as the girl silently approached us. Still Mother couldn't see her. The girl kept her head down, not looking at us, and when she got so close that I was afraid she would bump into us, I jumped off the tracks into the mud to let her pass. My mother was furious that I had dirtied my shoes, but the girl continued down the tracks and Mother never saw her. Only years later when I was old enough to ask questions did I learn that a white girl had run away from a birthday party dressed in a white gown and had been killed by a train on those very tracks.

"When I was seven years old I started reading cards. I managed to get a deck of tarot cards and spread them out on the table and was amazed that they told me things. I didn't really read them. What was happening was that there was a voice inside me that told me what they meant. The voice is still with me. It's like an old-fashioned phonograph record. I don't know whether it is a male or a female voice. And it's not as if I 'hear' the voice as much as I 'feel' it. I'm sorry, but I can't explain it any better than that.

"The first time I read the cards for somebody else I got into a lot of trouble. There was a neighbor girl named Jacy who came with her younger brother and wanted me to tell her future. I was only seven then and the voices told me that Jacy was pregnant. I told her: 'The cards say you are pregnant, whatever that means.' Jacy became indignant, slapped me across the face and went home. That evening her mother complained to my mother that I was spreading lies about Jacy. Her little brother had asked her mother what 'pregnant' meant and the mother demanded that I be punished. My mother burned my cards and locked me in my room. Two weeks later Jacy went to a doctor and he told her she was going to have a baby. She was only fifteen and had no idea what caused babies. She thought they came with a kiss. She would let an older neighbor boy sleep with her, but not kiss her.

Drum and Candle

"After that someone gave me another deck of cards and Mother let me keep them. I was enrolled in the first grade of school but only wanted to read the cards. I quit after eight months. My mother said it was okay, but I had to get a job if I didn't want to study. A family in town hired me as their maid. I was only eight years old. When I wasn't washing clothes or dishes I would read the cards for them. My boss had a tobacco-exporting business and he used to consult the cards about it all the time. When I was only ten he made me his secretary and I was in charge of the safe and the mail. One day the cards told me that a man was going to steal a valuable letter from the post-office box that my boss used. I got up very early the next day and went into the post office as soon as it was opened. The man I had been warned about was right behind me. I raced to the box and took out the letter. He tried to grab it from me. I screamed like crazy and it frightened him away. My boss said that he would have been ruined if that letter had fallen into that fellow's hands.

"I worked for two years for them and they moved away. I took a job in the kitchen of a Methodist school. The directors were very strict and didn't want to know anything about my cards, but at night the students would come to me and I would tell them who was going to pass and who was going to fail. I stayed on there until I became kitchen manager, then I left to work in a fish cannery in the town of Rio Grande. I took my mother with me because I was tired of seeing her washing other people's dirty clothes. I don't know how old I was. Maybe nineteen or twenty.

"The humidity of the packing plant gave me chronic asthma, but I needed the job. I worked there eight hours a day and would read cards for people every night until midnight. I never charged them anything, they just gave me whatever they felt like. Soon people began coming from other towns to consult with me, and on my vacations I would travel to other cities and take along my deck of cards.

"My mother never liked the idea of those cards. She always said they were the work of the devil. She would never let me put the cards for her. Often she would turn people away from the house, telling them they should be ashamed of themselves as good Catholics coming to consult the spirits.

"When I was twenty-six I met a man and felt 'something different' inside me when I was with him. He said it was love and so I married him. He took me to live in the city of Santos but once there he treated me badly and had other women. Those women in Santos are tough! They walk around with knives in their shoes!

"After a couple of years of this, I returned to Rio Grande. Everyone was glad to see me back. My house began to fill again with my old clientele. I was glad to be back with my own kind. I never married again. Like my mother, one bad man in my life was enough.

"The mayor of Rio Grande was waging a campaign to shut down the spirit centers and he asked me to come to his office to talk to him about it. I told him that I thought he was playing with fire. He asked me what would happen to him if he closed the Umbanda and Spiritist temples. I placed the cards on his desk and saw a tragic death for him if he continued with his plans. He laughed at me. He closed the centers. He was killed exactly as I had predicted.

"Many people would like to have my gift of voices but at times it can be terrible. My mother and I were very close, and every year, around November, we would start buying Christmas gifts for each other. It was a wonderful game of buying and hiding them. We got more enjoyment from searching the house for our presents than actually opening them on Christmas Eve. Then one year my voices told me that my mother would die on the eleventh of December, just fourteen days before Christmas. So instead of gifts, I put all my extra money into a graveyard plot and saved for her funeral. It was awful to see my mother going around the house looking for her hidden Christmas presents. It was all I could do not to cry in front of her. She died on the eleventh. It was the saddest Christmas I ever spent.

"With my mother gone, I moved to Pôrto Alegre. Rio Grande was going into a business decline and many of my clients had moved away. Also, I hoped that the weather in Pôrto Alegre would be kinder to my asthma. No sooner did I move here and start to look for an apartment than a voice told me the number of the state lottery that would win that week. Never before had I been given such a clue. I searched all over town and found the number. I bought it and waited. It was third prize, and the amount was just enough to buy this apartment.

"In 1969 my voices told me that my husband was living with another woman in a town in the interior. I hadn't heard from him in years. They said that he would die at four-thirty one Wednesday afternoon and that the woman would leave him to die all alone. I shut up my apartment and took a bus to this town. I had never been there before yet walked straight to his house. Sure enough, there he was, sick in bed and all alone. I went and bought a casket and arranged for his funeral. I told the local padre to show up Wednesday around 4 P.M. My husband died at four-thirty; the padre was there and so was the undertaker. When the funeral was over, I returned to Pôrto Alegre."

Had she ever been able to use her powers to avert a tragedy, I asked.

"Once a client came to me and I read the cards. I saw her young son in a burning school building. I told the mother the exact day of the fire. She told the principal and he just laughed at her. On the day I predicted she refused to let her son go to school. A fire broke out that afternoon, but fortunately all the children managed to escape.

"The saddest experience I ever had came when a woman arrived to have the cards read and brought along her two

Drum and Candle

small daughters. One was very much prettier than the other and I jokingly said, 'This one will stay with me.' The mother laughed and asked for a reading. The first thing I saw was this beautiful child drowning in a large body of water. I could see the location and even the time it would happen. Her mother became furious and said that I was trying to use witchcraft to force her to give up her little girl. She left in a rage. The next day the family went out on a picnic. The little girl wandered away. At 6 P.M. they found her dead at the edge of a lake. I felt terrible about it because if I had gone after them maybe I could have saved the child. I don't know. I just don't know."

Dona Leda says that she has her best readings with people who are completely unknown to her and that often a spirit friend or relative will accompany a new client on a first visit. The spirits talk to Leda and try to get their messages across to their still living loved one.

"*Talk* to you?" I asked.

She shook her head in the affirmative. "Oh yes. Some say they are free and happy. Others are not doing so well. Most of them have not conformed to their new situation. They come sobbing sometimes and I have to tell them that they are dead and should go to the place of the other spirits."

"How do you know they are dead? What makes you sure they are not just ordinary human beings?"

"Oh, that's easy. They are always about a foot off the floor. They are dressed and I am able to completely describe their clothes and their features, but they just can't seem to put their feet on the floor. I remember one woman who came to me, I had never seen her before, and she said her husband had died and her problem was should she remarry and sell her house. I looked at the man who had come in with her and saw that he was floating about a foot off the ground. I asked her if her husband had been tall and thin, if he had blue eyes, white hair and a small scar on his left hand. She was amazed that I made such an accurate description. I didn't dare tell her that it was quite simple on my part, that her dead husband was standing right beside her. That might have frightened her too much. It's never good to tell the living about the dead that are near."

What about her religion? Is she a Catholic?

"Oh yes. I go to Mass every Sunday. I even have priests and nuns coming to consult me. One padre comes late at night and asks me to read his cards. A nun wanted me to teach her how to talk to the spirits. I told her it was something that couldn't be learned. It must just be there."

11

Everybody believes in spirits in Brazil. Those who say they don't are either very strong Christians or else kidding themselves while they try to kid you. It is extremely common to be talking to an upper-class Brazilian or a university-educated man and have him tell you that he doesn't believe. Then if you push the subject he will admit that while *he* doesn't believe, this and that happened in his family or to a very good friend, and he will then admit that "maybe there is something to it after all."

There is not one Brazilian who doesn't have a "spirit story" to tell, be it something that happened personally or else to a friend or a member of the family. The spirits have taken over Brazil and they seem to be entrenched for a long stay.

There was a man in Rio who openly said he didn't believe. He was rather wealthy, rather well educated and white. He lived in a good neighborhood in a house and not an apartment. His daughter was engaged to a young fellow whom he did not approve of. He made the girl break off with the young man. The wounded suitor went to an Umbanda priestess and a curse was put on the father's head. When he heard about the curse, he scoffed and telephoned the young lover. "Tell your witch that I'm not afraid of her charms and chants. She is a humbug and, frankly, so are you for trying such a low trick on me and my family."

The young man told all this to the priestess and she herself went calling on the man. She marched into his office, past his two protesting secretaries, and shouted into his startled face: "You dare to doubt the powers of my spirits! You dare to call me a fraud, *I* who have been calling upon the powers of good and evil for more than twenty years! I who have the respect of thousands who have visited my center and who have asked me to intercede with the spirits! I who . . ."

But the man rose and hustled her from his office. She kicked and screamed and as he shut the door she predicted: "You will see! You will die! There will be a man watching your house day and night. He will make you die! You will see!"

What the irate businessman shouted in return was not recorded, but his secretaries burst into tears and begged him to be careful. *They* believed, even if he didn't.

That night he drove home and, sure enough, there was a strange man sitting on the curb across the street staring at his house. He noticed the man but said nothing to him. There is no law against curb sitting in Brazil.

In the morning he drove out of his garage and there was the same man, still sitting and staring at his house. He went to his office, thinking about the stranger and intrigued at the coincidence. That night the stranger was there staring at the house.

The father parked his car and crossed the street, standing near the unknown man. "Just what do you want here?" he asked. "You don't live in this neighborhood. What are you doing spying on my house?"

But the man, pale and badly dressed, only raised his huge eyes and looked at him. He didn't reply.

"If you aren't out of here within a half-hour, I'll call the police!" said the father. "This is a decent neighborhood. Not made for the likes of you!" With that he went into his house.

A half-hour later he looked out the front window, and there, sure enough, the man still sat. Fuming, he picked up the phone and said to his wife, "I'm calling the police. That tramp across the street is up to no good."

The wife looked out the window. "What tramp?" she asked.

"That man sitting on the curb! The one with the old clothes and needing a shave."

"I don't see anybody," she replied. "Sitting in front of *our* house?"

He slammed the phone down. "Of course! Over there," he pointed; "the lone man staring at this house!"

His wife looked at him. "Dear, are you feeling well? There is nobody sitting on the curb. The street is empty."

Rather than call his wife an idiot, he stomped upstairs and said he didn't want any dinner. In the morning he shaved (his hands shook, it had been a night of nightmares and rolling and tossing) and drove out of the driveway. The stranger sat there awaiting him.

"Get away from here!" shouted the businessman, and when the stranger only gave him that silent stare he grew furious and gunned the accelerator and rode the car over the stranger's body. The automobile crashed into a tree and stopped. The noise brought his wife running. The husband was hugging the steering wheel and sobbing. "I killed a man," he groaned. "My God, I've killed a man!" But when he and his wife looked under the car, there was no corpse to be found.

He spent the rest of the day in bed, under sedatives from the family doctor. During the night he awoke and looked out the front window. The strange man was still sitting there staring at the house. The businessman began to curse and cry and beat on the walls. His wife and a maid managed to get him back into bed and the doctor was called for a stronger sleeping potion.

For three days the man moaned about a stranger that no one in the house could see. He cried that the man wanted to kill him. The wife tried to get her husband to eat but he refused. The calming injections became stronger. The patient became weaker. They began to lock his door at night so he couldn't get to the window and make those scenes that the entire neighborhood was gossiping about. Then one night, exactly one week after the visit of the spirit medium, he shouted for his wife. She went to his bedside and noted that he was thin and suddenly so tired and old. "I'm going to die," he told her in a hoarse whisper. "That man across the street is killing me. I don't know how, but he is forcing me to die."

"There is nobody across the street," she told him for what must have been the hundredth time. "It's all in your imagination."

"I have to go to the bathroom," he said. "Help me there." She supported him while he walked haltingly down the hall toward the bathroom. As they passed a front window he pulled back the curtain, then shouted, "He's gone!"

And he fell to the floor. Dead.

Imagination? The power of suggestion? Or spirits?

Juremira Pimenta de Morais is an attractive, educated widow who also did not believe in the spirits or an afterlife until she married a medium. She didn't suspect it, for he came from the best family in the small town of Nova Iguaçu. They owned great hunks of the place. What was not owned by them wasn't worth having. Juremira (whom everyone calls "Juju") had been raised a strict Catholic. She also came from a good family. Her husband Athayde, knew he was a medium but he hated the idea. When his spirit would arrive and take over his body he would speak in an old man's voice and use profanity that he never used when he was normal. It bothered him and he didn't like to discuss it.

One night, a few years after they were married, Juju and Athayde were visiting her mother's home in Copacabana. The family sat in the living room after a full-course Brazilian meal and talked "family talk." Suddenly the dining-room table shook with a loud, heavy blow. It was as if someone had pounded his fist against the table with all his force. The family froze, then Juju, braver than the rest, went into the dining room to see what had caused the noise. Again, the table resounded with a heavy pounding noise. Juju, who was not a spiritist but after living with her husband was interested in the subject, said half in jest, "If you are a good spirit trying to tell us something, knock three times."

Immediately the table shook with three firm blows.

"Athayde," she shouted. "Come in here. Get a pencil and paper and open yourself to this spirit. I think there is a message for us."

Her husband did as he was asked and sitting at the table, held a pencil lightly over a sheet of paper and began to concentrate. There was a minute's pause, then the pencil started to write. In swift, clear sentences the message filled the paper. Athayde's head went backward and his hand wrote with a speed that he had never used before. The signature was his signal to come out of the trance and that the message was over.

Eagerly the family crowded round to read it. It was from Juju's aunt (her mother's sister), who had been dead for fifteen years. The message said that there was strife among her children and she was very upset about it. After her death the family had managed to stay together in the old home. Now the eldest son was about to be married and wanted to bring his wife to the house. But that meant the other children would have to leave. He didn't want to start a new life surrounded by his brothers and sisters. They quarreled with him, saying that they had a right to stay there and if he was going to be so selfish then they would sell the house and each go their own way. The dead mother did not want them to separate, nor did she want them to sell the house. She begged Juju's mother to go and have a talk with her children. Maybe she could get them to come to a more rational agreement.

The sister hadn't seen her nephews or nieces for over two months, and she didn't know anything about the upcoming marriage, but taking the paper, she went the next evening to the old house and managed to find all the children together. "Sit down," she commanded, "and explain what has been going on in this house."

In those days Brazilian children still had respect for their elders, and when their aunt ordered them to do something, they did it. One by one they told her about their problems with the impending marriage. It was exactly as the spirit had written. When they were finished the aunt told them that she knew all about their problem, whipped out the message and showed it to them. "It's Mother's signature," one of them said, and they all began to weep. The conflict was settled. The new bride came, but she shared the house and family harmony returned.

Now Athayde had never met the woman who sent him the message: She died years before he married Juju. No one had any idea of what was happening to the children in the old house. The only one who knew was their dead mother. And she was concerned enough to come back and dictate a message. It was the first and last time she ever returned.

In 1957 Athayde died suddenly, at the age of forty-eight. A few minutes after his death Juju felt a hand caress her hair several times as she mourned. She knew it was Athayde's touch. He has appeared to her several times. They were a very happy couple and she feels that his appearances are those of a protective husband and are not intended to frighten her. "Sometimes at night I will hear a loud knock on my wardrobe closet door and I will call out: 'Athayde, if that is you, please go back and rest in peace. I am happy and well. There is nothing you can do for me. And anyway, you know I'm frightened of ghosts!' Then I will say one or two Our Fathers and ask Athayde to go back where he came from." Then she falls asleep.

She has seen her husband (always a white blur) on several occasions, but more often others with her have seen him. Once she was visiting a relative and a repairman arrived to fix the relative's television set. Juju noticed that he kept glancing at her, but she didn't give it much thought. The next morning the repairman returned with a needed part and asked the relative: "That woman who was here yesterday, she's a widow, isn't she? Was her husband tall and dark and did he etc. etc. . . ." and he went on to describe Athayde perfectly. The repairman admitted he was a Spiritist and said that all the time Juju was in the relative's house, the spirit of her dead husband was standing right behind her.

Television is a most modern and scientific invention, and those who make their living from it must also be modern and scientific. Yet the following happened in Rio in 1968:

A TV producer was having a run of bad luck. He had one of the best-known names in the business, but it seemed that everything he touched went wrong. One evening, after a miserable day in the studio, he returned home ready to take it out on the first person who crossed him. That person happened to be his wife, who is a well-known Brazilian actress. She was also six months pregnant. She said something and it was just the spark to set him off. In a rage he slapped her and she fell against a table. Almost immediately blood began to run down her legs. The husband was frightened that his wife was going to have a miscarriage and yelled for the maid to call a doctor. She, a spiritist, called a medium from an Umbanda center. He arrived and gave the wife some green leaves to chew and ordered her to soak herself in a hot tub that he filled with a special yellow liquid. The bleeding stopped shortly after she got into the water.

Then the medium told the producer that the evil eye had been put on him by someone who was jealous of his professional prestige. He said that if he lit three candles at seven different crossroads, walked away and never looked back his luck would change. Grateful that his wife had improved, he did exactly as the spirit doctor ordered. One week later he was promoted, over incredible odds, to director in chief of one of Rio's most important television networks.

Sometimes the seeker has more faith than the medium. In 1959 Maria de Lourdes Rosa da Cunha was having trouble with her husband. He was lazy, wouldn't work and had another woman. He also beat her and mistreated the children. As there is no divorce in Brazil, Maria de Lourdes resolved to kill him off and sought the services of priestess Cesarina do Nascimento, a black magic worker whose specialty was errant husbands. Cesarina took about $75 from Maria de Lourdes and promised her a speedy release from her spouse. She gave her a bottle of sugar-cane alcohol that had a dead coral snake in it as well as the parings from the fingernails of a recent corpse. Maria de Lourdes gave this to her husband but he didn't die. He didn't even go away. Back she went to Cesarina complained: Either you get rid of my husband or give me back my money. This time the alcohol bottle contained ground glass.

Still hubby hung on, and the third time around Cesarina gave her a bottle of alcohol that was more than three-quarters filled with a liquid rat poison. Maria de Lourdes filled her husband's breakfast coffeepot with the mixture. When she saw him drink it down, she left the house and started playing the part of the inconsolable widow to the local parish priest. Her man was dead, she moaned. Whatever would she do now? The padre went back with her to bless the body but instead found the husband agonizing but alive. The priest called an ambulance and the hospital called the police. Maria de Lourdes confessed and named Cesarina as her mentor. Cesarina was sentenced for attempted murder, and while she confessed that she didn't know how many husbands she had gotten rid of over the years, she pleaded innocent to any wrongdoing. "I gave the necessary potions, that's true. But I had nothing to do with it. I was only carrying out orders from the spirits."

If spirits can upset a family, imagine what they can do to an entire town.

Martinópole is a small village 211 miles inland from the seaport town of Fortaleza, the capital of the poor northern state of Ceará. It contains a public square and a Catholic church, six elementary schools and a doctorless hospital, plus a business area that has about fifteen shops and stores. It burst into Brazilian national prominence in October of 1969 when spirits began telling the good citizens of the town where gold and jewels were buried.

The first man to hear the news said that a friend of his, who died in 1962, appeared in his home one night and told him where to dig to find a ceramic jug filled with money. He dug in the exact spot and unearthed a pot of silver coins and a gold button. The news spread all over town and the search was on. Three other men found their own treasures, so they say, but since the spirits who gave the locations warned them that they could not open the jugs for at least six months after digging them up, they sold them to buyers from the capital. Since none of these dealers have returned asking for their money back, the townsfolk are sure that there really was a treasure in each jug.

Of course, con men moved in on Martinópole. One businessman was awakened one night by a stranger with a battered and dirty ten-gallon tin can. He said he had been told by a spirit where to dig and had found this near a huge mango tree. But he couldn't wait the six days that he was told should elapse before opening it. He needed the money now. He asked for $150 for the can; the businessman got him down to $85. The man took his money and went away. Six days later the can was opened: It was full of stones.

The local padre says there are many jugs buried in the area. Years ago there were no banks in town and safes were

Drum and Candle

imported and expensive. Many people, fearing thieves, buried their money in places known only to themselves. When they died the secret went with them. "I hope the spirits point out all the jugs in town," the Catholic priest was quoted. "This place needs all the money it can get."

If the spirits can get into one human town, then what happens when a human gets into a spirit town? Senhor Mozart Bastos Ferraz has the answers. So many answers that he wrote a book about it and called it *The True Glory*.

Sr. Ferraz is a medium who worked in many centers around Brazil. He was raised a Catholic and called upon his Catholic spirits when it was necessary for an especially difficult cure, but over the years he came to the conclusion that Catholicism was pure fantasy, and he determined to "present the facts and not a philosophy to the spirit believers in Brazil." His book represents *the facts* as personally verified.

One night his soul left his body and floated around his small town of Ribeirão Prêto, in the state of São Paulo. It's a rich coffee-growing town and Sr. Ferraz was pleased that he could enter so many homes and see so much going on without being observed. Then after praying for guidance, one night his soul took him straight out of town and up, up, up into the town of Aurora, which was located exactly over Ribeirão Prêto. He was allowed to move around, see things and ask questions. He came back with a notebook full of facts.

First of all, the city had no cars or buses. It didn't need any because the streets moved by themselves. You just stood on them and they took you wherever you wished to go. He never came to the end of a street because it "seemed to undulate off across the horizon." There were no animals of any kind there, but there were lots of birds in the town woods "who are there to carry out the cycle of evolution." It never rains, the wind doesn't blow and nobody works for anyone but himself. Every one of the one million inhabitants wears the same kind of clothes: white full shirts or blouses and dark trousers or skirts. They are all thirty-three years old, too. No babies are born there but there is a sex life for those that want it. The women "have an eternal air of unsatisfied sensualism." There are private residences, a school, a theater and a library. Writers and painters create their books and paintings while up there and then, once they have been reincarnated on earth, copy their celestial works on earth. There is a huge "Department of Reincarnation," where he learned (to his amazement) that there is no such thing as freedom of choice. "We are all fatally subject to the cycle of reincarnation. We are who we are and have a private will because there exists a general will." It is here that past lives are summed up and future lives chosen. The dispatching section of this department is one of the busiest places in town.

Senhor Ferraz also got the journalistic scoop of the century while up there; for who else did he interview but the Virgin Mary herself! She said that most of what is written in the Bible is "foolishness" and told him the true story. "I was the flesh-and-blood mother of Jesus and nothing more than that. I married Joseph and we were both illiterate, boorish and unthinking people. We had six sons and two daughters. The oldest was Jesus, who was easy to get along with and wasn't interested in fast living like His brothers and sisters. He courted several girls, but it wasn't His destiny to marry. Then one day when He was thirty years old He decided He was going to go out into the world and see what it was like. On the first night of His travels He fell asleep against the trunk of a big tree. At that same moment, in Jerusalem, Mary Magdalene and Judas Iscariot were dancing together in her luxurious home. Jesus slept on and His fluid spirit left His body and went to investigate the music at Mary's place. Just then the Christ descended on earth and He cut the fluid's umbilical cord and entered into Jesus' spirit. From then on, who was walking in my son's body was not Jesus, but the

Christ." Senhor Ferraz' book has sold—in Rome's biggest Catholic country—three separate editions.

Often it helps to be a spiritist in Brazil, especially if you are anxious to be in the public eye. Moab Caldas, for instance, was a radio commentator in Pôrto Alegre who gave news of spirit centers while disc-jockeying with the latest record hits. He decided to become a politician and turned to his spirit contacts for help. By slanting his campaign in 1960 heavily toward the spirit centers, he got the votes of all those who frequented the 12,500 different groups. This pale-faced man with light blond hair was elected state representative by thousands of other white-skinned gaucho spiritists. He was the first man ever to be elected on a spiritist ticket in Brazil. He wanted to be sworn into office wearing his white Umbanda outfit, but the state ruled that he had to dress in a suit and tie like all the other deputies. Caldas kept his word to his constituents and worked hard at getting new schools, clinics and rest homes for the aged built. He would openly call upon the spirits from the floor of the House of Representatives while his followers lit candles and burned incense in the galleries. A good man (and a clever politico), he was only put out of office when the revolutionary military government took away his political rights for ten years.

Maria Bethania is one of Brazil's top entertainers. A slim, supple girl with a big, full voice, she hails from Salvador, Bahia, and her night-club numbers alternate between the latest Beatles hit and songs of praise to her Candomblé gods. The public loves her and buys all her records. She has made a fortune and a national name for herself, yet she consults the gods each time she plans on starting a new venture. If the gods say no—even to a lucrative Hollywood contract—she also says no.

Jorge Amado is Brazil's best-selling author. He has published five books that have been translated into sixteen languages. He gets royalties from such scattered places as Russia, the United States and Greenland. His book *Gabriela, Clove and Cinnamon* sold out in the United States both in hard cover and pocket book. MGM bought the movie rights with the idea of having Sophia Loren play the leading role. His name has been submitted for the Nobel Prize for literature and he jets around the world signing autographs and contracts. Yet he is an ordained priest in the Candomblé of Achê do Opô Afonjá and is considered one of the most powerful spirit intellects in Brazil.

Even the Brazilian post office believes in Spiritism. In 1957 they issued a brown postage stamp with Allan Kardek's portrait in honor of the hundredth anniversary of the publication of his first work, *The Book of Spirits*. In 1964 they issued another stamp with Kardek's picture in honor of the hundredth anniversary of his book (highly contrary to Catholic doctrine) *The Gospels According to Spiritism*. They will probably issue another stamp in 1983 on the centennial of his death. In 1969 a postage stamp came out (this time in two colors) in honor of L. O. Teles de Menezes, who in 1869 published the first Spiritist magazine in Brazil, *The Echo from Beyond the Grave*. Brazil is the only place in the world where you can mail a letter by sticking a picture of a Spiritist on the envelope.

In the port city of Santos, there is a spirit first-aid station. Set up in 1969 by the Guardian Angel Spirit Society, it has listened to hundreds who are at their wit's end and don't know where to turn. "People used to go to confession and hope for a solution," staff counselor Vicente de Silva told me, "but the priests could only offer biblical lectures and admonitions against sin. Here we offer hope for this life and get our advice directly from the spirits. It's no wonder we have been a success." The station does not charge anything for its celestial advice, but it will accept donations to keep the humble converted store going. On the walls signs get to the patients while they await an adviser: "You, distant creature of Jesus, know what a gigantic labyrinth awaits a suicide.

Before you commit such a meaningless act come to the spirit first-aid station and you will find a friend to help and understand you. When you feel down, defeated and wish a friendly word, we are here to give it." And if you cannot muster the strength to come to the station, the gods will talk to you over the phone if you just dial 2-3313.

Jurema Tavares is one of the most indomitable little women I have ever met. Born some fifty years ago into a gaucho family that had been ruined by civil strife and revolutions, she married early and moved to the port town of Rio Grande. Her husband was an expert carpenter and soon they owned three houses in the booming city. She became pregnant and the first child died when he was just months old. Her second son lived for almost a year, then he died. Her third son was strong and as stubborn as she was, and although he caught all the diseases that plagued children some thirty years ago, he lived and was her joy.

Then she was stricken with tuberculosis. A doctor put her into a rest home and sent her small son to live with friends. She came out, lasted about three months, and was sent to another t.b. home. Again she was allowed to leave and pronounced cured, but in less than a year she was confined to still a third hospital. There they operated and removed one lung. Months later she left, thin and weak, but even worse, her husband had to sell their houses to pay the doctors' bills. A strong man who had worked all his life, this continuous series of setbacks forced him to drink. Soon he wasn't working at anything, and she, ill and feverish most of the time, had to sell ready-made clothing from door to door on credit. Over the years she managed to give her son an education and keep the family together, but it was a never ending hand-to-mouth fight.

The town of Rio Grande went into sudden decline. A leftist state governor closed down all the British- and American-owned meat-packing plants, which forced thousands out of jobs, and sent other industries, like cigarette manufacturing and sardine packing, into near-ruin. Dona Jurema resolved to move to Pôrto Alegre, where, maybe, she could start in again. It was a bigger city and there should be more customers for her small line of merchandise. In two years' time she had a long list of steady clients and things began to improve.

Then one night she awoke with terrible pains in her chest and something clogging her throat. She gagged and coughed up a clot of blood. Each night the coughing became worse and finally one night she coughed a piece of her lung into a handkerchief. Frightened, she went to a doctor, and after much X-ray examination he told her that her old tuberculosis problem had returned and infected her only remaining lung. Other doctors told her the same thing. There was nothing they could do; they would not operate, for there was no way to stop the eating disease. There was not much time left, they told her. It would only be a matter of months.

She cried during the night, not afraid of dying but afraid of what would happen to her husband and son. Neither of them were working and the only money that came into the house came from her small retail sales. One day a woman came into her tiny shop. The woman was a complete stranger to her and seemed to be more interested in her than in the merchandise. Finally she said, "You are not well. You are going to die."

Dona Jurema, taken aback, admitted that it was true.

"There is no need to suffer any more," said the unknown woman, "and no need for you to die. You have many things yet to do on this earth. There is a spirit doctor visiting Pôrto Alegre. His name is Gerson. Go see him. See him tonight. He can save your life if you really want to live." She wrote down the address of the spirit center and abruptly left the shop. Dona Jurema never saw her again.

That night, without telling her husband or her son where she was going (both of them fear spiritism and therefore deny it), she found the right street and number and went into the building. After the drumming and dancing had stopped and the healing session was about to begin, she got into a long line and awaited her turn. "When I finally got to Gerson, I saw that he was a stumpy, dark-complexioned mulatto. His face looked as if it never smiled and he had huge green eyes. I never saw eyes that shone the way his did. He didn't say a word to me. He didn't touch me. He just stood there and stared at me. Then, very slowly, he started to run his eyes down my body. When he reached my feet he started back up again. Then he looked deep into my eyes and sighed."

Gerson quickly scribbled a prescription for various pills and inhaling powders. She had been told by her medical doctors not to take anything that wasn't prescribed by them, but she was desperate, for nothing that any of them had given her had helped. A drugstore filled Gerson's prescription and she started taking the medicines. The second day the pains went away. The fourth day the coughing stopped.

Two weeks later she got a telegram from her niece asking her to come for a visit. She was afraid to make the trip for fear her niece's small children might contact her deadly t.b. She went to one of her doctors and asked his advice. She told him the pains had gone but didn't tell him about the visit to Gerson. The doctor sat her before the X-ray machine and exposed a plate. When he came out of the laboratory, developed plate in hand, he was puzzled. "Let's take another picture, Dona Jurema. The first one didn't come out right." The second plate puzzled him even more than the first. "I don't know what happened," he said, "but your body is absolutely clean of any tuberculosis and your one remaining lung is strong and healthy." Her disease never came back.

There is a sequel to this true story (by "true" I mean the X rays, hospital reports and doctors' files are available to anyone who wishes to verify it). One night several years later Dona Jurema was visited by her sister, Nair. Nair is one of those fantastic bubbly creatures who, in spite of her sixty-odd years, makes friends wherever she goes. One of her new acquaintances was a spirit medium in a local center. She had been invited to a special celebration at the center and had stopped by to see if Jurema wanted to go with her.

Jurema didn't want to go, for all day she had been suffering from a terrible stomach-ache. The pains had started a few days earlier and became more intense with each new day. Pills, special foods and injections had done nothing to make them go away. "Aw, come on," insisted Nair. "The fresh air will do you good. Anyway, who knows, maybe someone there will have a cure for your troubles."

Because they are not members of this center they sat in the very last row. The organization was enormous and at least eight hundred people were there that night. They watched the opening rituals but for Jurema it was pure agony. Her stomach was throbbing worse than ever and she sucked on a painkilling lozenge. Then the drums rolled, a side door opened and in came the specially invited guests. As they took their places near the altar Dona Jurema said in surprise, "Look, Nair, you see that ugly mulatto there? That's Gerson, the one who cured me of my lung disease. I haven't seen him in years."

"Good," replied Nair. "Maybe tonight he'll cure you of your stomach pains."

"Don't be silly! There are too many people here, and anyway this is a special celebration. There won't be any cures tonight. This is not his center. He doesn't have any powers to work here."

Gerson sat way up front and watched the ceremony. Dona Jurema sat in the very back row and concentrated on Gerson. Then suddenly he turned and looked at the audience. He rose from his chair and stared over row after row of people to where Jurema sat. "I rose too," she recalls, "and looked at his face. It changed from round and healthy into a skull.

There were deep lines around those blazing green eyes. I gasped because there came a deep, stabbing pain in my stomach and then nothing more. Nothing more ever again. He just looked at me and every bit of pain went away. For good."

Now one would think that something like this happening twice in one's family would be enough. Few are the American families that have even half as interesting a story to tell, and in this new age where we all are searching for ghosts and ESP sensations, this kind of tale is excellent cocktail party talk. But Dona Jurema has a niece. She lives in the city of São Paulo and has died three times.

Rejane Izaguirre, born Rejane da Silva, was always a rebellious girl. Even when she was small she was against authority and seemed even to be "against life itself," as one relative put it. Her father was Dona Jurema's brother. He died when Rejane was very young. Her mother followed soon after. Jurema, in spite of her bad health and the constant fight for money to pay bills, took Rejane and her sister Ione to raise as if they were her own children.

They were living in Rio Grande when Rejane became ill. She was seventeen and a tall, lanky teen-ager who was dissatisfied with everything. A sudden asthma attack hit her and a doctor was called. He examined her and found nothing wrong. He advised rest and fresh air. That evening the attack hit again, but this time she moaned and gasped for breath. Again the doctor came, said there was nothing organically wrong and prescribed a sedative. Early the next morning she began to shout and cry. Her fingers clutched the blankets and tried to grasp something in the air. She coughed and choked and between the spasms gulped "like a fish that had been thrown up onto a beach."

Dona Jurema hurried to her room, as did Jurema's husband, Ivo. The girl seemed to be drowning in air, and Jurema

Drum and Candle

picked her up and cradled her in her arms. Then Rejane "gave one last gasp, rolled her eyes upward and died."

Jurema began to cry and call her name. "Rejane! Rejane! Don't go, Rejane! Please don't go! Rejane!" Ivo tried to console his wife, while younger sister Ione ran crying from the bedroom into the kitchen and fell sobbing across the table. "Her heart had stopped beating," remembers Jurema. "Her body no longer showed the slightest sign of life. Then about three minutes later she began to stir and came to in my arms. She was exhausted, but completely coherent."

Rejane told them a strange story when her strength returned. She said that she had been gasping and trying to breathe when she decided that it didn't matter any more. That she was sick of the whole thing. At that moment she suddenly left her body and walked right through the bedroom wall into the kitchen. She said that she saw Ione sobbing at the kitchen table, looked at her for a few seconds and turned back toward the front of the house. She walked down the hall and passed her bedroom. There she saw Jurema cradling her body in her arms and heard her saying, "Rejane, don't go!" She says she watched the scene impassively and remembered thinking: "My, how long and thin I was." Then she continued toward the front door.

At the door she was stopped. There stood the spirits of her mother and father. They said nothing to her but grasped her arms and led her back into the bedroom. She saw her own body once more, heard her name being called and entered her body. Then she awoke.

The doctor arrived afterward, for the third time that night, and gave Rejane another sedative. On the way out he asked Jurema to come to his office in the morning. He said he wanted to hear the entire case history. Jurema appeared and related it all to him exactly as Rejane had told it to her. He listened and finally said, "Dona Jurema, I am a Spiritist as well as a medical doctor. I knew when I saw that girl's first attack that it was nothing that medicine could cure. What you have told me bears it out. Rejane *did* 'die.' She *did* leave her body exactly as she described it. Rejane has been through many incarnations and is exhausted by the world. This incarnation is undoubtedly her last one. After this life she will find eternal peace. She senses that. It will not be easy to hold her here on this earth."

"But if she is so strong, why did she come back? Why did her parents stop her?"

"Because her time was not yet up. While she is advanced, she is also rebellious and wants to get it over with as soon as possible. But she is not supposed to leave yet. She has to carry out a few more months or years here before she will be completely free to leave. Her mother and father know that. They undoubtedly have been watching over her. She came back because of them and because you, a mortal, kept calling her to come back. It was your voice pleading with her that made her spirit obey her parents and re-enter her body once more."

"And if she tries to do this again, doctor, what shall I do?"

"Exactly as you did before. The entire family is to start shouting, 'Rejane, don't go! Think of the consequences over there when you appear before your time. Think of the penalties you will have to pay! Don't go, Rejane!' And she will not go. Not if you are cautious."

Rejane married a good man who was told the entire story. They have three children. Sister Ione has never married, preferring to stay near Rejane to help her with the housework and to be there when she is needed. Rejane sees into the future and will sometimes write out predictions that always come true. She doesn't like it, for she knows what is happening to friends and relatives even in other countries.

Twice since her marriage she has tried to leave her body. Twice she has been called back from the dead.

12

What kind of stand does the Catholic Church take in all this? A very uncertain one.

The present Pope (and many before him) likes to refer to Brazil as "the biggest Catholic nation in the world." It is that, if he is talking about square miles of land. And it is that if he means that the eighty million inhabitants of Brazil are all born Catholics. Few are the children in Brazil (the numerous Protestant sects not counting for much numberwise) who are not baptized into the Catholic Church. Those born of Catholic parents are automatically considered Catholic. Yet (and the Pope never mentions this) Brazil is the largest "spirit (i.e. pagan)" nation in the world, and the majority of His Holiness' subjects attend spirit sessions, listen to drumbeats, light candles to the dead and wear magic charms. The Pope would be shocked if he could see the same fervent faces who asked Oxalá for a cure and Yemanjá for a sweetheart on Saturday night sitting and chanting the praises of Jesus and the Virgin Mary on Sunday morning. He would be amazed to see the Spiritist social centers, the free clinics and the orphanages filled with so many "good Catholics." It would appear to him as if Brazil, one of the first bastions of Rome in the New World, was in need of being converted all over again.

The Church probably made its first mistake when it allowed the African slaves of the colonial plantations to keep their own rites. The bishops of the era should never have left the religious education of the blacks to their white masters. The bishops obviously thought that the heathen blacks would take to Christianity the way the heathen Aztecs and Incas did. They did not consider that the blacks had a strong *personal* set of beliefs (rather than a state-organized religion like the Indians') or that the Portuguese owners themselves were such weak Catholics. The Spanish were harsh masters and firm believers. The Portuguese were easygoing masters and almost indifferent to High Church dogma.

Civil authorities weren't much help to the Church either. When the first spirit groups openly set up shop and the priests complained, the police did raid a few sessions and throw a few believers in jail. But after a while the policemen themselves (not to mention the mayor, the senator and the governor) began to believe in and respect the spiritist beliefs. A policeman will not break up a session if he feels the curse of Exú will be put on him. A judge will go easy on a Mother of the Saint if he suspects that she is capable of putting the evil eye on him. A politician, needing votes, will not come out openly against spiritist beliefs.

Anyway, the constitution of 1946, paragraph 7, article 141, clearly states that Spiritist sessions, be they Candomblé, Kardek, Umbanda or what-have-you, are legal. "The freedom of conscience and belief is inviolable and the right to exercising religious creeds is assured, except those which perturb the public order or public morals. Religious associations are judicial entities under civil law." The new constitution, drawn up under the military strong men of 1969, retains all the old Spiritist privileges. All religions have free rein in Brazil. The *official* religion is Roman Catholicism, but it's not the *only* religion of the land.

"We are a nation of folklore Catholics!" insists Padre Boaventura Kloppenburg. "We have all the hybrid religions. There is the Catholic-Spiritist, the Catholic-Umbandist, the

Catholic-Mason, the Catholic-Rosicrucian, the Catholic-theosophist, the Catholic-astrologist, the Catholic-cartomant, and on and on. But this type of folkloric Catholic demands all the rights of the authentic Catholic: He wants to marry in the Church, wants to have his children baptized in the Church, he wants to be a godfather and belong to the various brotherhoods, he wants a religious funeral and he wants a Mass on the seventh day of his death. And when I, or another priest, tell him he cannot have both religious worlds he says: 'The Church is intolerant. The padre is old-fashioned.'"

Padre Kloppenburg is a priest who knows his subject. He has been cursed and hexed and harangued by some of the most powerful spirit leaders in Brazil. He has been preached against from Umbanda altars, has had his effigy stuck with pins in a public square and was declaimed against in a state assembly. For over ten years the spiritists of Brazil actually and literally "hated his guts." He had the duty of investigating the spirit cults. He was given no help and very little money. He was one lone man representing the Vatican against a turbulent ocean of ghosts, devils and magic rites. He was Rome's single crusader against the heresies of the spiritists. It eventually turned his hair white, got him in trouble with his bishop and made not a ripple on the spiritist movement.

The padre came from Germany when he was just four years old. His parents settled in the peaceful farming state of Rio Grande do Sul and he grew up speaking German at home and Portuguese in the streets. He also grew up a good Catholic, so good that he entered a local seminary and was ordained a priest.

He looks as if he might be Irish. He is short and slightly chubby, with a soft chuckle in his voice and a bright twinkle in his eye. He is a scholar (his small room in the Franciscan seminary in Petrópolis is crammed with books) and he is also a doer. He runs the Franciscan publishing house of Editôra Vozes ("Voices"), edits dozens of books yearly, writes another dozen tracts and pamphlets, oversees book distribution and still has time to act as Latin America's co-ordinator for the ideas set down in Vatican II. He jets from Brazil to Venezuela to Argentina to Haiti to Rome to Chicago the way other priests go from rectory to chapel to rectory. He doesn't like to talk about his fight against the spiritists today. "It was ten years ago," he says. "I've been doing other things since then. I stopped investigating Umbanda and Kardecism when Pope John XXIII asked me to come to Rome and help with the organizing of the First Vatican Congress. I have been too busy since then to think much about spiritism."

Does he consider the Church's work against spiritism finished? "No."

Is there any priest seriously investigating it today? "No."

Does he, personally, believe in Brazilian spiritism? "What I saw I could not, as a Catholic, believe. I did hear many stories of things I did not actually see. If those stories were true, then there are many things that I cannot explain."

Padre Kloppenburg began his studies innocently enough in 1951 when he was sent from Rio Grande to Petrópolis, near Rio de Janeiro, to teach in the Franciscan school. "I had to celebrate two Masses every Sunday and the services were broadcast over the local radio. One day a man came to me and told me he was afraid his wife had been given the evil eye at a spiritist session. He asked my advice. I, even though a Brazilian, had no advice to give him. I had never been exposed to spirit practices and had never considered spiritism as any kind of threat to a true Catholic. I asked him for time to investigate.

"All that week I read spiritist books and talked with people who professed to be spirit believers. The next Sunday I let them have it! I preached against the evils of spiritism and gave Scripture citations of why spiritism was a sin.

"The reaction was violent. Even before the service was over there were angry people outside the church door. I was stopped on the street, was telephoned all hours of the day and night and was openly told that I was treading a dangerous path and that I should be more careful of my facts before I started condemning the spiritist religion. They called it that, a 'religion.' As far as I was concerned there was only *one* religion, and it was based on the words of Our Lord Jesus Christ, and not on the gyrations of some pagan jungle deity."

He began to study seriously the various brands of Brazilian spiritism. He surrounded himself with books written by spirit chiefs and by supposedly dead but still writing entities like Emmanuel and the Old Black Slave. He read all of Kardek's works and searched for the Bible's answer to Kardek's charges. At night he would take off his brown Franciscan robe, put on a dark suit and a black beret and drop in on Umbanda and Kardek sessions. "I was probably the first priest in Latin America to remove the habit," he says with a laugh. But it was worth it, for he saw with his own eyes exactly what his fellow Catholic priests were up against, and he also saw "many of my parishioners consulting the devil" instead of trying to lead a Christian life.

Through his position as editor of the publishing house he is able to get his ideas against spiritism across to priests all over Brazil. Much to his surprise, padres and bishops began writing him, telling of the problem in their area. There was not one corner of Brazil that did not have spiritist sessions, and not one large city church that was not in open competition with the spirits for the souls of their congregation. He finally asked his bishop—who had to ask Rome—for permission to combat openly these pagan beliefs. Both gave their grudging consent. The bishop did not want to get involved and the Vatican had no idea just how serious the situation was. Brazil was Catholic. There was nothing more to say.

Armed with a Bible and a lot of courage, the youthful

Padre Kloppenburg started on a tour around Brazil. He went from the Amazon to the pampas and from small crossroads to industrial centers. Everywhere it was the same: large crowds, public support, studio and town hall broadcasts and spiritist damnation.

When he was in Belém (on the mouth of the Amazon) he got carried away over the local radio and announced boldly: "All the spiritist priests and Fathers of the Saints as well as Mothers and Daughters and Sons of the Saints as well as all Umbandistas, drum beaters, witch doctors and magicians, listen to me!

"Whether you be in Brazil, Africa or anywhere else in the world I beg of you to unite in one vast international congress. Call upon your strongest Exús, demons, evil spirits and astral powers. Offer them your most valuable gifts and sacrifices. Draw your most powerful hex signs, beat your biggest drums, light boxes of candles! Ask these forces, all of these terrible forces, to hurl themselves upon me! And I will remain calm and at peace in the hands of divine providence."

The next day the local newspaper published a reply. It was from the Father of a large Umbanda center called "King Xapaña of Belém." It read: "Brother Boaventura: The High Council of Exús accepts your challenge, so that you can know the truth about spirit forces. I see that you are ignorant of the truth and that's why you have come to this earth to provoke creatures whose forces react upon the human body and who are already possessing your body and mind. Let it be known, Brother Boaventura, that the following list of demon Exús has accepted your challenge: Skull, Filth, Hunger, Sloth, Blind, Liar, Drunkard, Bloodsucker, Excrement, Jester, Sadness, Cancerous, Leprous, Weak, Maimed, Despair and several others. They have appeared spontaneously to me and demand that you also accept their challenge. They want you to know that the force of the spirits exists and can be used for good or for evil. Since you wish these forces to be used against you strictly in their capacity for evil—wait! Within a few days you will have ample physical proof that the powers can act upon you. Within a few days a frog will appear in your stomach and will refuse to leave by any other means than a complicated surgical operation. Then all the world will see the frog and will know who is right!"

Says the soft-spoken priest today: "The frog never showed up. I don't know how much longer I'm supposed to wait. I hope it's not too long, for an operation now would delay my schedule."

In another town candles were lit and spiritists chanted that the rain that was falling would turn to blood over the monastery where Kloppenburg was staying. But they wanted the bloody rain to be *his* blood.

A national congress of Umbanda meeting in Rio de Janeiro in 1961 passed a resolution against the investigations of the young priest. The motion was to ignore his work completely rather than to urge united spiritist action against him. One of the Umbanda big shots told me personally (I was there covering the story for *Time*) that they could easily call down his guardian angel, who "being a higher spirit would therefore agree with us, when we explained the situation to him, that his protégé was not doing right. We would not ask his guardian angel to do him any harm exactly—perhaps just to relax his watch every now and then . . . when the padre was crossing a busy street, for instance."

What was upsetting the Umbandistas (and the high spirit Kardecistas as well) was the fact that the padre was taking his message of "Catholics cannot be spiritists" directly to the people. He was actually appearing on theater stages and television screens and doing things that supposedly only highly attuned mediums were able to do!

One of his more impressive demonstrations was table rapping. He would have a light four-legged table onstage (or in front of a TV camera) and call upon four or five people from the audience. Then he would ask them to place their hands, palms down, on the table and to wait for a few seconds. "I know that Kardek said there had to be silence and concentration upon the spirits and that within ten or twenty minutes the rappings would begin. Well, I deliberately kept on talking, refused to let anyone think of ghosts and always within *one* or *two* minutes the table would lift up and start tapping out intelligent answers to questions put to it. Each time the impromptu helpers declared that they had not moved the table deliberately, that all they had done was place their hands on it. But there was no doubt: The table moved because of unconscious muscular movements that controlled their hands. This can be easily verified with special apparatus that registers muscular reaction. When a person receives the suggestion that he will move a table, his muscles subconsciously go to work through his hands. The movement is so slight that the mind is never aware of it. Kardek's theories and all his answers came from muscle movement and not the spirits of the dead."

The padre also declared that there was no such thing as spirit healing. He once told an audience that nervous disorders could be cured by suggestion because the mind had to hear that there was really nothing wrong. Organic diseases were curable only by medicine. A woman in the audience arose and brought her young son to the edge of the platform. He had become blind about four years earlier, she told him, and doctors had been unable to do anything. Padre Boaventura reached down and touched the boy's closed eyelids. "In the name of Jesus Christ, open your eyes. You can see!" he shouted. "Then much to my surprise the boy *did* open his eyes and began to look around. His sight had been restored! Of course, there was general pandemonium over my 'miracle' and the next day my lecture session was filled with the blind, the crippled and the diseased, all wanting me to perform a 'miracle' on them too." He had to leave town.

When he wasn't lecturing in public squares, he was busy writing a four-volume exposé of spiritism which he called *Orientation for Catholics*. The first volume was *Spiritism in Brazil* and dealt with Kardek and his teachings. The second was *Umbanda in Brazil* and was concerned with the Exús, the organization of a spirit center and the dire side effects of many of the cures. The third was a slim volume written to help priests. Called *Pastoral Action in the Face of Spiritism*, it is heavy on philosophy and Scriptural refutation of spirit doctrine. The fourth was *Reincarnation in Brazil* and was more a history of why the Church did not believe in the matter of various lives than an exposé of any definite system.

The books are well written, in an easy, almost conversational tone. One theme keeps running through them all: "A man cannot call down a spirit. A spirit can never be called down by a man. There is a difference between man calling a spirit/angel to earth and God sending one to earth as he did to tell Mary that she was with child."

Padre Kloppenburg never denies that there are spirits—"to do so would be to deny one of the basic tenets of the Bible and to deny the angels and the Trinity." What he does deny is that these spirits work for ordinary human beings. And why he is most emphatically against this idea is because God himself said: "See that I am who I am and there is no other God but me." He adds that Christ said: "I am the way, the truth and the life. There is no way to reach my Father except through me." And later: "God gave us eternal life and this life is in His Son. Who believes in the Son has life, who does not have the Son of God also does not have life." In 1917 Pope Benedict XV was asked if Catholics were permitted to watch or assist mediums at work or to seek advice from the spirits or consult them on spiritual matters. His official pronouncement: "Forbidden in every case without exception."

Therefore, reasons Padre Kloppenburg, a Catholic who believes or practices any of the spiritual creeds, who lights a

Drum and Candle

candle to a spirit instead of to Jesus Christ, who seeks spirit help instead of calling on Jesus to be healed or who deliberately calls upon the devil to castigate an enemy is committing a grave sin against the Church.

Umbanda, high spirit Kardecism and Candomblé (he seems to be saying) are all right for those who do not wish to be Catholics. But Christianity and spirit religions are incompatible.

He is, naturally, 100 per cent against the use of Catholic saints in those "pagan" rituals and is also against giving spirit centers such names as "Temple of Mary Magdalene and Yansá," "Spirit Center of the Divine Light of Jesus" and "The African Cult of Our Lady of Lourdes Congo." He has tried to get the plaster statues of the saints barred from sale in the spirit shops but it has been to no avail. (In 1957 the Umbanda Federation of São Paulo held a session on the beach at Santos and paraded many Christian images. The local bishop complained to the local police and started a legal suit against "the use of Catholic images" in that sect's sessions. A year later a priest in the small and almost unpronounceable town of Pindamonhangaba processed an Umbanda center for the same reason. Neither of the two cases could find a judge who would back up the Church's point of view and order the images taken away from the spiritists.)

Padre Kloppenburg was called to Rome just before his books were published, and he gave a lecture on Brazilian spirit religions at the Gregorian university. He also had a private audience with Pope Pius XII about the subject, but "I don't know how much of it he understood. I was only given fifteen minutes and His Holiness just sat there shaking his head and smiling."

Back in Brazil his works hit the bookshops and were immediate best sellers. Obviously empowered by Rome to come to some sort of conclusion and to set up a list of rules for

Brazilian Catholics, his volume on Umbanda contains "Rules for a Catholic Position in the Face of Umbanda."

1) *In the face of Umbandistas, the Catholic attitude is of Christian respect and prudent discretion.* He claims it is a waste of time to discuss religion with these people and that "the best thing we can do is to pray, begging God to grant them a conversion."

2) *In the face of Umbanda as a doctrine, the attitude of a Catholic is frank and total condemnation.*

3) *In the face of Umbanda as a practice, the attitude of a Catholic is energetic and declared repulsion.* "It is inconceivable that someone truly loves God and at the same time practices necromancy and magic that has so often and so severely been forbidden by God. For this reason a Catholic may never be a member of any group, confederation, society, fraternity, center, church, tent, temple or hut of Umbanda."

4) *Concerning Umbanda sessions, the attitude of a Catholic is complete abstention.* "To assist an Umbanda or a Spiritist session is a grave sin of disobedience against the Creator. Still a worse sin is if the Catholic asks to call a certain spirit or the soul of a deceased person."

5) *Regarding the books of Umbanda, the attitude of a Catholic is disapproval and unrestricted censure.* "The Catholic who, without due permission of his bishop, reads, keeps, sells or reproduces such literature commits a grave sin and immediately incurs the punishment of excommunication."

6) *In the face of an Umbanda medical diagnosis, the attitude of a Catholic is absolute reserve.* Deuteronomy 18:12-13: "For the Lord abhorreth all these things, and for these abominations he will destroy them at thy coming. Thou shalt be perfect, and without spot before the Lord thy God."

7) *In the face of Umbanda cures and medicines, the attitude of a Catholic is absolute repudiation.* He is against burning incense, crossroad candles and special herbs but does allow homeopathic medicines because "they are prescribed

Drum and Candle

by the spiritists but have nothing in common with magic or necromancy."

8) *In the face of the cult of Umbanda Orishas, the attitude of a Catholic is one of decided refusal.* "Our saints are used only as bait, as a façade. Idolatry is one of the gravest sins that man can commit against God."

9) *In the face of the cult of Exú, the attitude of a Catholic is one of holy horror, and he will repel it always with apostolic vigor.*

10) *In the face of despachos [offerings to the spirits to obtain favors], the attitude of a Catholic is reigning disdain.* "When you find one of these works, even if it is in front of your own house, make the sign of the cross (because you are in front of an object consecrated to the Enemy!) and calmly remove it. You may even use the useful things found with it, without fear or scruples (plates, money, cigars, matches, beer, chickens, etc.)."

11) *In the face of fetishes to ward off evil spirits, amulets, figas [the clenched fist], chalked symbols, the spade of St. George, etc., the attitude of a Catholic is simple and formal disdain.*

12) *In the face of Spiritism or Umbanda, therefore, the attitude of a Catholic is absolute, total and open opposition.*

Those were the rules and attitudes up until Vatican II. The Church of Rome had a second thought (or maybe a *first* thought) about so-called paganism, and poor Padre Kloppenburg was forced to revise his point of view. In 1968 he published a short paper and hid it away in the June issue of the *Brazilian Ecclesiastical Review*. There was no fanfare when it came out. Few Brazilians know about the change in attitude but there has been a very great change.

Padre Kloppenburg, after lamenting that in the last ten years "more and more European-type Brazilians have become adepts in spirit practices," wrote that Umbanda "now gives one the impression of being a popular means of protest against all the creeds that have been imported and insufficiently adapted to the local scene." In other words: Vatican II is sure that somewhere along the line Catholicism has failed to win over the majority of Brazilians, that the imported religion of the white masters has done nothing "to solace spiritually" the African slaves and their descendants in Brazil.

Pope Paul IV published his *Africae Terrarum* in 1967, "accentuating [in the words of Padre Kloppenburg] and even exalting the positive values of the antique and non-Christian African traditions." Many traditions and rites are of value, the Pope wrote, and it is up to the new Catholic mentality to look into these rites and to use the best ones for "a newer approximation to the Church." There are many things to be learned from the Africans, the Pope implied, and therefore the priests and bishops should "look anew at the non-European mentality."

Padre Kloppenburg must have had to swallow hard when he wrote: "By his nature the Negro man demands his own ritual litanies. We must respect, rise up and consummate in Christ everything that we discover as being truly good, beautiful, just, holy and lovable in Umbanda! [The exclamation point is mine!] As the Church, at the Council, changed its attitude and its mentality, so have I. I must now feel as the Church feels and so have changed my attitude and mentality as well."

His old enemies and detractors are delighted that he no longer comes nosing around their spirit centers and that his lone voice of Catholic opposition has been silenced by Rome itself. Amazingly white-haired now (when compared with his photos of just a few years ago), the padre spends all his time explaining the rules and regulations of Vatican II.

"Of course, I am still interested in Umbanda and the spirits," he told me the last time I saw him, "but I have new duties now and they take up a great deal of my time. I don't know if I accomplished anything or not in the ten years that I investigated the spirit religions. At the time I was sure I was on the right track. Now I don't know any more. I saw many things then that I cannot explain. Perhaps if I had been given more time I would have been able to explain them all. But you know how fast time runs out on a man."

He walked me down the steps of the huge Franciscan seminary and down the thickly shadowed driveway to a taxi stand. The trees were in full leaf and a welcome relief from the hot sun. As he shook my hand and put me into a car I got that old feeling of goose bumps on my scalp and arms. The feeling I always get when I'm in the presence of a strong spiritist person. Then I remembered what Dona Leda had told me months earlier: "You are going to interview a man for your book who lives in a big house. There are also many trees around his house. Oh, what beautiful trees! Pay attention to what he says, for he is a very wise man. He is also a very powerful medium, but he is afraid to admit it even to himself."

13

Then it happened to me.

I didn't expect it, of course. In fact, I didn't even know when it hit. I was amazed to hear of it and for quite a while didn't believe it. I just didn't expect it, that's all. People never expect to be in an automobile accident until the car actually crashes. Then often they don't believe it even as they climb from the wreckage. That's the way I felt, but the pieces were all around me for everyone to see. A promise to Exú—against me!

When it all started I had been living in Rio de Janeiro for eight years. I had a very nice apartment with three bedrooms and a terrific view across the rooftops, just two blocks from the beach. I was happy there, I did a lot of carrying-on there, I got a lot of work done there.

Now every bachelor in a three-bedroom apartment needs someone to look after it and look after him. I had a series of maids who took care of things for a while until they got better jobs or else got married. Then I got a new maid. She was young, well curved and a soft, dusty brown. She was single and full of life. She was intelligent and clean. We became good friends even while maintaining the boss-employee relationship. (And before tongues start wagging—that's all it was: strictly boss-employee.) I will call her, to avoid future legal problems, Edna.

Edna has a personal story typical of many Brazilian domestics. She was born in the interior to a poor family who already had five children when she arrived. Her mother washed clothes for a few of the wealthy white people in town and her father (ah, her father! A novel could be written about him!), her father was a professional killer. For a few dollars he would go away and bump anybody off. All you had to do was to tell him the victim's name and address and pay him half the agreed fee. When he came back with proof that his work was done (an ear, a ring on a severed finger, a sliced-off tattoo), then you paid him the balance.

Edna often told me how her father would go away for days at a time, dressed always in a spotlessly white starched linen suit and how he would return and the suit would be caked with mud and green with grass stains, as he slithered through the forests and across the fields always running from the police. As if her mother didn't have enough to do, the suit had to be scrubbed white again, restarched and hung ready to be worn as soon as the next job was offered.

One day the man left on a new assignment and never came back. The mother and children lamented and mourned until a neighbor told them he saw their father in another town living with another woman. At this Edna and her brothers and sisters helped to pack their few belongings into cardboard boxes and took a bus (on borrowed money) to Rio.

The mother found an available shack in one of the city's more disgusting *favela* slums and looked around for a job. She got a position with a white family who needed a cleaning woman three times a week. On her free days she washed clothes for other white families. One by one the children grew up and, illiterate though worldly-wise, left the *favela* to better themselves. One girl married a man who immediately put her into another *favela* and gave her a new baby each year. A boy became a truck driver, took the truck and never came back. A sister went to stay with an aunt and vanished in the vastness of Brazil's interior. Edna stayed on with her mother, helping with the piles and piles of other people's laundry and working (for a while) in a factory that glued butterfly wings on wooden trays for tourists.

Then her mother died. Edna borrowed money to bury her and took a full-time job as a maid for a middle-class white Brazilian family. The woman treated her well, let her sleep in the cramped maid's room off the apartment's laundry area and gave her her food and an occasional castoff dress.

The job meant getting up at six to buy milk and bread and to have breakfast ready for the two smallest children. Then she walked them to school, making sure they were there by seven-thirty. At eight the oldest boy had his breakfast and went off to high school. At eight-fifteen the husband had his breakfast and went to his downtown office. At ten the "madame" of the house arose and had her coffee and hot rolls. With breakfast out of the way, Edna cleaned the house, put the clothes into hot, soapy water and went out to buy food for lunch. She prepared it and went to pick up the two elementary school children, brought them home, gave them their lunch and then walked them back for the afternoon classes. Then she washed and hung the clothes in the open area off the kitchen, ironed those she had washed the day before, went back to the school and picked up the two kids, bought food for dinner, prepared it, served it, washed the dishes and fell into bed. For this she got fifteen dollars a month.

Edna wanted to stay on because it was the first clean, dry place she had ever lived in. But finally she was forced to leave. The teen-age son began making advances to her when the family wasn't looking. One night he pushed his way into her tiny room and tried to rape her. Her screams of protest brought the madame running, and, of course, Edna was fired on the spot.

A friend, another maid, took her in that night and she stayed there a few days. Then through a friend of a friend she heard that *um Americano* was looking for a maid. She came and talked to me, we liked each other on the spot and she moved in that afternoon.

The apartment began to shine. My clothes were always pressed, the food put upon the table was delicious. She knew how to answer the telephone and (even rarer in Brazil) how to write down the name and number of the person who had called while I was out. She defended me against unscrupulous salesmen, butchers, plumbers and dry cleaners. I, in turn, never came back from a trip without a present for her, always gave her more money at the end of the month than we had agreed upon, paid for her doctor and dentist appointments and introduced her to all my friends. Soon people who wanted to get through to me knew the best way to do it was by being nice to Edna. She had an uncanny eye for phonies and freeloaders and more than once tossed out an acquaintance who she felt was using me or had overstayed his welcome.

While she never went to Mass and hated the trappings of the Catholic Church (a self-important priest had refused to bury her mother), she was also adamant in her disapproval of Umbanda and Spiritism. "I won't have anything to do with it," she told me time and time again. "It only works for evil, I don't care what they say about it doing good. It is bad and dangerous. I know too many people who have suffered from it. Stay away from it, Senhor David. It can't help you."

Once I came back from Bahia with an iron statue of Exú. Edna hated the thing and one day it mysteriously disappeared. Later she told me that she had been discarding some of the junk in the apartment and that the Exú must have gotten thrown out "by mistake." Another time I came proudly home with a magnificent plaster wall plaque of the Old Black Slave. He sat in all his glory on a tree stump, smoking a pipe and surrounded by the symbols of Umbanda. Edna refused to have it in any of the front rooms and (since I *was* the boss) I finally managed to get it hung on the wall in the library. One day, while I was out of town, the nail "came loose" and the plaque "fell by itself" to the floor and shattered.

In 1968 I subletted my apartment and went off to the mountain village of Teresópolis to write a book. The house I rented was small and well furnished and in the middle of a huge grassy yard surrounded with shady trees. The air was crisp and invigorating. It was a most pleasant change from muggy Rio de Janeiro. I loved it. Edna hated it.

She had gotten involved in a folklore dance group that practiced three nights a week. They had danced on television; once, after her picture appeared in a Rio newspaper, a woman stopped Edna on the street and asked her for her autograph. After that I was living with a "star" and had to put up with the fact that a star needs extra money for clothes and make-up, cannot be expected to cook and prepare three meals a day and never washes other people's underwear. I went along with all these demands and changes because I felt that Edna was a new and different person, that because of me she was living better and doing things that she never would have been able to do with another household or factory job. I had seen her grow from a shy waif into a secure and attractive woman. I felt like a poor man's Pygmalion and (silently) took all the credit for her metamorphosis.

So sure was I that she was ready to fly on her own, i.e. get a better job and raise her social status, that I told her I thought she should look for something that paid more. I explained all the reasons why a person had to keep advancing in life but instead of inspiring her to new heights, I caused her to break into tears.

I tried new tactics. I read the Help Wanted section of the newspaper aloud whenever I found something that she could do. I talked to her about getting a bank loan and putting a down payment on a house of her own, and when she had enthusiastically agreed I told her that to get such a loan she had to have a steady job and that no bank ever gave a hunk of money to a domestic servant. Then one day I decided that I was going to leave Brazil as soon as the new book was sold. I set my heart and sights on going to Greece and began to annoy the Greek embassy for brochures and a friend at a travel agency for prices and itineraries.

Edna saw the literature and asked what it all meant. I told her that I was going to leave Brazil and go to Europe.

"What about me?"

"I'll give you half a year's salary when I leave."

"No, what about me when you are gone? Where will I go?"

"You can get a hundred jobs, Edna. You are young and intelligent. You'll make lots more money with a company than you're getting with me and you'll even be able to buy that little house we've talked so much about."

Her reaction was to burst into tears and to slam the door behind her as she went to her room.

Later, when I told friends that I was going to Greece, they all said, "What about Edna?" I would reply, "She knows about it. It had to be done, you know. I feel better now that it's out in the open."

My Brazilian friends would only shake their heads and smile at me as if I was a hopeless mental case.

I blithely went on with my plans, openly talking to Edna about Greece and all the changes that were going to take place just as soon as I sold the book.

But the book didn't sell. First of all, the girl who was supposed to type the manuscript made such a terrible botch of it that she had to type more than half of it over again. Then she got sick and the pages sat locked in her desk while I fumed and snorted but could do nothing to help. Then when it was finally ready and in my agent's hands, he took forever to read it (granted, it was an overlong tome), and every editor who did glance through it took ages to report back on it. One New York publishing company held it for four months before turning it down!

Meanwhile, I was desperate for money. I am the world's worst businessman and had been walking a financial thin edge ever since I started writing the book. I refused all outside assignments and stuck with the novel. I had pictured an easy sale, an easy pay-off of all my debts and an easy quick exit from Brazil.

But it didn't happen that way. The book money never came and an inheritance that I was expecting around the first of February still hadn't been cleared through all the legal processes by the end of August! Instead of jetting off to Greece I was stuck down in Rio two months behind in my rent, my telephone cut off for non-payment and everybody and his brother wanting their IOUs made good.

As if that wasn't bad enough, I had been carrying on a flirtation with a most lovely Argentine. We had been sending each other love letters for months and straining toward the day when we could be together. I had a good friend in Buenos Aires who earned lots of money. I managed to get a plane ticket (more IOUs) and flew to Argentina to be with my beloved and to hit my friend for a loan. But the person to be hit was I. My beloved spurned me and walked off with another in a sudden lightning-bolt decision that sent me reeling. My friend refused to lend me a cent. He did it with great charm, but it was nevertheless a refusal.

I returned to Rio with no lover, no money and no way to pay off the new IOU for the airline ticket. I was broke, miserable and alone . . . except for Edna. "Don't worry about things, Senhor David. It will work out all right. So what if you don't have the rent and the phone has been cut? You still have your health."

Two days after returning from Buenos Aires I had a relapse of malaria!

Telephone calls (on other people's phones) to New York,

Chicago and London about my book and my inheritance all brought negative results and deeper debt. For some reason everything had come to an impasse. There was nothing I could do to break the barrier I had come up against. Healthwise, moneywise and lovewise I was in a bind. It was an incredible run of bad luck.

Or was it more than that?

One day while walking nervously on Avenida Copacabana I met an old friend, a Brazilian woman from the city of Belo Horizonte. After the usual greetings at such an encounter she pulled back and stared at me. "What's wrong with you?" she asked. "You look terrible."

I thanked her for the compliment but told her that everything was fine.

"No it's not," she insisted. "Let me look at you." She walked around me, never taking her eyes from me. I felt like a piece of steak in a butcher's window. Finally she said, "I didn't think you had any enemies. This is terrible!"

"I don't have any enemies. . . . *What's* terrible?"

"Someone has put the evil eye on you. Your paths have been closed!"

"Nonsense," I protested. "I don't believe in all that! I'm just having a run of bad luck, that's all."

"That's not all! Someone has closed your paths. You are in a terrible situation! You must do something to break this evil spell you've been cursed with."

I started to laugh but she cut me off quickly. "Never laugh when Exú is at work! I am a spiritist. I know what I'm talking about. Get rid of that hex before it breaks you down completely!" She hurried away and I stood watching her, admiring the fact that she could get so concerned over some silly idea.

A few days later I got a letter from another friend, this time in far-off Mato Grosso. "David, I went to an Umbanda session last night and the Old Black Slave who spoke through the medium asked me if I had a friend in Rio who was a foreigner. When I told him that I did have such a friend he warned me that you are in grave danger. He said someone has made a 'work' against you and that all your paths have been closed off. Please, dear friend, go to a session and have them take this thing off you." After she had signed her name she added a PS: "When I asked him who did this to you, he said it was a Negro woman who shares your apartment. I *know* Edna would *never* do a thing like this, but I thought you should be told of his answer. Please burn this letter. I wouldn't want Edna to see it."

More phone calls and more telegrams about the book and the inheritance, and more negative answers. The rent was due for the third month, and that, in Brazil, is legal grounds for eviction.

Then an actor friend came from another town to spend a few days with me. He was to start a soap opera on TV and to finish shooting a feature film. He is a good person and a good actor. He is also a spiritist. I didn't know that detail.

The night he arrived Edna served dinner and then left for a rehearsal with her dance group. As soon as she had gone my friend started talking. "That woman is ruining your life."

"Now wait a minute," I replied. "She treats me better than anyone in the whole world. She would do anything for me."

"No matter what she *was,* she is *now* your enemy. She has put a curse on you. Your paths are closed."

"That woman has been with me for five years," I objected. "She has been through the good and the bad times with me. She wouldn't do a thing to hurt me. Where do you get off making accusations like that? You never even saw her before tonight. You didn't even know she existed before you came in here!"

"I heard about her three days ago."

"From whom?" I demanded.

Drum and Candle

"Sister Magdalena," he replied.

I froze. Sister Magdalena is one of the strongest spirits in the huge city of São Paulo. I had heard about her long ago, but her sessions are exclusive and secret. The medium through whom she works bars almost everyone who is not known to her. "Sister Magdalena," I gulped. "*She* told you about Edna?"

"I went to consult her at the last session," he explained, "and I asked her if the TV series was going to be successful and if the film was going to be completed on time. She told me that both would be exactly as I wanted them. Then I told her I was going to be staying with an American writer who wondered about his new book. He wondered why it wasn't being sold. The table began rapping softly. Out came the phrase: 'Is this writer's name David St. Clair?' I told her that it was."

He jumped up quickly. An actor is always an actor. "Then the table made a violent movement! It came pressing toward me and then against me and finally knocked over my chair and pressed me to the floor! Then it scurried to the other side of the room and those sitting around it felt it tap out: 'Stay away from that apartment! It has been cursed! There is a curse on your friend!' When I got up and went back to the table I was still shaking. I never saw Sister Magdalena so agitated before!"

"Oh, come on now," I scoffed. "The table didn't do all that."

"You don't believe me? You are calling me a liar? You are doubting the truth of Sister Magdalena? David, I'm really surprised at you!" He was truly offended. "You know I would *never* lie where Sister Magdalena is concerned."

I apologized to him and asked him to tell the good dead Sister that I was sorry the next time he "spoke" to her. That seemed to calm him.

"She told me that you have an enemy in your own household. A Negro woman who is jealous of you. This woman does not want you to leave her. She wants you to marry her or else buy her a small house. Only when you have done one of these two things will she unblock your paths and will you be able to continue your own life. Until then you are stuck," and he jabbed a fork into a boiled potato and held it dramatically aloft, "stuck like this!"

I saw myself at the end of his fork, all white and starchy, and wondered what Pygmalion would have done in such a situation.

"But *if* Edna is doing these things," I asked, "*how* is she doing them? Did the Sister tell you that too?"

"She goes once a week to a Quimbanda session and—"

"Quimbanda? Black magic? My Edna worships at Quimbanda? I don't believe it!"

"She goes to a Quimbanda session and she takes a piece of your clothing. Not a new garment, but something you have been wearing. She gives it to the priest and he buries it, spills some cane alcohol over it and lights candles to guard it and keep *you* from escaping. He also sells her some special black pepper that she puts in your food. Your paths are closed, aren't they? Are you missing any clothing?"

I started to say no, when I suddenly remembered how my socks were disappearing. For the past couple of months it seemed that no sock had an identical mate. One time I even had to wear one dark blue sock with one black one and hope that nobody noticed the difference. When I had asked Edna about it she said that it must be the wind that carried them off the line in the laundry area. I told the actor about the missing socks.

"You see!" he said triumphantly. "That's even stronger Quimbanda. While one sock stays here, the other is buried in the ground. You are being held to the earth and to this apartment. You'll never get to Greece at this rate."

I'm stubborn. It's not one of my better qualities and it gets worse with age, because while I was coming around to believe that *perhaps* someone *had* put the evil eye on me and closed off my paths, I just could not believe that it was Edna. I refused to believe it.

Soon after, my friend left for his own apartment, I decided to put Edna to the test. "Edna," I said, "everyone tells me that my paths have been closed, that Exú is working against me. What do you think?"

"Oh, Senhor David! Do you believe that? It's just a foolish notion of your superstitious friends. Don't listen to them."

"But maybe they're right. Who knows? Maybe all this bad luck I'm having is because someone put a hex on me. In Brazil it's impossible to really know what is fact and what is imagination. I've given it a lot of thought. I've used all my rational American logic and it comes out only as being a bad period in my life. But as a person who's been in Brazil for almost ten years and who *thinks* like a Brazilian, I've come to the conclusion that something has been put on me."

"You believe that?" She leaned against the kitchen wall and tried a half-smile.

"As a Brazilian I believe it," I said. "There is nothing else to believe. The facts this time are heavier than the imagination. I've got to do something to get rid of this curse."

"What can you do?"

"I'm going to a session and have the curse taken away." Her eyes widened. "And I want you to take me there!"

"Me? But Senhor David, *I* don't know anything about those places. I've never been to an Umbanda session. Why me?" Her eyes were wider now, but this time with fear and doubt.

"You have many friends who know about those places," I replied. "I want you to ask them to take me to a good strong Umbanda center this Saturday night."

"But this Saturday is so soon . . ." she begged off. "I don't know whether it will be possible in such a short time. . . . I may have a rehearsal of my dance group and maybe I—"

"Edna," I said in a tone I hardly ever used on her, "*I* want you to take me this Saturday!"

"But it's impossible, because—"

"Edna! This Saturday!" And I walked out of the apartment.

The rest of the week I was served badly cooked meals by a sullen-faced Edna. I knew what she was getting at but pretended not to notice. Then on Saturday morning she went away for a few hours. When she came back she said, "I talked with Anna Maria. Her mother knows such a place as you want. You can go to their house this evening and they will take you to the session. But I warn you, it's far out in the suburbs. You have to take two buses to get there."

"You mean *we* have to take two buses. *You* are going with me!"

That evening we went to the *favela* slum shack of Anna Maria and her mother. To reach it we had to leave the main road and wander up a set of rock steps that were slippery with water and garbage. There was an electric lamppost every hundred feet or so and while insects crowded around the light, the slum inhabitants crowded around the base. It was Saturday night and there was nothing to do (and no money to do it on) but to stand around and gossip. Later there would be a card game somewhere or a bring-your-own-bottle party that would probably end up in a knife fight and the sirens of the police ambulance.

The shack, nestled among dozens of others in the muggy, fetid darkness, was about the size of my living room and was constructed of castoff wooden planks and kept dry by a roof of flattened tin cans. I had met Anna Maria before when she came to help Edna prepare a dinner party I once gave. She was short, fat and very black. Her mother, a thin old lady in her sixties, was light chocolate in color and had a ready smile. They both seemed glad to see me and to welcome me to their home. "Sit down, Senhor David," the old lady said. "We will be ready in a few minutes. Would you like a beer? Shall I turn on the television?"

Not waiting for an answer, she flicked on the huge screen

and opened the small white refrigerator that stood beside it. The beer was cold and delicious after the climb up the hill. Then she excused herself and went behind a brightly colored curtain that separated the "living room" from the "bedroom." Edna sat poised and chic on the very edge of a plastic-covered chair, wearing a pink two-piece light woolen suit I bought for her in Buenos Aires. She was out of place and felt it. She had come a long way since knocking on my door to ask for a job.

After much drawer slamming, paper rustling and lowered conversation Anna Maria and her mother, Dona Julia, were ready. They had put on clean, brightly printed cotton dresses and leather sandals. Each carried two bulging shopping bags. "Our things," they said when I asked what was in the bags. I would see soon enough.

Edna had been right. We did have to take two buses. One brought us to the silent Saturday night downtown commercial section of Rio and the other took us far away from the city and out into an area of small houses lit by lanterns, pitch-black skies and barking dogs. I had never taken this route before in all the years I had been in Brazil. It made me realize that in spite of the fact that I probably have traveled over more of the giant nation than any other American (and most Brazilians), I still had many places to go and many things to see.

Anna Maria shouted something to the driver and he stopped at the next crossroads. We got out. There was nothing there but trees, muddy ditches and a feeling of utter desolation. "Here?" I asked. Dona Julia shook her head and took my arm. I followed as Edna and Anna Maria walked ahead.

The women chattered about a dress sale in Copacabana as my eyes tried to accustom themselves to the blackness. Finally I realized that this must be some humble, far-off workers' suburb, one of those patches of humanity that dot the area outside fashionable Rio de Janeiro with small houses, garden plots and numerous children. We walked down a dirt road for about fifteen minutes. In front of a high wall of trees and vines Dona Julia stopped. "In here," she said.

There was a huge area behind those trees, an area that held a long, low, one-story house made of cement blocks painted white and with a red tiled roof. Around the house was a sidewalk of pink cement leading to another low shed-type structure painted with various magic signs and symbols and thatched with banana leaves. The nearest side was open and there a Negro woman brewed coffee and sold small triangles of meat- and chicken-filled dough, deep-fried and delicious. There were about a dozen other people already there, milling around the food stall or else sitting on several green wooden benches under a huge mango tree. All the others were black. I was the only one with even a drop of white blood. They looked at me curiously, then when I was introduced by Anna Maria or Dona Julia they accepted me and ignored me.

Edna and two teen-age girls got into an immediate conversation about Carnival, and she seemed to be enjoying herself. While the girls were neatly dressed, it was obvious that Edna was the best-dressed. In fact, of all the other Negroes there, Edna stuck out like a fashion model. Her shoes, her purse, her gold bracelets and her elaborate hairdo made her look like a madame rather than a maid. But (and this is to her credit) she introduced me to people as "my boss" Senhor David.

When 11 P.M. came and went and there was still no action inside the long white house I wandered around the grounds, inspecting the various designs worked in cement between low shrubs or trying to figure out the meaning of the wrought-iron symbols that had been nailed to the trunk of the old mango tree. At the base of each tree several candles burned. They, and the naked bulb from the food stall, were the only illumination in the pitch-black night.

Drum and Candle

There was a small cement house, complete with tile roof, blue shutters at the windows and a white picket fence, on the far side of the property. The house was like a doll's house, reaching only to my waist. I knew it must be the home of Exú. I bent down to see what was inside the open front door and a dog's angry face, sneering and with bared fangs, made me pull back rapidly. Then I looked again and saw that it was only the severed head, and not the whole animal. From the way the eyes still freshly gleamed, I realized it had been killed quite recently.

When I returned to where Edna was still in conversation, several of the others had disappeared, including Anna Maria and Dona Julia. "Where are they?" I asked. I was told they had gone to change.

At eleven forty-five (I kept glancing at my watch wondering when the ceremony would get under way) three young men wandered out of the shadows carrying drums. They were drums made from long slabs of curved, polished wood, wider at the top than at the bottom. The mouths were covered with some kind of animal skin tied down with a thick rope and secured with the same kind of pegs that the Frankenstein monster had in his neck. The appearance of these three drummers was the signal for the spectators to move toward the meetinghouse. As each of us filed in the small side door we removed our shoes and had to be cleansed by incense fumes. One of the girls who had been making the little hot pies was now dressed in an ankle-length satin dress with several flaring skirts, and she held the censer as we turned one by one through the heavy lilac smoke. Then the females went to one side of the room and the males to the other, near the drummers.

I made a sign to Edna to notice the wall paintings, but she scowled and shook her head. All the inside walls were covered in bright primitive paintings. Three of them were of the devil, Exú. In one he ate fire, in another he held a grinning skull and in a third he lit candles as a naked blonde fought off a host of lesser demons.

There was St. George (a familiar figure by now) on his white horse spearing the horrible monster. There was the Old Black Slave sitting on his tree stump. There was a woman who might have been St. Barbara except that under her richly ornamented garments she had no flesh, only bones.

Red and black paper streamers crisscrossed the ceiling, and in the far right-hand corner a many-platformed altar reached to the roof covered in artificial flowers, Christian images, burning candles, Umbanda deities and ceramic bowls of cooked and raw foods. There was a throne in front of the altar, facing the spectators. It was painted black and the seat was covered by blood-red velvet. On the floor against the far upper wall rings of burning candles separated offerings of food, opened bottles of *cachaça* sugar-cane alcohol and individual plaster images. The floor was of beaten earth and cold to my stocking-clad feet.

The drums began. I looked at my watch. It was exactly midnight.

They started slowly, almost listlessly, and gained momentum with each passing minute. Then from outside came a woman's raucous voice. She shouted something that I was sure was not Portuguese, and a chorus of female voices answered her in song. I turned to look out the window to see what was going on, but there were no windows. The shutters on the outside of the house opened onto nothing. The only entry to the building was that one lone door.

The chanting grew louder as the drums increased in tone, and by the voices I could tell that the procession (I could only imagine the dancers placating Exú by weaving and bowing around the house with the severed dog's head) was coming my way. The singing was milder now and the strident voice had lowered a few octaves. Then through the only door they filed in, thirteen women dressed in long-sleeved blouses and multiple satin skirts. Some wore white, others pale blue, some were in yellow and others in green. None wore jewelry, all had their hair loose and hanging down their backs.

With a start I saw Anna Maria and her mother in the procession. The daughter was dressed in pearl white and her mother in blue with white trimmings. Anna Maria, already fat, billowed out like a black-faced gas balloon, while her mother had a majestic dignity that was only hinted at in her everyday cotton street clothes. They were barefoot and moved in small, quick steps to the beating drums. Their skirts swayed and they chanted in some African dialect. They were oblivious of their friends who stood against the walls. They were working for the spirits now. They had no time for mortal acquaintances. Forming a semicircle, they swayed to the rhythm and gestured toward the door. They held out their hands, palms upward, and did a funny backward hop, then a forward step. They seemed to be beseeching someone to come into the room.

Then with a loud guttural cry she came! Dancing in circles and shouting hoarsely, the woman entered the house like a satin-clad whirlwind. She was Negro but not the jet-black of Anna Maria. She was, I guessed, somewhere in her late forties. She wore a spotlessly white ballooned-sleeve blouse and an equally white full skirt. It hung all the way to the floor and was created of layers and layers of dainty lace. It billowed as she spun, but never showed more than her ankles. Her hair was hidden under a white silk turban. Her face was free of make-up and her only jewel was a magnificent gold cross that hung from a gold chain around her neck. The cross bounced on her enormous bosom and picked up reflections from the candles along the wall. As she entered, the dancers clapped their hands and kept it up until she had reached their midst and embraced each of them.

The drums changed pace and she began to chant. It was a prayer to God the Father to grant His blessing to the services about to be held. Then another change of pace and a chant to Jesus for guidance and comfort. Then another change and a new chant to the Holy Mother. Then one to St. Peter, St. George, St. Sebastian and on and on until I lost track of which saint was being honored.

One by one the women around her began to be possessed. They shook, shivered, jerked, leaped and moaned as the spirits came into their bodies. They danced slower now, or else stiff-legged, going around the room peering at the spectators or grinning at some monster only they could see. The Mother kept her saints under control, and since I had been given the number 1, I knew that my case would be the first to be listened to by the spirits. I was ready and willing to ask them about my evil-eye hex, because it was way past one-thirty in the morning, my legs were tired from standing and my feet were freezing on the earthen floor. I was sure that as soon as the ritual dances and possessions were over with that the spectators' turn would come.

As at so many other times in Brazil—I was wrong.

No sooner had all the women become ridden by their spirits than one by one they were relieved of them. The Mother invoked the closing rituals of Umbanda and the girls came out of their trances, their eyes glazed and their hair awry. Before I had a chance to wonder what was going on, they all filed out the door and we stiff-kneed and shivering-footed spectators were left to ourselves.

I looked across at Edna and hunched my shoulders. She made a sign that I was to wait, for she thought (rightly) that I was ready to get out of there and go home. Then we heard singing from outside the hut. Once again the drummers began their beat and the girls danced back into the center of the house. The second act was to begin.

The drums beat slowly, then faster and then at breakneck speed. The dancers whirled and stepped, gaining momentum each minute. They chanted and shouted and twisted and applauded. It was more pagan than I had ever seen in any other center before. I glanced at Edna but she was watching everything so solemnly that she didn't notice me. The faces of those around me were turned toward the door. They were waiting for the Mother. So was I.

She came in.

With a terrible cry the door burst open and she bounded in. Gone were the white blouse and the white multilayered lace skirt. Gone were the white turban and the gleaming gold cross. In their place was a blood-red blouse with sleeves that ended it tatters. The skirt was wine red and filthy dirty. It hung to her knees and was made from dull satin. Under it several pink, red and wine-colored crinoline petticoats rustled with every movement. Her hair was topped by a red and black peaked nurse's cap and her feet were bare, toenails painted red. In place of the cross now hung a polished skull. It must have belonged to a child of one or two years. A black ribbon held the jaws together, a dead snake was tied between the two eye sockets.

I was fascinated but just a little bit uneasy, for she had changed from the white of Oxalá/Jesus to the red of Exú/Satan. I was in the earthly presence of the Lord of the Darkness and I wasn't sure that I liked it.

Her gestures were broad and masculine. She stepped as if she wore thick boots and she danced across the room and over to the altar whirling and chanting like the demon she was representing.

She stood and looked at the altar and let out a loud, long laugh. She picked up the image of the Virgin Mary and pretended that she was going to throw it down. She sniffed at the bowls of food and taking a mouthful of corn meal, made a face and spat it into the air. She shouted that she was thirsty and one of the women left her place in the dance group and hurriedly opened a bottle of *cachaça* sugarcane alcohol for her. She filled her mouth with the fiery liquid, spat it on the ground, then took another swig. This she swallowed and let drip from her grotesquely painted lips. The dancer then opened a small wicker basket and removed a snow-white, freshly ironed and starched linen napkin. It had flowers and songbirds embroidered on it. The Mother of Exú grabbed the napkin and smeared it across her mouth, wiping the dripping alcohol. Then she crumpled it and tossed it to the floor.

Then she called for a cigar. A fresh box was brought to her and she chose one, demanded that the golden paper wrapper be removed and stuck it in her mouth. A fresh box of matches was produced, and the cigar was lit. She took two or three puffs at it, smiled with satisfaction at the aroma and then turned it around and stuck the lit end into her mouth. From out of her nostrils blue smoke appeared. She grinned and spat on the floor. Then she signaled to the drummers and the rhythm began anew.

The dancers began to sing and move with the beats and the priestess danced right along with them. But she was no longer the devoted white-garbed leader of the first half of the ceremony. She was now the devil and in complete command. She bawled out orders to the drummers and berated a woman who was out of step. She called for another swig of *cachaça*, and another freshly laundered and starched embroidered napkin was used once and tossed to the floor. I wondered how many hours had been spent—by what poor Negro woman in the dance group—in washing and ironing those mistreated napkins that week. I considered it a waste of time and effort. They obviously considered it as much a part of their ritual as the fresh white cloth the Catholic priest uses in each Mass to cover the communion chalice.

The music was building up to a pitch that I hadn't noticed in the other session. The dancers became possessed again, one by one, but this time their faces were contorted in what looked like horrible pains. Their fingers were twisted and their elbows pushed out like bat wings. The priestess called for another swig on the bottle and drained it dry. I watched closely, but not the slightest emotion flickered across her face as the strong and outrageously bad-tasting alcohol emptied into her stomach. (My father, who claims he can drink anything, once took two slugs of *cachaça* and admitted defeat. Here this woman had just drained a complete bottle as if it had been soda pop!)

She called for another cigar, and stepped over one of the dancers who had fallen onto the floor. I looked and it was Anna Maria who was now groveling in the dirt. The priestess reached down and scratched Anna Maria's head as if she were a pet dog and walked toward the altar and the open box of cigars. Anna Maria began to yelp and, just like a dog, crawled by digging her elbows and toes into the earth over to the priestess. She reached her and sniffed at the hem of her filthy skirt, then just as happy as a little puppy began to lick the priestess' bare feet. The woman paid no attention and stepped over her, returning to the center of the room to relight her cigar. Anna Maria, yipping and panting, dragged herself back across the floor.

The woman went to the drummers and said something, then looked at the three men who were standing beside me. She stared at them and approached one. She embraced him, then spat on the floor. It barely missed his stockinged feet. "Are you back again?" she roared at him. "What's the matter, don't you want the girl now?"

He blushed under his light Negro skin and muttered something just for her.

"You stupid ass! You didn't do it right! F——ing bastard! Why, if you had done it the way I, Exú, told you she would have been in your arms by now. Of course she won't leave her husband with a job only half done! I should throw your ass out of here! You come and beg me and make all sorts of promises to me and then you only do things by half measures!

What are you? A man or a half-man?" Her voice rose into the rafters.

He, ashamed, muttered that he was a man, but . . .

"If you are a man, let's see the proof!" Her hands lunged for his trousers and started working at the buttons on his fly. He pulled back and pushed her away. She let out a roar of pleasure and danced back into the center of the room, laughing and pointing a bony finger at him. "A man! He says he is a man!" The women spectators on the other side of the room laughed nervously, trying to pretend they thought it was funny.

Then another bottle of *cachaça* was called for. This time she drank it down without stopping. A fresh napkin was used, crumpled and tossed to the floor. She looked at the cigar she was smoking and made a face. She shouted to her assistant, who came running with another one. The first one she threw to the ground (almost hitting Anna Maria, who was licking her ankles) and stomped out with her bare feet. The new cigar was lit and immediately the hot ash end was popped into her mouth. That was when she stared at me.

"You!" she called. "What are you doing here? Who are you?"

I started to speak when I saw Edna shaking her head. I was not supposed to answer, I gathered. The woman who had been supplying the cigars and the booze whispered into the priestess' ear who I was and, obviously, who had brought me. "Do you like *cachaça*, Americano?" she called. "Have a drink with me! I've never met an Americano yet that didn't like a drink!"

Her assistant ran for a fresh bottle and handed it to her. She skipped over to me, extending the bottle. I reached for it and she laughed and pulled it away. "Me first," she said and plunged the neck of the bottle deep into her mouth. Then she swallowed long. The bottle came out half empty and she licked the rim with her tongue several times before handing it to me. I knew what she was trying to do. I, as a white American, was not supposed to want to put that saliva-gleaming bottle to my lips. To do it would be to push aside many home-grown prejudices. Not to do it would give her every reason to torment me. The entire room watched as I took the bottle, stuck it into my mouth and took a long, full drink. Then I passed it back to her.

"Very good," she said with a laugh. "I like to see a man like me who knows how to drink!" She came closer, her face just inches away from mine. "I am a man, you know. I am more of a man than that nervous character over there," and she pointed to the spectator whom she had groped a few minutes earlier. "Do you know what my name is?" I shook my head. "My name is Exú! I am the God of Evil! I can kill you if I wish! Does that make you afraid?" Again I shook my head. "Good!" she said. "I don't like people who are afraid!" and she opened her mouth to laugh. It was then I saw that each of her teeth had been capped in gold and that a small diamond gleamed in the center of each gold cap! She took another draw from the *cachaça* bottle and instead of swallowing, suddenly spat it into my face!

I pulled back. My first reaction was to strike back at her, but instead, I reached across and grabbed her long, ragged sleeve. I pulled her closer and wiped my face on her blouse. The hush in the room could be tasted.

She glared at me, glared at the damp spot on her sleeve and after a second's pause broke into another laugh. Everyone relaxed, including myself, for I had no idea where all that courage had appeared from so suddenly.

"I like you," she said. "You are Americano?" I nodded yes. "Do you know what nationality *I* am?" I paused, wanting to get it right, and knowing that "Brazilian" was too pat an answer for her, said, "African?"

"No! Why do you say that? Because of my skin? I am Jewish! Don't you know that the devil is Jewish? I am the one that killed Christ! So I must be Jewish, right?"

"If you say so, Senhora," I replied.

"No! Don't call me Senhora! Call me Senhor! For I am Exú and Exú is a *man!*" She turned a half circle and clutched herself between her legs. "Maybe I don't have the equipment down here that he has," again pointing to the poor fellow in line with me, "but I am more of a man than he is!" She glared at the drummers. "Play those f——ing things, you animals!" Immediately the beats resumed and the dancers (now all possessed and staggering under the weight of their individual demons) began to move with the rhythm.

Anna Maria was still crawling around the floor; her pearl-white gown was smeared with dirt, *cachaça* and cigar ashes. Her elbows were bleeding from having dragged herself across the floor so often. Her mother, Dona Julia, was almost stock-still. She was standing by herself with her feet wide apart and her hands on her hips. Her hair was a mess and her eyes were turned back into her head. All I could see were the whites. The pupils were completely hidden. I felt sorry for both of them, yet I had to tell myself that they knew what they were getting into. Dona Julia had told me earlier in the evening that since joining this spirit center her life had improved tremendously. She never had money worries any more. She was in perfect health and her husband, who had been a stone around her neck for years, had suddenly abandoned her. Yes, she had many reasons for being glad she had joined this particular group. "You'll see how it is," she told me, "and you too will become a steady visitor."

The drums stopped and I was glad, for my ears were aching with the noise. My feet were cakes of ice and I was tired from standing for so long. I looked at my watch. It was almost 4 A.M.! Time had flown, but not fast enough. I wanted to get out of there. To hell with knowing about some superstitious curse. I was a twentieth-century American and I was tired and hungry!

It was at that moment that the small round bench appeared.

Drum and Candle

It was placed in the center of the room and Exú made a motion that I was to come over to it. She told me to sit down, which I did. Then lighting a fresh cigar she began to blow the smoke in my face, on my chest, around my legs and against my back. She yanked off my socks (my only protection against that cold earth floor!) and blew smoke between my toes.

"Now tell me why you are here," she said. My first impulse was to tell her that if she was really the spirit of evil she would *know* why I was there, but I didn't want to become involved in a long conversation, I just wanted to get the thing over with and get out of there. "Someone has closed off my paths," I said. "I want to know who it is."

She clapped her hands as two dancers came near. One of them was Anna Maria, but to my surprise she was no longer possessed by the spirit of Satan's dog. When she had returned to normal I couldn't say. It must have been when the drums stopped and I was going through the fumigation process. Anna Maria took my right hand and the other woman took my left. Then the drums began to beat, Exú began to chant and the spectators began clapping their hands.

I had seen this before. When a spectator was between two mediums he usually began to twitch and writhe with them. I was hoping that I would start the same gyrations because I wanted to feel what it was like. But to my disappointment the women shook and moaned but I felt nothing. Not even a tiny electric charge.

"What did you feel?" the priestess asked.

"I felt that something was leaving my body," I lied, hoping to shorten the whole affair.

"You felt nothing! Don't invent things!" she said in a loud voice. "Now let's try it again."

Once more the drums beat, the chants came and the hands clapped and once more the two mediums clutching my hands jerked and groaned as if they were holding a bare electric wire. I again felt nothing, but Exú didn't question me this time. Both mediums were flat on the floor, their dresses up above their knees, their eyes and their mouths open and gasping. The priestess seemed satisfied with the results this time. She puffed the wrong end of the cigar and spat on the floor. I pulled my feet back just in time.

"Hey," she yelled and pushed at Anna Maria with a dirty bare foot. "Can't you talk?"

Anna Maria laughed a high-pitched laugh and said, "I know who put the evil eye on this Americano. I know, but he doesn't want to be told. It will hurt him too much, he thinks."

"Is that true?" asked the devil. "You don't really want to know?"

"Of course I want to know," I said with exasperation. "That's the reason I'm here!"

"Then what is the name of this person?" Exú shouted at Anna Maria. "Tell us!"

"He doesn't want to know!"

"I *do* want to know!"

"Tell us, you stupid demon! You have been brought up from hell to tell us! Stop acting like a silly virgin with a secret!" The bare black foot gave Anna Maria a sharp kick.

"Very well," Anna Maria giggled, "but he won't like it. The person who put this curse against him and who has closed off all his paths and is making him suffer is the very same person who brought him to this session tonight!"

Everyone stopped breathing and looked at Edna. I also looked straight at her. She paled and weaved for a second as if she was about to faint. Then she composed herself and glared at Anna Maria on the floor.

When my voice returned, I was able to say, "That's impossible! The person who brought here this evening is a good person. She would never do a thing like that to me!"

"That's what you think," said the voice from Anna Maria's

body. "She is not *that* good. You told her you were going to leave the country. She wants you to marry her. Either that or buy her a house and a piece of land before you go. She doesn't want to be left alone. She has become greedy over the years that she has been with you."

"I don't believe it!" I shouted. "This woman is my friend!"

"Everybody is everybody's friend when they want something," said Exú. "No one stays with anyone just for the pleasure of it. There is always a reason. In this case the reason is a marriage or a house. Did you promise to marry her?"

"Of course not!" I protested.

"But she cooked for you and made your bed and cleaned your house and kept away your enemies all the time, didn't she?" The priestess looked from me to Edna and back to me.

"Sure she did," I answered, "but I paid her to do all those things. She is my maid. Those are her duties. She is my maid and *nothing* more!"

"Just a maid," mused Exú. "Dressed like that with those jewels and *just* a maid? You don't expect me to believe that, do you?"

"Listen," I said, "I don't care what you believe. That woman is my maid. We are not lovers. We never have been. And I don't believe that she would do a thing like that against me."

"Then you are saying that I'm a liar?" the priestess shouted.

"I'm not saying anything," I said wearily. "All I want to do now is go home." I started to rise but the devil pushed me back down. "You stay," she said, "but you," pointing to Edna, "can leave."

Edna glared at the woman and then glowered with hate at Anna Maria as she walked across the room and out the door. "I'll wait for you outside, Senhor David," she said.

"Good. She is gone. Now we will get rid of the curse." The priestess ordered the drummers to begin their work, and as she sang and chanted and blew smoke in my face the entire corps de ballet danced around me chanting and waving their arms. It must have lasted for a good ten minutes. I was cold and getting more impatient by the second. When the chanting stopped the priestess said, "Okay. You are free. The curse has been lifted and it will now come down doubly hard upon the person who placed it on you. The person who wished you evil will fall ill and suffer."

I rose from the bench. "But I didn't ask you for that! I only wanted you to remove the curse from me! I don't want anyone, no matter how mean they are, to suffer because of me." I was furious at her and surprised at myself for taking everything so seriously. Was I starting to believe all this mumbo jumbo?

"It is too late," the devil said smugly. "Your curse has been taken from you and is now upon the one who started it. Evil must be handled intelligently. If not, it flies right back in your own face."

"May I go now?" I asked.

"You may. And go away blessed."

"By the devil?"

"The devil is not always evil. I work for good as well. You will see how my work is good when you start to live again with your paths open and freedom ahead of you."

I started toward the door. "How much do I owe you?" I asked.

"Put your donation in the box beside the drums. Anything you wish to give." I folded a few cruzeiro notes and put them into the box. She came over and embraced me, her breath smelling of cigar smoke and alcohol. "I like you," she said, "but you don't like me. You think I'm a fraud. You will see. The future will show you that Exú can be your friend."

I went out the door and turned to look at her for the last time. She was already placing one of the woman spectators on the bench and lighting a fresh cigar. The sun was just beginning to come up across the open fields and everything looked new and naked in its strange light. Even the old priestess looked different from outside. Her filthy clothes, her lined face, her tired eyes. Edna and I walked for a few blocks and caught a bus into town. We didn't say anything the entire trip.

Call it whatever you will ("coincidence" is probably the strongest word in English) and believe it or not, three days after having the curse taken off me I got a telegram from a big U.S. magazine. They wanted a story and were sending me the necessary expenses via Telex. It was a story that I had suggested months before and that they originally had turned down. Their expense money paid the back rent and the telephone bill.

One week after the visit to the priestess the U.S. judge freed the inheritance money I had been waiting for and I was able to repay everyone I owed.

Ten days after the hex had been removed I got a letter from Argentina saying that the breakup in the love affair had been a horrible mistake and would I be willing to start where we had left off. I didn't even reply.

And two weeks afterward, Edna—for the first time in five years—became deathly ill. She lost weight, took on a sallow color, couldn't eat and went about her work nervously and always at the point of tears. Finally I sent her to a doctor. He said there was a growth in her stomach that had to be cut out. Okay, I agreed to pay the bill. They opened her and found nothing. She came back from the hospital even weaker.

One night I heard her moving around in her room. When I went to see if she needed anything I saw that she was packing her suitcases. The room was littered with the dresses, shoes, coats and scarves that I had given her over the years. Through her tears she said she was leaving.

"Why?" I asked. "I mean why *now*, when you are so sick? I've put off my trip for a few months. You don't have to go now, *tonight*."

"Yes I do. My health is getting worse. The stitches from the operation are hurting me and I can't sleep or eat. Only when I leave this apartment will I get better." She folded a blue silk blouse and placed it into one of the bags. "He told me that I could not hope for one minute's peace as long as I stayed here with you."

"Who told you that?" I was indignant.

"A Father of the Saints, an Umbanda priest I went to see tonight. He said that the curse I had put on you had returned onto me twofold. As long as I stayed near you I would suffer. I'll only get better by leaving."

I was stunned. "Edna, did you have my paths closed? Was the old priestess and everyone else right when they told me that you were working a curse against me?"

She sank onto the bed and sobbed. "I didn't mean to hurt you. But they told me that I was foolish to let you go without your buying me a house, without your giving me some security. They told me that I should try and marry you, but when I told them that we had never had anything between us they said it didn't matter. That by burying one of your socks each week and putting special pepper into your food you would think you were in love with me and would marry me."

I wanted to hold her and comfort her and yet at the same time I was repulsed at what she had done *against* me. She had been my friend, at times my only friend when the chips were down. I felt responsible for her even though she had done black magic against me. "Well, if it will help," I stammered, "I do have some of that inheritance money left, maybe I can buy you a small house or an apartment if you think . . ."

She got up and wiped her eyes with a handkerchief. "No.

Drum and Candle

It wouldn't be any good. Any house you would buy me would be filled with the curse of that woman. That awful Exú woman! No. I have to go away and start everything over again away from the evil influences that I put on you."

About an hour later she called me. The door was open and her bags had already gone down into a taxi. She embraced me, trying to say something, but only tears came. Then she closed the door and was gone.

Then I cried.

Now the big question must be answered. Do I, a white, educated Christian American believe in the powers of the Brazilian spirits? I cannot truthfully answer no. I must answer, truthfully, that I do.

There it is.

In print.

I do believe in the pagan spirits that inhabit that vast South American nation called Brazil. I have seen too much *not* to believe. My mind has reeled at spirit manifestations, at table rappings, at spirit operations, at prophecies that have come true, at cards that foretold exactly what would happen and at events that cannot be explained any other way.

If this brings derision and laughter down upon me, I can't help it. I went into Brazil with an open mind. I wanted to see everything and learn the truth about things. I couldn't accept the idea that people returned from the dead. I doubted the theory that we have a soul that pays for our misdeeds in this life through suffering in the next.

Perhaps the biggest stumbling block I had to get over was the fact that maybe—just maybe—these uneducated black-skinned descendants of illiterate slaves have something we modern sophisticates do not. That these people have managed to stay pure and natural and close to Nature in such a way that the secrets of Nature are revealed to them. Now maybe the ways they *interpret* these secrets are not 100 per cent correct. Maybe they see spirits and demons and talk to dead friends because this is the way that the Great Force of Nature (God? Buddha? Jesus? Oxalá?) can get through to them. Maybe this is the way that the Brazilians *understand* things we *refuse* to see.

There were great secrets the ancients never passed on to us moderns. Or if they did, we pooh-poohed them in the name of Christianity first and science second. We shut our minds to things that went against the New Testament and what the boys in the laboratories couldn't prove in their test tubes. I grew up knowing that ghosts did not exist because we can't see them. That was the explanation I was given. All well and good. But also, in my formative years, I learned that we cannot see things that are happening in places where we are not present. Yet when I was about fourteen or so my aunt bought the town's first television set and there I was watching things happening in New York City, some two thousand miles away! Beliefs change with each new generation. The impossible becomes the possible. My great-grandfather would have called you an idiot if you told him one day he could bring sunlight into his farmhouse at night just by pushing a button on the wall. My grandfather was incredulous that man had the audacity to think he could fly! I am still amazed that I can pick up a piece of black plastic and talk with someone miles and miles away. A man walk on the moon? Impossible!

Okay, all these things are the work of science. Science and the atom. Yet the great minds of today still don't know what an atom *is*. They know how it works and how to make it work, but as to what it *is* they are still ignorant. Science has made great leaps forward in the past one hundred years. It has filled the world with gadgets and objects, and only recently have men of learning (Professor Rhine at Duke University, for example) become interested in bettering man's *mind* through science.

Drum and Candle

We now—all of us—take extrasensory perception for granted. It has moved out of Poe into modern-day fact. We are starting to believe in the powers of the mind. Thoughts can make us nervous, make our heads ache and upset our stomachs. That we all know. But we don't know why or how. Someday we will. Someday, in the not too distant future, we will know what we have under our hats. We will know how to use those mental powers (for "good" or "evil" if you like) and we will believe them when we see them in operation exactly the way we believe a television receiver when we see it turned on. Nobody doubts a television wave any more. You can't see it. It can't be held in the hand or put into a test tube. But it's there. It's the outcome of one small gift of Nature that we somehow stumbled across. Imagine what is inside that most marvelous of all Nature's gifts: the human mind!

Yemanjá grants her salty favors because those who ask her *believe*. Exú is feared because Brazilians *know* he is dangerous. Arigó cuts through flesh and the patient feels no pain because he has *faith* that Arigó is doing the right thing and would never hurt him.

Somehow and from somewhere the spirit mediums, doctors, believers of Brazil reach into the known-unknown and bring about a miracle. Someday we will be able to do the same. We probably won't beat drums or light candles as we do it, but to our present way of thinking it will be a miracle.

Do you believe in *miracles*? I do. I've seen so many in Brazil that they've become commonplace. Go down there. Take a look for yourself. Learn to live with and love the Brazilian people and you will learn to live with and personally experience everyday miracles.

One high spirit medium told me: "To progress along the path of spiritual evolution, there are two main requirements. The first is to love one another. The second is to acquire knowledge. Love with your eyes open," he said, then added, "and with your mind open as well."

DATE DUE

TL747 7450
5-5-95